UGLY PREY

UGLY PREY

An INNOCENT WOMAN and
the Death Sentence That
Scandalized JAZZ AGE CHICAGO

Emilie Le Beau Lucchesi

CHICAGO
REVIEW
PRESS

Published by Chicago Review Press Incorporated
814 North Franklin Street
Chicago, Illinois 60610
ISBN 978-1-61373-696-8

Library of Congress Cataloging-in-Publication Data
Is available from the Library of Congress.

Typesetting: Nord Compo

Printed in the United States of America
5 4 3 2 1

To my "Tana," Nella Lucchesi Thalji

And to my husband, Michael Lucchesi,
for many, many reasons

CONTENTS

KEY FIGURES

SABELLA NITTI: Real name Isabella Maria Travaglia. Immigrant from Bari, Italy, about age forty-four in 1923. Lives with family in Stickney, Illinois, on a truck garden farm.

FRANCESCO NITTI: Sabella's first husband. Deceased or missing as of July 1922. Immigrant from Bari. About age fifty-six when he disappears from the Stickney farm.

PETER CRUDELE: Real name Pietro. Immigrant from Bari. About age twenty-two in 1923. Works on Nitti family farm as a farmhand. Becomes Sabella's husband in March 1923.

JAMES NITTI: Real name Vincenzo. Immigrant from Bari. About age twenty-five in 1923. Sabella's oldest son. Married but a wanderer.

MICHAEL NITTI: Real name Michele. Immigrant from Bari. About age twenty-one in 1923. Sabella's second son.

CHARLEY NITTI: Real name Pasquale. Immigrant from Bari. About age seventeen in 1923. Sabella's third son. Lives on family farm in Stickney.

FILOMENA NITTI: Called Philomena or Fily. Born in the United States. About age six in 1923. Sabella's fourth child. Lives on family farm in Stickney.

MARY NITTI: Real name Maria. Born in the United States. About age four in 1923. Sabella's fifth and youngest child. Lives on family farm in Stickney.

DEPUTY SHERIFF PAUL DASSO: Cook County deputy sheriff. Son of Italian immigrants. Leads charge against Sabella.

EUGENE A. MORAN: Sabella and Peter's first defense attorney.

HELEN CIRESE: A member of the defense team representing Sabella and Peter on appeal. Young, beautiful, and Italian, Cirese was shut out of the major Chicago law firms.

MILTON SMITH: A prosecuting attorney.

MICHAEL ROMANO: A prosecuting attorney.

GENEVIEVE FORBES: A *Chicago Daily Tribune* reporter who covers Sabella's case.

MICHELE DESANT: Farmhand who lives in a shanty behind the Nitti family farm with his wife. Immigrant from Bari, also serves as a translator during the trial.

JAMES AND ANNA VOLPE: Bari immigrants, witnesses for the prosecution.

Part I

GUILTY

THAT MEANS A HANGING!

July 9, 1923

IN THE EARLY AFTERNOON, the jury filed back into the courtroom with a verdict. The twelve men kept their eyes low, diverted from the defendants' table. They knew they were sending this middle-aged woman, Sabella Nitti, and her young husband, Peter Crudele, to the gallows.

They had made the decision in the deliberation room, voting a dozen times until they came to agreement. It was the right thing to do, they believed, to bring Francesco Nitti's killers to justice. But it didn't *feel* right to send a woman to the gallows. She would be the first woman to hang in Cook County, and that was a heavy burden on the jurors' consciences.

The audience in the courtroom read the jurors' faces, trying to get a sense of what they decided. One man, a regular murder trial attendee, voiced his veteran opinion to the other courtroom enthusiasts. "That means a hanging!"

Peter stiffened in his wooden chair at the defendants' table. At twenty-two, he was almost two decades younger than his wife, and he had picked up the English language soon after emigrating from the Adriatic Coast to the Chicago area a few years back. He understood what the observers were saying. They believed he was a doomed man and they talked about the possibility of him hanging as if they were watching a motion picture or reading a detective magazine.

Peter had a long oval face, dark hair, and pale skin. He hardened his jaw and locked his dark eyes on the desk in front of him. He was a handsome young man, and his good looks contrasted with his aging wife. Peter and Sabella had been married only two months when they were arrested, along with Sabella's youngest son, Charley, for the murder of her former husband. Prosecutors claimed the mismatched couple had killed Francesco Nitti the previous July so they could be together.

Peter likely sensed how the spectators at the trial thought the worst of him and Sabella. The charges against Sabella's son had been dropped just days before, and the boy sat in the gallery with the rest of the audience, eager to hear the fate of his mother and stepfather. The boy might have been one of the few people in the courtroom not hoping for a conviction.

From the audience, reporter Genevieve Forbes studied the defendants, paying attention to every foreign detail about the woman in particular. If it were up to Forbes, she would find Sabella guilty and hang the old woman that very night. Forbes was disgusted by Sabella. This little Italian woman was everything that Americans reviled about these invading Southern Europeans. Sabella didn't speak English. She was dirty. Violent. Ignorant. Uneducated. She clung to her backward ways, and she clearly cared nothing for American rules and order. Maybe in Italy a woman was free to bludgeon her husband to death and marry a much younger farmhand. But there was a proper justice system in Cook County, which Forbes wrote about for the *Chicago Daily Tribune*. Later that day, she would sit at her portable typewriter in the newsroom on Madison Street and describe Sabella as the "dumb, crouching, animal-like peasant."

At first glance, Forbes appeared to be Sabella's polar opposite. Forbes was slender and light. She was not particularly pretty but she had fine features—a slender nose, thin lips, and light eyes. To Forbes, Sabella was a peasant who looked—and smelled—like she had just walked out of a field. Sabella was a compact woman with a muscular frame built during a lifetime of work. Her olive skin had deepened like tanned leather after years of toiling in the Mediterranean sun. She had long, thick black and gray hair that she piled onto her head in a messy bun and secured with pins and combs. Across the courtroom, her hair looked filthy, and several times Forbes wrote the word "greasy" in her notebook as a description of this little woman's appearance.

If Sabella had been born under different circumstances, it would have been easy to describe her as pretty. She had fine, arched eyebrows and round, close-set eyes. She had a slender nose, a wide mouth, and a defined jawline. In another life shaped by school or cotillion, a young Sabella might have charmed men by looking up at them with a wide smile and long, fluttering eyelashes. But a lifetime of desperation and work under the sun made it easy for Forbes to call Sabella "grotesque" in the news reports.

It was not just her appearance that irked Forbes—it was her manners. Sabella appeared in public without a hat, which proved to Forbes that this murderer lacked any tact or class. And she showed up to court as if she was ready to work on a corn row. Sabella wore a long-sleeved dark work shirt to the trial and a heavy, long dark-blue skirt. Her skirt was full, but it had been shortened for work in the field. Her attire was far too heavy for a hot courtroom in July, and Forbes watched as the doomed woman took out a small square of fabric and wiped sweat off her brow.

Judge Joseph David peered down at the packed courtroom. The gallery was crowded with spectators who had read about the murder trial in the newspapers and wanted to be there for the big moment. Many of them were Italian, and Judge David suspected they might disrupt the courtroom after the verdict was read.

"Deputy Dasso," Judge David ordered. "Tell your people in their language that if there is any noise or demonstration, the guilty person will be sent to jail."

If Deputy Sheriff Paul Dasso cringed at the comment "your people," he kept it to himself. He was not from Sabella's home province of Bari, in southern Italy, nor was he even Italian born. He spoke the language of his parents' homeland, but these were not his *paesani*. Sabella and Peter were dark, thin, and hardened by labor. Dasso was a round man who wore a three-piece suit that made him seem even larger. He was light skinned and his hair had turned white over the years. No one passing him on the street would have thought he was an Italian. It was probably a surprise for most of the spectators to see such a prominent man stand up and address the court in an Italian dialect.

Judge David looked at the jury. He was a slim man with downturned eyes that gave him the appearance of being sad or even sympathetic. He was neither. At times during the trial, he tried to warn Sabella's attorney against making poor choices during questioning. But Judge David was primarily irritated during the trial, particularly with the difficulties in finding a proper translator. He frequently snapped at the Italians watching the trial from the gallery, and gave the impression he wasn't fond of these people.

"Has the jury reached a verdict?" he asked.

The foreman, Thomas Murtaugh, stood. "We have, Your Honor."

Murtaugh passed two sheets of paper to Matthew Vogel, clerk of the court. Vogel unfolded the papers, and the crackling sound rolled around the quiet courtroom. The room was perfectly still. No one breathed loud or shuffled their feet. After a pause, Vogel spoke and his voice vibrated clearly around the courtroom.

"We, the jury," Vogel read, "find the defendant Peter Crudele guilty of murder, in manner and form as charged in the indictment, and we fix his punishment at death."

Peter stared ahead and did not blink. But Forbes was watching every move he made, looking for muscle reaction and vein bulges. She scribbled in her notebook how his skin looked gray. He had white pox marks on his forehead, which contrasted against his skin.

Vogel moved the papers around. He brought the page with Sabella's verdict to the top and read: "We, the jury, find the defendant Isabella Nitti, otherwise called Sabella Nitti, guilty of murder, in manner and form as charged in the indictment, and we fix her punishment at death."

The stunned courtroom sat in silence. Sabella patted her hair and looked hopefully around the room. She hadn't understood a word. Forbes inspected her from across the room. *Stubby fingers,* she wrote, *ingrained dirt in finger nails.*

The silence in the courtroom broke. Defense attorney Eugene A. Moran blurted, "Motion for a new trial."

"Denied," Judge David responded. "Clear the court."

Forbes watched as the Italian women who sat in the back of the gallery avoided looking at Sabella as they filed out. Forbes didn't speak a word of Italian, and she certainly had no knowledge of Sabella's distinct Barese dialect. She eyed them as they left. *They grinned at the verdict,* she noted, *they spent their days listening to the testimony and speculating on "how she got that young man."* They didn't support her, Forbes assumed. They were against her and she was guilty.

No one seemed to remember in the moments after the verdict was read that Sabella did not speak English. Or at least no one bothered to translate the verdict so she would understand it. And there was nothing in anyone's behavior that might have suggested to her that something was different about the day. The jury filed out of the courtroom, as they did at the end of each day. The women who sat in the back rows like they were patrons at a free opera had walked out without looking in her direction. That was typical, too. Her lawyer left abruptly, but he couldn't communicate with her anyway. What clues did she have?

Sabella saw her oldest son, James, push his way through the crowd of spectators and burst out the courtroom doors. Her middle son, Michael, was notably absent. Her youngest son, Charley, calmly wandered into the hallway and bought an orange from the peddler.

The defendants were separated. Peter was led away to his cell in the men's jail, and Sabella was led back to the women's section on the fourth floor, just as she had been each day for the previous week.

Until someone translated the verdict, Sabella would not know she was scheduled to hang in just ninety-five days.

2

GIVE THEM
THE EXTREME PENALTY

To the victor goes the courtroom. The attorney for the loser in a court case usually rushes off to appeal, but the winning side has the privilege of lingering to soak in the moment. Prosecutors Milton Smith and Michael Romano stayed to enjoy the accolades. Colleagues shared their congratulations, shook their hands, slapped their backs, and filled their ears with compliments. *Well done. Excellent work, gentlemen. That was justice.* They had just done what too many prosecutors before them had failed to do—convict a woman of murder. Almost every woman who had killed a husband or boyfriend in the past few years had walked free. More than two dozen times, prosecutors had stood stunned in the courtroom when the jury returned a not guilty verdict. It was as if juries in Chicago didn't believe a woman was capable of murder. Prosecutors' losing streak ended with Sabella Nitti's verdict, and Smith and Romano were heroes.

At twenty-six, Romano was at the beginning of his career and this was a major victory. He had graduated from law school at Northwestern University only a few years back, and he was already trying—and winning—cases that captured national headlines. And what a case to win. The verdict was more than a victory. It was a new precedent. Women needed to take heed—no more slipping arsenic into your husband's pie and then smiling sweetly at the jury to get an acquittal. Those days were gone.

Romano must have felt as though his life was proceeding as planned—a law degree, a prominent career, and a wedding planned for the next month. His fiancée, Cecilia Volini, was certain to be impressed. Cecilia's father was a prominent physician in Chicago, known for his philanthropic work. He rushed back to Italy several times to tend to humanitarian crises. Cecilia even went with him after the big earthquake hit Messina, and she saw her father lead Red Cross relief efforts. The Nitti verdict confirmed that she was indeed marrying an important man next month, one whose work made a difference.

Romano stepped to the side to speak with *Chicago Daily Tribune* reporter Genevieve Forbes. Forbes was tall, but Romano towered over the woman, like he did most people. He leaned in to speak, and referenced the rash of cases from the previous several years when women who murdered their husbands or boyfriends were set free. These women were very often beautiful or charming, and Chicago juries didn't seem to think an attractive woman was capable of murder. Not today. Today, justice was served and the late Francesco Nitti was vindicated. "The verdict has made husband killing no longer the safest sport on the continent. It was a cold-blooded murder, horrible, and she was treated like a cold-blooded murderess. That was just," Romano said.

Co-prosecutor Milton Smith didn't need to add a quote to the story. Already in his early thirties, he was quickly becoming the star prosecutor whom the state chose for its most important cases. And Sabella wasn't the first person he sent to the gallows. He was part of the two-attorney team who convicted Carl Wanderer two years earlier. Wanderer hired a hit man to shoot his pregnant wife during a fake holdup. After his wife was shot in the doorway of their home, Wanderer killed the hit man to make it look as though he was defending his wife. At first, it seemed as though his claim of self-defense might work. The newspapers ran a picture of him and his late wife along with headlines claiming a Great War vet tried to defend his wife. Then, things started to look suspicious. Why was the gun found in the hit man's hand? The police dug deeper and Smith presented Wanderer's elaborate plan to the jury. Newspapers across the country reported the story. Wanderer was a decorated lieutenant in the army, promoted and rewarded for killing in the open fields of France. Some newspapers opined that war was the reason a man like Wanderer didn't value human life. He was desensitized and unprepared for civilian life. But the jury didn't agree that Wanderer's "war insanity" was reflective of a societal ill. A few months later, Wanderer was hanged shortly after sunrise.

Sabella's verdict was another victory for Smith to bring home to his family. Another reason for them all to raise their glasses that evening around the dinner table. Still single, Smith lived with his parents on the South Side of the city. He would marry just a few years later and treat his bride to the most exclusive apartment building in Lincoln Park. At that point, he would be a state senator and the Smiths would fit in nicely with their neighbors—company presidents, physicians, and members of boards of directors. The Nitti verdict brought him one step closer to that life of prestige.

———

The Cook County criminal courthouse connected to the jail through a covered walkway. In the courthouse, the secretary typed the day's verdict, and it was further processed with signatures and official stamps. Across the walkway, Sabella Nitti sat in her jail cell, unaware that her fate was sealed with the ding of a typewriter and the squish of a rubber stamp. The stamp read FILED in large, hollow letters above the line CRIMINAL COURT OF COOK COUNTY. The date and the clerk's signature followed.

And then the workday drew to a close and the secretarial staff began their shutdown procedures. The ink pens were capped. The typewriters were blanketed with a dust cover as if they were going to sleep. Chairs were pushed under the desk. Fans were silenced. Lights were turned off. The secretaries clicked down the halls and out into the early evening sun. There were streetcars to catch. Elevated trains to ride. Speakeasies to visit. Dates to think about. Jazz records to play. Dinners to prepare. Lives to live.

Across the walkway from the courthouse, Sabella waited in her cell. Her small cot was positioned low to the ground and gave the appearance that she slept on the floor. The mattress was stuffed with hay and covered by a sheet topped with a blanket. In the corner of the barred cell was a single toilet where Sabella relieved herself in full view of any inmate, reporter, or guard walking past. There was also a small sink where she washed her hands and splashed water on her face.

In the early evening, Sabella went to the dining room for her meal. The food was limited, and a good dinner was a bowl of soup with bread and a mug of coffee. A disappointing night was when the kitchen worker had only a loaf of bread and a mug of coffee to hand out. Some women received meals or treats from family members, and that helped with the hunger. Sabella was alone; she had no one to bring her food—and no one to tell her the verdict.

"Sabella," someone should have said, passing her a cookie or wedge of cheese to fill her empty stomach. "The jury reached a verdict this afternoon. I regret I have bad news. The jury found both you and Peter guilty. The sentence is death. They will hang you in early October. You will stay here until your execution date." But what were her fellow inmates supposed to do? Have someone gently hold her hand while another woman acted out choking noises? There needed to be a translator. Someone to tell her the verdict and then calm her down with hope—her lawyer was working on an appeal. There was a chance.

When a translator arrived, he would have much to tell Sabella, filling her in on the trial proceedings she had not understood and warning her about what was to come. In October, Sabella would be led up a staircase onto a wooden stage and positioned above a trapdoor. Her hands would be tied behind her back, and her legs bound together. A noose would be tied around her neck and a hood positioned over her head. The charges against her would be read to her in English, along with the jury's verdict. After the charges were read and prayers offered, the trapdoor would drop, sending Sabella plummeting to her death.

Cook County officials used, or at least intended to use, the "long drop" technique when hanging an inmate. There were many ways to hang a person, and this technique was meant to be the most scientific, precise, and humane approach. An experienced executioner calculated the condemned person's weight and height and determined the ideal length for the rope as well as the amount of tension around the neck. When these were properly estimated and the trapdoor opened, the force immediately broke the person's neck. The result was instant death—no strangulation, no unnecessary suffering.

If the long drop was the enlightened ideal, the suspension technique—in which a rope was placed around the person's neck and he or she was either pushed off a platform or pulled into the air—was the barbaric opposite. It was not unusual for the suspension technique to take up to twenty minutes to slowly strangle the person, who suffered greatly, particularly when the smaller bones in the neck were crushed or the larynx was damaged.

Cook County had officially stopped using the suspension technique, but that didn't mean all hangings were quick and humane. Almost half the men executed from 1920 to 1923 did not die from a broken neck and were instead slowly strangled. Some officials blamed the rope. In the years preceding Sabella's conviction, Cook County had switched from a rope made from hemp to a coarser, stiffer option. The stiff rope tended to hold the head in place, like a seatbelt, even after the trapdoor dropped. The victim then suffocated to death from the pressure of the rope.

Slow strangulation was not the county's intention, and the execution process was subject to criticism. Other states were beginning to consider all hangings inhumane. Several states began using the electric chair instead. Ironically, this technique was demonstrated by revered inventor Thomas Edison, who invited the press to watch him electrocute unsuspecting horses, dogs, cats, and cattle. Edison's public spectacle of animal electrocution occurred in the late nineteenth century, when a new technology required public demonstration to be considered credible.

Over the years, more US states were requiring executions to take place behind a wall at a jail or other private space. Public behavior at these events had grown increasingly dangerous. Executions had become a spectacle. Crowds gathered as if they were there to be entertained by a show, and many people were excited—if not delighted—by the thought of watching a condemned person hang. Many revelers spent the prior evening drinking and celebrating the event. By the time the condemned was walked up to the gallows, there was an angry, alcohol-fueled current flowing through the crowd. Fights broke out among spectators, and the hostile atmosphere surged like a riot.

Private executions were meant to embody justice quietly served but were frequently as brutal as public hangings. The few select witnesses present were either lawmakers or politically connected spectators who were motivated to see the condemned hang. They felt no sympathy for the accused and did not worry about whether the long drop technique was employed properly or it failed and the person suffered a traumatic death.

Whether Sabella was to die instantly or suffer silently under her hood for twenty minutes, the jury believed she deserved to be the first woman executed in Chicago.

––––––––––

The reporters lingered in the hallway, walking past Sabella's barred cell as if she were on display at Lincoln Park Zoo. They carried small notepads in their hands, jotted down information and sprinted back to the newsroom when they were ready to write. Sometimes, they moved as a pack, descending on the same public phone and pushing to be first. Without an exclusive interview or informant, they all had the same story to tell, and the only thing that distinguished one hungry reporter from the next was being first.

Some of the more opportunistic reporters probably wouldn't have hesitated to tell Sabella the verdict if only they knew how to speak to her in Barese. Hell, they would tell her in Italian if they were able. Instead, they looked at her face for signs. Did she know she was going to hang?

No, not yet. She seemed to have the same expressions and worries as she did the day before. Certainly, someone would tell her soon. How would she respond? Cry? Scream? Go into fits of hysterics that would make a tremendous headline? Or accept the news stoically, as if she knew all along that her day of reckoning was coming?

Genevieve Forbes was one of many Chicago sensationalists who wanted to see Sabella's reaction. Forbes might have pretended otherwise, but she wanted to see this woman suffer. It was a great story. A woman in Chicago had *never* swung. And the fact that the condemned woman didn't even know her fate was headline news. Forbes held a lot of power. She didn't tell people what to think, but she told them what to think about. And at Forbes's direction, readers thought about Sabella's greasy hair and stubby fingernails. They thought of the evidence Forbes described, along with the reporter's assurance that Sabella Nitti was a violent woman.

Forbes and the other reporters left the jail that night disappointed. Neither the courthouse nor jail officials had arranged for a translator to come to Sabella's cell and tell her the verdict. The reporters abandoned the jail hallways reluctantly. They'd be back first thing tomorrow to catch her reaction.

3

I'LL TELL HER IF I HAVE TO

July 10, 1923

COOK COUNTY JAIL WARDEN Wesley Westbrook didn't know what to do. It was not *his* responsibility to tell Sabella Nitti the jury had found her guilty and sentenced her and her new husband to death. Still, he felt uncomfortable. He knew someone should tell her—perhaps her lawyer or someone from the courthouse? But not Westbrook; his job was to make sure that Sabella was safe and unharmed until her execution date.

Westbrook was a barrel-chested man with a square jaw, a cleft chin, and a full head of light brown hair. He had been hired to bring order to the chaos his predecessor caused. But Westbrook was struggling to assert control over the thousand or so inmates awaiting trial.

Anyone building a case against Westbrook's competence might have started with his appearance. His uniform looked as though it belonged to someone else and he had pulled it on quickly and tried to assume the role. His wide girth pulled on the four buttons running down his tight jacket. The sleeves stopped inches above his wrists, while his pants were loose and wrinkled.

Whether dealing with uniform or inmates, Westbrook tended to take the path of least resistance, particularly when his own self-interest was involved. The following year, the county would fire Westbrook after he allowed two jailed bootleggers to come and go as they pleased.

Westbrook would claim in court that one of the deputy sheriffs forced him to give these two men a free pass, and he had no choice but to go along with his superior. The judge wouldn't see Westbrook as an innocent bystander—probably due to one of the bootleggers' testimony that he paid the corrupt warden thousands of dollars each month for the privilege to come and go—and would send Westbrook to jail for four months.

For now, Westbrook had other problems, and the female inmates weren't his main concern. Compared to the men, the women were far easier to manage. They kept their cells relatively clean. Most washed the floors and their own uniforms, and hung their laundry on clothes-lines running from one steel wall to the next. They made their beds. And for the most part, they avoided fighting with each other. When the women behaved, Westbrook let them move freely in their section. They ate their meals in a dining room and visited the recreation room to read or exercise.

But the men were trouble. They required constant surveillance. They fought with each other. They ran bootleg booze operations from inside the jail walls. And they had an attitude of entitlement, as if the jail *owed* them a cup of coffee and roll each morning. The men were contained in dimly lit cells, eight tiers high. They lived their lives almost entirely in these suffocating cells, which was a drastically different situation than in the three dozen cells that made up the women's section. Sabella moved freely about the women's block, and she likely did not know that Peter was restricted from doing the same. The only time he left his cell was when the men in his cell block were ordered to the recreation room. But there were no means of recreation, and Peter crowded with hundreds of other men in a bleak room with nothing to do but stress and maybe fight.

Sabella kept busy. She asked for work and was assigned tasks such as laundry or cleaning. She volunteered each day to wash the floors in the women's cell block, and she did so without any regard for her appearance. When Sabella cleaned, her focus was on scrubbing the dirt and the stains off the cement floor. If the dirt migrated from the floor onto her hands or her face, so be it. Then everyone knew she was working as she should. She wore her prickly gray uniform without complaint. She took her shower each week. And she reduced herself to a small shadow that moved about the jailhouse quietly, asking for nothing and interfering with no one.

Sabella didn't have to work, and many of the women chose an idle incarceration. Some stretched on their straw beds, visited the recreation room to read or write letters, or talked to the reporters and tried to create public sympathy. But Sabella was used to being in the background. Not being able to read, write, or speak English meant she had nothing to say to the other inmates or the reporters and was unable to pass her time with a book or newspaper. Before her trial, she had no expectation that anyone should ever pay attention to her—especially a crowd of people. And so she did not seem to realize she was being watched that morning. Reporters were lurking about in the hallways, waiting to see her reaction in case someone described the long drop.

Genevieve Forbes was eager to see how Warden Westbrook handled the situation. She was pressing him, treating the matter as if it were his responsibility. Westbrook reminded her and the other reporters that it was the court's responsibility to inform an accused person of the outcome of the trial. Eventually, he conceded to Forbes, he would tell Sabella if he must.

The temperature in the jail rose as Sabella scrubbed. The day was expected to be hot, and it was already in the eighties by midmorning. Warm Chicago summers made this new land feel familiar, but the bitterly cold winters were like nothing she experienced at home in Bari, where temperatures rarely fell below the freezing mark, and the palm and olive trees were almost never iced with snow. The year of her arrest, the temperature in Chicago kept dropping below zero in January and February. All of Sabella's time was spent trying to keep warm. When she had to venture outside, she trudged through inches of snow wearing only scraps of carpet for shoes.

The rising heat in the jail didn't affect Sabella much. She didn't need to collapse on her bed like some of the other women to avoid sweating. She worked and remained productive. She was in the midst of her chores, unwashed and sweaty, when someone motioned for her to get off her hands and knees and leave the bucket behind; she had a visitor.

Sabella found her lawyer, Eugene A. Moran, waiting for her in the designated cell for attorney-inmate meetings. Although the cells in Cook County Jail were separated by solid steel walls, the women had little privacy. The cells had open fronts with steel bars running floor to ceiling that only the guards unlocked. The women heard each other through the walls—crying, complaining, or producing the sounds a person made when she thought no one was watching. The open fronts allowed anyone to stand and stare, and indeed the reporters were watching when Sabella was led to the meeting cell. They had been waiting for this moment since the verdict was handed down almost twenty-four hours earlier.

Sabella's face brightened when she saw Moran. She had been wondering when the trial would end and she might return home to her two little girls. She hoped Moran might have good news. Moran stood with another man, a translator named Charlie Molinelli, as well as Warden Westbrook.

Forbes and the other reporters stood in the hallway. They didn't need to be close to hear what was said. They didn't understand Sabella anyway; all they needed was her reaction, which they hoped would be dramatic. There was another type of hope in the room, too. The attorney, translator, and warden were likely bracing themselves for an emotional reaction. Who wanted to tell a condemned woman that she was going to die? Perhaps they hoped her reaction wouldn't be *that* bad. Two jailhouse matrons had also been summoned to the cell. It was better to have female staff handle these types of scenes.

Although the translator was a native of Genoa, Italy, he could communicate only minimally with Sabella. Despite the fact that Sabella would barely understand him, Molinelli was still not looking forward to his task. He kept looking for a reprieve, even as they stood before Sabella, ready to deliver the news.

"I'll tell her if I have to," Molinelli said as he swallowed hard.

"The court should tell her," Westbrook reminded.

But they were here now, and there was no sense in making the woman wait any longer. And so Moran began. He spoke in English, and Molinelli repeated his words in a dialect of Italian Sabella did not fully understand. *The trial ended yesterday. The jury reached a decision. They found you guilty in the death of Francesco Nitti. The punishment is death by hanging. The hanging won't happen right way. There is time to appeal. We're working on an appeal. We will try to get you a new trial.*

Sabella's face transformed as she sensed the news was bad. She was not going home. Those men from the court were going to kill her. Sabella was quiet as she absorbed the verdict. Then she took a step backward from Moran and Molinelli, as if the distance protected her from the news. She slinked back to the corner of the room and tried to make herself smaller. The weeping began. Slowly, softly at first and then building in a crescendo.

Forbes stood in the hallway and watched Sabella crouch in the corner, weeping with her back against the wall. Perhaps it was the cell bars that made the reporter feel as though she was in a zoo. She saw Sabella as an animal. *She's cornered,* Forbes wrote in her notepad. *Tortured by a new kind of trap.* The sounds of her weeping were animalistic. *Frenzied pleading of a cruel animal.*

Sabella could not breathe through her own tears. Her fear caused her to hyperventilate. As she took quick, fast breaths, she began to feel lightheaded. Then Sabella stopped and there was a moment of quiet before she dropped to the ground. A pause and then a plummet—she fainted.

For the assembled reporters, it was a great reaction. Representing the city's biggest dailies—the *Chicago Daily Tribune, Chicago Daily News, Chicago American, Chicago Courier, Chicago Evening Post, Chicago Herald-Examiner, Chicago Journal,* and *Chicago Post*—they were competing with each other but also with every reporter in their own newsroom who wanted the top stories and best assignments. They really couldn't have asked for more.

But each reporter still needed an edge. An exclusive with Molinelli or Moran. Perhaps a private talk with Warden Westbrook. The reporters dispersed to pursue their own angles. Some migrated to the hallway outside Sabella's cell, where she had been moved, to watch her wake up. When she did she cried into her pillow, speaking in Barese and whimpering. *She prays in Sicilian*, wrote one reporter, who wrongly thought Sicilian and Barese were one and the same.

For Forbes, Sabella's reaction was an indicator of guilt. She wrote in her front page story how hearing the verdict changed the "cruel, dirty, repulsive woman." Forbes thought Sabella showed no mercy the night of the killing, and she expected readers to feel no mercy for a murderer: "She was not the calm human who, the state charged, held her husband's head in her gnarled hands while her lover, 23 years her junior, pounded the sleeping farmer over the head with a six pound hammer."

Perhaps it was for the best that Sabella was illiterate. She already knew the jury, the sheriff, the judge, and the lawyers were against her. She didn't need to know how the next morning, a farmer in Freeport, Illinois, might open his newspaper and read how hard she cried when she learned she would die. Or how a housewife in Des Moines could study the picture that accompanied the story—under a headline labeling Sabella a HUSBAND KILLER.

4

SEND A WOMAN TO THE GALLOWS?
HOW COULD YOU?

July 11, 1923

ALL THE NEWSPAPERS HAD a girl reporter to handle the society pages, the fashion updates, and the tips on childrearing. *Chicago Daily Tribune* reporter Genevieve Forbes always wanted more challenging assignments than writing recipes or women's club updates, and in the seven years she'd been at the paper, she wasn't afraid to create stories for herself in order to be taken seriously. Just two years earlier, the *Tribune* had run her series in which she went undercover as an "immigrant girl" from Ireland to report the conditions newcomers faced when coming to Ellis Island. She sailed first to County Cork, Ireland, and then returned on an immigrant ship, posing as a young woman hoping for a new life in the States.

In her stories, Forbes revealed how vulnerable immigrants were being harassed and broken by the Ellis Island overseers. Some of the worst examples came from the numerous medical examinations immigrants were subjected to. Upon arrival, males and females were separated and inspected individually by a doctor or nurse. Overseers scared young women into thinking they would be stripped naked and violated. Forbes described how the men in charge enjoyed terrorizing females who had no power to fight back. She also detailed the fear faced by many parents whose children were being examined without them. One Italian man was a widower with a four-year-old daughter. The overseers forced him to surrender his little girl to unrelated female passengers during the exam. Forbes described these parents' fear that their children would be lost in the crowd and never seen again. Two Czech men cried as they were dragged up a flight of stairs, protesting in broken English, "My fam-lee, my fam-lee!"

Forbes's series was a success, and federal officials investigated abuse and corruption at Ellis Island following a heated public response. For Forbes, the story must have brought a sense of vindication for all those she saw abused on the voyage. In the moment, she had been powerless to help the shaking young women or the crying fathers. She avenged them through her writing. In this sense, there was a selfless quality to the series. But her immigration series also proved to the men in the newsroom that she didn't have to write about fashion or luncheons in order to handle women's issues. Stories about women were a profitable part of serious journalism.

That was Forbes's new role—serious stories about women. She began working her way into the political arena by interviewing—or at least trying to interview—candidates' wives in order to offer a woman's political perspective. Most of the wives were uneager to talk to the press. So whenever possible, Forbes covered women who ran for office or had political involvement. But such women tended to be harder to come by, and more often her editors assigned her to cover murder trials, especially the sensational trials of women accused of murder.

There was no shortage of these assignments. The previous year, two dozen Chicago men were killed by women. Only two of these women went to the penitentiary. Most had their cases dismissed by the coroner, grand jury, or a sympathetic judge. When a woman did stand trial, it seemed the whole city was watching. Forbes typically wrote about these women as if they deserved an assumption of guilt, and this was particularly true of her work covering the Nitti-Crudele trial. These stories read like a campaign against Sabella.

Readers weren't blind to Forbes's bias. Her version of Sabella was a caricature whose grotesque features communicated evil, even though Forbes knew full well that evil was rarely obvious. She had sat through trial after trial in which a guilty but beautiful woman somehow convinced a jury to acquit her. It was almost as if she wasn't taking chances with Sabella. Forbes labeled her gnarled and dirty, and described her language as a series of grunts and moans—as if she were a demon. At times, the photos that accompanied the stories advanced Forbes's argument. Sabella appeared hunched over with her head hung low.

Forbes clearly wove fictional elements into her stories about Sabella, although readers focused on the excitement of the trial likely did not notice. She wrote about events that happened simultaneously as if she were witness to both. On the Monday evening after the Nitti verdict was handed down, Forbes was at the courthouse and then the jail, both on Dearborn Street, just north of the Loop. She heard the verdict, watched as the courtroom emptied and the prosecutors were congratulated. Forbes took notes as Sabella returned to jail without any understanding she had received the death penalty. Forbes then lingered around the jail to see if defense attorney Eugene A. Moran or some court representative might come to the jail and give Sabella the bad news. But the story she filed that evening also suggested she was seven miles away on the South Side of Chicago. Forbes wrote as though she was with the jury foreman, Thomas Murtaugh, when he returned home from the trial and was confronted by his wife.

Murtaugh was a cigar salesman who lived with his wife, Catherine, and their eight-year-old daughter, Margaret, on Forty-Second Street on the South Side of the city. Mrs. Murtaugh worked part-time as a cashier in a restaurant and Forbes's story suggested she heard the news about the verdict while at work.

The story read as if Forbes stood in the living room, chatting with Mrs. Murtaugh when her husband walked through the door. And Forbes's descriptive and dramatic style made readers feel as if they did the same.

"Send a woman to the gallows! How could you? Hang a woman! Tell me you didn't really vote for it," Mrs. Murtaugh accused as her husband walked through the door.

"But the evidence," Mr. Murtaugh defended. "That woman's a fiend. She held her husband's head while her lover beat out the man's brains with a six pound hammer. I saw the hammer."

"Yes but they are going to hang her. Oh!"

Mrs. Murtaugh reportedly collapsed into a chair at the thought of Sabella Nitti hanging for her crime. Forbes's story claimed that Mrs. Murtaugh threatened to return home to her mother if Sabella Nitti did indeed go to the gallows. Mr. Murtaugh, in fear of losing his wife, begged his fellow jurymen to reason with his wife, reveal the evidence, and explain how the decision was rational and just.

Anyone reading closely could deduce it was unlikely that Mr. Murtaugh connected with his fellow jurors and begged for help—all in time for the press deadline. Those men were at home on a Monday evening, and Mr. Murtaugh did not ride the streetcar around the city, visiting these men's homes while Forbes or a scout watched on. Besides, anyone who personally knew the Murtaugh family could tell Forbes took liberty with the story. Mrs. Murtaugh's two younger sisters lived with her and Mr. Murtaugh. Her mother was actually dead, as was her father. There was no childhood home to return to if Sabella Nitti did hang.

————

What sold newspapers faster than a headline about a husband killer? A headline about two husband killers. On the Monday the jury reached a verdict in Sabella's trial, another capital case in New York City came to a conclusion. Only hours before the Chicago verdict was read, a judge in New York set an August execution date for Anna Buzzi to go to the electric chair. It was a stunning headline—*two women slayers given death*.

Anna had received the death penalty a week earlier in the murder trial of her married, much older boyfriend, Frederick Schneider. The two had lived together for the previous eight years, until he was found shot in his car on a quiet highway.

Frederick had paid for his wife's upkeep in another residence. To keep up appearances, Frederick and Anna sometimes told people she was his housekeeper. The press saw her as a social climber. One New York reporter wrote how she "pathetically" called "herself 'Mrs. Schneider.'" The same story suggested that Frederick and his wife had decided to reconcile. Perhaps angry or fearful of being booted from her lavish apartment, the police alleged, Anna had gone for a drive with Frederick, pulled a gun, shot him twice on the side of the road, and scurried away while he died. Newspapers across the country plucked the story off the wire and put it on their front pages.

Anna had an alibi, but she also had a lot of enemies. Her brother-in-law testified that he had lent her the gun that matched the bullet shells found at the crime scene. He also said she confessed to him.

Like Sabella, Anna Buzzi was sentenced to die within two months' time. The two women received similar treatment from the press. The murder reports and trial updates were shaped to bring satisfaction to a public that felt increasingly uncertain about how women and men were to relate in modern life. It had been only a few years since women received the right to vote, and everything felt as though it was changing. Girls were cutting their hair to look like boys. They reduced their weight until they were willowy and lean and resembled young men. They were going to school and moving into apartments on their own. It was as though the order to everything was changed, as evident in how women were now *killing* men.

There was a contingent of men in the country that was unnerved by these changing norms. Some argued that Sabella Nitti and Anna Buzzi were symbols of female advancement gone wrong. Others felt that if women wanted equal rights in voting and political participation, then they must take the good with the bad. If a woman insisted on pulling a lever in a voting booth, she must accept the possibility of having a noose wrapped around her neck. One Chicago editorial made its way across the country with side-by-side photos of Anna and Sabella. "If the feminist movement has given women equal rights," the author opined, "it has also made them equally responsible for their wrongs."

The papers reported how Anna took her verdict stoically. She paced around her cell and joked with visitors on the condition of the accommodations. She was raised in America and had more understanding of the court system than Sabella. Sabella, readers learned, did not take the news well, and soon reporters stopped telling the two women's stories together. It no longer made sense to compare the women or run their photos together. Anna was a plump woman whose wealthy beau funded her beautiful wardrobe. Though muscular, Sabella was thin and ragged, worn down by years of malnutrition. They just didn't compare well. One woman had a sense of what was going on, and the other was confused and terrified.

Anna was likely guilty of her crime, but doubt shadowed Sabella's sentence from the start. The newspapers continued in the following week to report Sabella's growing fear, and it struck many readers as sad. Others in the jail also seemed shaken by the verdict, particularly the jailhouse matrons. These seasoned guards were jarred by Sabella's despair, and such an atypical reaction on the part of the matrons was interesting to the reporters. They wrote how two of the matrons were tasked with carrying Sabella back to her cell after she heard the verdict and passed out. Her fear and her vulnerability were so upsetting that even the matrons began to cry.

Jailhouse matrons rarely displayed emotion; that was a key part of the job. They knew that being manipulative was a natural reaction to being incarcerated. The inmates were desperate and some of them were very conniving. They wanted more of everything. More food, more letters, more newspapers, more bedding, more visits with family, and more information about their trials. Some clamored for more attention from the reporters in the hope that newspaper stories might help their case. Sabella had shown none of this desperation. She was nothing but a quiet shadow in the jailhouse who did her chores, avoided conflict, and stoically lived her days without her children.

Now, in Sabella's mind, death was certain. She knew nothing of the appeals process. In contrast, Anna Buzzi waited calmly after her execution date was announced, knowing she wasn't going to be strapped to any electric chair until the appeals court had viewed the court transcripts and scrutinized the proceedings for wrongdoing. Even if that failed, the governor could grant a stay of execution up until the last moment. Her sentence wasn't final, she knew, until the lever on the electric chair was pulled.* None of this information was revealed to Sabella, who sobbed on her cot. She spoke to herself in Barese, muttering her questions and concerns to her own ears. There was no one for her to speak to, no one who would understand her if she tried to confide. The other inmates brought their soothing tones and sympathetic looks to Sabella's bedside. There was comfort in their care and kind gestures, but there was a limit to how much a person could be soothed in the absence of words.

The idea of execution was completely foreign to Sabella. She was just a young girl when the newly unified Italy banned capital punishment. Convicted killers in Bari were not marched through the narrow, cobblestone streets and onto gallows constructed in the town square. The people of her province did not gather excitedly to watch someone hang, nor did they look forward to reading about the details in the newspaper the next day.

But if execution was foreign to Sabella, violence and physical pain were normal. She had been beaten her entire married life, and knew the hanging would be her worst punishment yet. She accepted that she was to die, but she refused to suffer the way the county intended. And she couldn't wait weeks or months, anticipating the impending agony.

Sabella stood and bowed her chin so the top of her head faced forward. She pushed forward, as if she were running, and slammed her head against the wall. Crumpled on the ground, she waited for a darkness to confirm she was dead. But the only thing she saw through the streams of blood were the jailhouse matrons, carrying her to the hospital unit. This attempt failed. She'd have to try again.

---

* Anna Buzzi received a second trial and was found not guilty. She promptly went shopping in Times Square to celebrate.

Part II

THE YEAR BEFORE

5

GONE

July 1922

ON A WARM SUMMER DAY, Sabella, Francesco, and their farmhands slipped in and out of the corn rows. It was a cicada year in Chicago. Every seventeen years, the winged insects emerged from the ground and took to the trees to find a mate and complete their life cycles. The droning song of the cicada during these years was incessant. The *Chicago Daily Tribune* called the bugs a type of locust and warned readers to cover young trees with cheesecloth to protect growing branches from the weight of a swarm of thousands. But the cicadas were actually harmless. They would not swarm on the Nitti family crops and cause devastation. They merely hid high in the trees, their vibrating calls muffling the sounds that Sabella and the work crew made in the corn rows—feet squishing in the mud, cornstalks rustling as bodies breezed past.

Sabella was barely over five feet tall, and the corn was already waist high, with the tallest leaves inching above her shoulders. Each member of the work group moved from one plant to the next, ripping off the tassel that grew from the top of the stalk. Sabella moved from stalk to stalk—bending the tassel, listening for the snap, pulling it from the plant, and dropping it on the ground. The two girls, Filomena and Mary, stayed close to their mother. There was no one to mind them, and they toddled around Sabella's skirt.

To a passerby flying past in a motorcar, the scene might have seemed as though it was from another century. Sabella was dressed in a work shirt and skirt. Her long, graying hair was typically pulled into a bun. Most Chicago women had taken to wearing sleek skirts and drop-waist tops. They colored their graying hair, trimmed their locks to their chins, and then wrapped their tresses around little rollers that set their hair into finger waves.

Sabella never fussed in front of a mirror. She never donned a cloche hat and posed in front of her reflection, carefully turning her chin to study herself from several angles. Her hats were strictly utilitarian and meant to block the sun while she detasseled the corn or yanked weeds. Her homemade carpet shoes were also functional, certainly not fashionable. Her loose skirt moved easily while she worked and hit around her knees, short enough so it didn't dip into the mud when she crouched next to a cornstalk. To a typical Chicago woman from Austin or Hyde Park, Sabella and the men who worked alongside her must have looked like pioneers or sharecroppers from the 1880s, hard at work on their primitive farm.

———————

Sabella was just fifteen when she married Francesco Nitti. He was already in his midtwenties, and the practice of marrying a teenage girl to an older man was standard in the Southern Italian provinces. It was meant to be for a girl's benefit. A girl who married young didn't shame herself with the local boys. And she was young enough to still be obedient, so her man could mold her into the type of woman he needed.

Francesco and Sabella lived together for a decade in Triggiano, a town built in the fourteenth century about three miles from the Adriatic Sea. She gave birth to Vincenzo when she was seventeen, and then Michele came when she was twenty-one. Pasquale was born when she was twenty-six. She lost an infant when the boys were young, and it wasn't uncommon for families to grieve several lost children. The age gaps between her children indicated that Sabella possibly miscarried other babies. Or she mindfully spaced out her pregnancies by doing what experienced women advised— fed the baby at her breast for as long as possible to avoid another pregnancy.

But then Francesco left and immigrated to America when his youngest was less than a year old. That stopped any more babies from coming, for a time. Francesco came to Chicago with thirty dollars in his pocket and a desire to find a *padrone* to connect him with a job. After five years, he returned to Italy and brought his oldest son, Vincenzo, back to Chicago to work. When Isabella came a few years later with Michele and Pasquale, she had been apart from her husband for almost a decade. She found that he was now Frank, not Francesco, and Vincenzo preferred the name James.

When they immigrated, Michele was fourteen years old and probably none too pleased to learn how Americans did not pronounce his name "Mick-el-ee." They said Michelle as if he were a girl. He opted to go by Michael. Pasquale switched to Charley. Within a year, Sabella gave birth to a daughter, Filomena, and then Maria, called Mary, was born in 1919.

Sabella and Francesco rented a plot of land and set up a small truck garden farm in Stickney, a rural area bordering the city limits. It was far enough away from the city that they had space to farm but close enough for Francesco to drive the carriage each week to a farmer's market in Chicago to sell their produce. It was a meager existence and the family worked from daybreak until after sunset, although the older boys slipped away from the farm on a regular basis. Sabella grew to resent her sons for leaving the family when their labor was needed, and then showing up when they ran out of options elsewhere. But she always let them reclaim their spot at the table, and they knew the boundaries of her forgiveness had not yet been exceeded.

Sabella toiled the hardest and her work was never done. A farm woman was allocated both indoor and outdoor chores. It was unheard of for a man to wash bedding or cook a meal when he had a wife to do it for him. There were times when his outdoor work was complete— the horses were fed and the barn door was shut, the tools were put away—and he rested. A woman never claimed the same. This was why so many men preferred a fifteen-year-old bride; they took her young, before she ever knew of a better life.

———

The Nitti farm was an outlier—separated and left behind from a city rushing toward progress. By 1922, Chicago had an extensive sewer grid and a fresh water system that had nearly eliminated diseases such as cholera and typhoid. Utility companies were well established and pumped gas and electricity into neighborhoods across the city. A typical Chicago home or apartment was heated by radiators, cooled by electric fans, and washed by fresh water poured directly from the tap.

Sabella didn't know the joy of running a tap and stepping into a steaming tub. She hauled in buckets of water to fill a bath or wash a load of laundry. When she had to use the bathroom, she moved through her darkened house and stepped out to the backyard privy. Such a lifestyle was near obsolete in Chicago, and the Nitti family's dated ways isolated them from a city advancing toward modernity. Sabella didn't even have a fireplace or an electric stove. All the appliances one expected to see in a Chicago home were notably absent. There was no modern stove in the kitchen, nor was there a radiator system to pipe heat into the various rooms. The only heat source was an old wood-burning stove the family used for both warmth and cooking. Food in the Nitti kitchen was kept cold with ice, a practice many Chicagoans were abandoning in favor of electric iceboxes.

The Nitti household looked different, and it sounded different as well. Sounds from a phonograph or an electric rug sweeper did not fill the house. There was no buzzing from a dough mixer or an electric washing machine. The sounds in the Nitti household were ones that were heard a century before: The candles used to light the dark evenings sometimes snapped and sizzled. The logs stuffed into the stove softened as they burned, shifted, and then made a thudding sound when they rolled off each other. A cast-iron pan filled with fresh-baked bread clanged as it was pulled from the stove. The cat meowed, allowed to come inside on a cold winter's night. Farmhand Peter Crudele's footsteps vibrated on the wooden ladder as he climbed to his mattress in the upstairs loft. And the feather-filled mattresses made crinkling sounds when a tired body plopped down to sleep.

These were the more pleasant sounds in the Nitti household. But they were frequently muffled by the clamor of violence, which confirmed the family was indeed living in another century. Few parents in the Chicago area withheld a spank or a slap when a child was impertinent. But the Nitti home was different. Francesco was violent, and he filled his home with sounds of skin being slapped, bodies tumbling backward, bones cracking, pleading, screaming, and weeping. In the aftermath, bruises and whip marks were illuminated in candlelight, perhaps as they were in generations before.

By the end of July 1922, the home was still shaken by the explosions of two violent episodes earlier that summer. In the first, disquiet brewed between sixteen-year-old Charley and his father. The fight had started when Charley voiced a complaint. He felt he was working too hard on the farm and it didn't seem fair. His older brothers, Michael and James, came and went as they pleased, and Charley also wanted a break. Other parents might have issued a stern warning or a light slap as a response. Some might have awarded Charley additional chores and given him something to really complain about. Perhaps others would have ignored the boy or even half-listened while he aired his grievances.

Francesco showed no such leniency, especially when his son implied that Francesco's job, taking the vegetables to market, was an easy one.

"Pa," Charley complained. "I can't do it anymore. The day is too long. You don't know how it is to work on the farm."

The accusation that Francesco did not know how to work on a farm sparked his fury. He slapped Charley, but the boy had received enough beatings in his life that one slap didn't deter him. Charley moved to hit his father back.

In the past few years, Charley and his father had fought increasingly. Once, Charley rushed for the shotgun and held his father at bay by threatening to shoot if he didn't back down. That victory had gone to Charley, but this one went to Francesco. When the beating became too severe, Sabella stepped in and tried to calm her husband. Francesco was too far gone in his rage and he turned his fury on his wife.

All the residents on the farm heard Francesco beat Sabella. Filomena and Mary heard their mother cry. Michele Desant, a farmhand, witnessed such abuse as a jarring part of his workday. And in the fields outside, farmhand Peter Crudele heard his kind friend Sabella being abused.

The aftermath of Francesco's beatings was always the same. People moved carefully, terrorized by the sudden violence. The dark light cast shadows on their bruises and hid Sabella's face as she kept her eyes cast toward the ground. This time, Francesco wasn't calming as quickly as he had in the past, and both Sabella and Charley anticipated another eruption. Charley wasn't American born, but he spoke English and knew such savagery wasn't the way other Chicagoans lived. Charley prodded his mother to follow him to the office of a local magistrate to report the abuse.

It's likely that Sabella thought the magistrate would simply speak to Francesco, much like a priest in Bari might do if a beaten woman appealed for help. It's also likely that at sixteen, Charley was wise enough to know he was getting his father into trouble. The magistrate saw a bruised woman and her beaten son, and promptly issued an arrest warrant for assault. Francesco seemed unprepared for his arrest, and he protested as the handcuffs were tightened around his wrists.

Sabella declined to press charges, and the arrest should have been short-lived. But Francesco was impertinent with the officers and they looked for an excuse to punish him. They searched his pockets and pulled out a pocket knife and a razor. He was promptly arrested on weapons charges and pushed into the police car.

Francesco returned to the farm within a few days after his arrest. A magistrate dismissed the charges and relieved him of his legal troubles. But his power over his family had been eroded by the police, the lawyers, and the humiliation that no one posted his bond. Perhaps his sons saw the old man as weakened when he returned. Perhaps Michael, who was young and strong at twenty-one, sensed his father's vulnerability. The moment felt right for Michael to approach Francesco and demand he give him the $300 the family had saved.

Michael wanted the money to fund his marriage. His request wasn't a mere want, it was an actual need. It was customary among Italian grooms in Chicago to pay for the wedding. It was also expected that a groom secure a residence and provide the furnishings. The typical bride and groom moved into a one-bedroom apartment, and the more moneyed found themselves in larger units, perhaps even a single-family home. Grooms then used store credit to select davenports, dinettes, rugs, and lamps for their new residences. The most fortunate brides were able to select the furniture and send their fiancés the bill. Few parents allowed their daughters to consider a man who didn't have the appropriate funds. Michael was at a disadvantage, and the jump from his parents' farm to a small apartment would be near impossible without the windfall of the family's savings. When Michael approached his father to ask for money, he must have decided that demanding was a better approach than asking.

It was the wrong strategy. Francesco refused and slapped his son for insulting him with such a demand. Michael responded with an intense fury that Francesco couldn't match. They pushed at each other, clawed at each other's faces, but then Michael beat his father into submission. He relented only when his father began crying and curled into a ball, holding his stomach.

Francesco emerged from the fight with two blackened eyes and what felt like several broken ribs. His pride was wounded and the fight wasn't over for him. When anyone asked about his bruises, Francesco quickly answered that it was his no-good son who had beaten him down. Francesco was shadowboxing, fighting back with blows to his son's reputation. But it was a performed arrogance meant to heal his pride. Quietly, Francesco had fears his son would return to finish the fight. After the fight, Francesco disappeared for a few days. There was a possibility that he was hiding from Michael. When Francesco resurfaced, he didn't tell Sabella where he had been, and she knew better than to challenge him by asking.

For the next two weeks, Francesco went to bed with two darkened eyes. The fight with Michael wasn't his only humiliation. There was a shameful rumor that his wife was intimate with one of the farmhands, Peter Crudele. Sabella told Francesco the rumors were false, and encouraged him to fire the young man if it made him feel better. But getting rid of Crudele wasn't an option. Francesco had fired him earlier in the summer and found the farm languished after a few weeks without his help. There was no point in letting him go when his help was needed.

By late July, Francesco's fight with Michael was weeks old, but it wasn't over. One Saturday night, Francesco sensed Michael might return to hurt him or damage their crops by setting them on fire. The family ate a late dinner with the farmhands. After dinner, Francesco sent Sabella to bed and told her he would be inside after he checked on the oats. While he waited and watched in the dark, Sabella fell asleep easily, but she woke up just before three in the morning, jarred by the realization that she was alone. Francesco was not in bed.

Sabella moved around the dark room, feeling her way into her shoes. She moved through the shanty and realized Charley was missing as well. His absence wasn't particularly unnerving; Charley, like his brothers, had taken to leaving home for days. No one knew what he did when he left the house. He went into the city and lived another life Sabella knew nothing about.

Sabella stepped outside to see if Francesco was with the horses or in the fields. The temperature was cool for July. The day had reached the upper seventies, and now the quiet early morning air required a light sweater or a shawl. Sabella blinked into the dark fields and toward the barn. There was no sign of Francesco.

Everything was quiet and untouched. Back inside, she woke Jennie, a farmhand, and asked for help. Francesco might be in trouble and she had to go to the police. Jennie needed to come and translate. The two women stepped into the darkened street. It was at least a mile walk to the residence of the police magistrate, Louis Kral. If they hurried, it would take them about twenty minutes to walk the distance.

Kral answered the door bleary eyed and surprised. He was a full-time restaurant owner, and police magistrate when required. He looked at the whimpering woman standing on his doorstep. Sabella was tearful and ragged in her carpet shoes. Her panicked gaze fluttered between him and the woman she brought to translate. Jennie explained how Francesco was missing and he might be in danger. Kral was unmoved by the sight of Sabella's panicked expression, and he referred her to Stickney's chief of police, Charles Eisele. The two women were given directions and told to walk the distance to Eisele's house.

Sabella was hysterical by the time they knocked on the police chief's door. Francesco had been missing for several hours and the police magistrate was indifferent to her pleas. Jennie translated over Sabella's sobs and again explained how Francesco never came to bed. Sabella pleaded desperately in Barese for the man's help. Eisele felt as though she was yelling at him, but he agreed to help with a search. He assured they would check the fields and ask around town to see if anyone had seen her husband.

When Sabella returned to the shanty, she looked around the house to see what might be amiss. The $300 was gone. Did Michael come back for the money and to finish his fight? Or did Francesco take the money and run off for a new life? Sabella feared both scenarios. Francesco had lived almost a decade without her when he first immigrated to the United States. He knew how to live life without his wife.

As the day progressed, the police saw no sign of Francesco. They looked over the fields to see if he lay hidden among the crops. Eisele came to the farmhouse at the end of the day to update Sabella. Someone translated, repeating all the chief had to say. *We've checked the fields. We've looked in nearby farms. We cannot find Francesco Nitti, he is gone.*

Sabella broke down in an explosive display of emotion. She wailed and then turned violent toward herself, as if it were her fault he was gone. The police chief watched as Sabella slid her fingernails down her own cheeks and the blood rose to the open wounds. He saw her pull on her own hair as if she wanted to rip it from her head. It was such an odd reaction to see a woman turn on herself when given such bad news. It was something he would not forget.

6

THE CRIME IN DASSO'S HEAD

ON SEPTEMBER 14, 1922, the *Chicago Daily Tribune* warned readers the day would be "unsettled," with strong winds and intermittent heavy rain predicted. There was never a newspaper delivered to the front porch of the Nitti household. Neither Sabella nor her missing husband could read. But it would have been nice to see some sort of warning that life, too, was about to become unsettled.

Ever since Francesco had disappeared into the night two months ago, the Cook County deputy sheriff, Paul Dasso, had been stopping by the farm to ask questions. Dasso was like the cicadas from earlier in the summer, constantly buzzing around. He interviewed the neighbors. He tracked down a few people whom the Nitti family knew from the old country, primarily James and Anna Volpe, and asked them about life on the Nitti farm.

Dasso buzzed closest to Charley's ear. He badly wanted to talk to the boy and find out what Charley knew about his father's disappearance. Charley didn't give the lawman anything helpful, and Sabella didn't have much to say to him either. But Dasso was relentless, and he would get his information elsewhere.

Sabella had little time for Dasso, nor could she sit idly by the window and watch for Francesco to return. She had to keep the farm alive, tend to the crops and animals. It was like all those years ago in Bari with Francesco gone. Year after year she had managed with her two young sons. Now she would find a way to manage with two young daughters and sons who were around to pitch in only occasionally, when they felt like it.

Sabella likely knew little about Dasso except that he was a lawman who caused her trouble. But there was a darkness to the man that the city seemed to have forgotten. Prior to becoming a deputy sheriff for the county, Dasso was the assistant superintendent of a juvenile jail for boys. In 1898, a former cook for the jail complained the boys were being treated cruelly. The city slowly began investigating allegations that the boys were either whipped with a leather strap or pushed into a dark cell for hours at a time.

Dasso believed the punishments were just and boasted to the *Chicago Daily Tribune* that there was an order to the system at the facility. In the mornings, the boys were lined up outside their cells. Boys who were accused of some sort of infraction—Dasso never described the offenses—were allowed to explain their side of the story. Dasso and another superintendent stood as the judge and jury, listening to the boys' pleas before determining a sentence.

The jail housed boys ages six to sixteen. Dasso found it was most effective to lock the little boys into a darkened room for hours. Little boys, he told the *Tribune*, were afraid of the dark, so the terrifying punishment was effective. Older boys, he believed, needed to be whipped.

A boy sentenced to a whipping was forced to undress, get down on his hands and knees, and receive up to eight blows with a leather strap. The other young inmates were forced to watch the punishment as a deterrent. Punishments typically occurred daily, with as many as five boys being whipped in front of the other prisoners. The boys howled during the whippings and pleaded for the lashing to stop.

The city was horrified by the news, and the aldermen rushed to tour the facility and evaluate the punishments. The city council appointed a special subcommittee to further investigate, and Dasso had to defend himself at an inquiry. The charges were true, the lawmen decided, and Dasso needed to be fired from the position. But Dasso was a connected man, and Chicago mayor Carter Harrison Jr. took eight months to review the council's recommendation. After a two-hour, closed-door meeting with the mayor, Dasso finally left his keys on the desk and resigned. Almost immediately, he became a deputy sheriff for Cook County.

Sabella was outside in the vegetable garden with Peter, her young daughters, and the farmhand Jennie. Sabella watched as Dasso sped in from the east in an automobile. Dasso assessed this crew of farmworkers as he approached and slowed to a stop. He saw Jennie wearing her khaki pants and noted that she was dressed like a man. He saw the two little girls near their mother. He didn't perceive any imminent threat in this arrest and decided to keep his gun holstered.

Dasso approached Sabella and Peter, speaking in the Italian dialect his parents had taught him. He oscillated to English when speaking with Peter, but spoke to Sabella in a language she did not comprehend. Dasso was convinced that if an Italian and Barese speaker just spoke slowly enough, they could understand each other. He failed to realize when he was not fully understood. He also thought he understood more than he truly did.

The nature of the charges against Sabella Nitti and Peter Crudele would have made some lawmen uncomfortable, but Dasso had little shame. He wasn't there to arrest them regarding the disappearance of Francesco. He didn't have enough evidence for that. He was instead arresting Sabella and Peter on adultery charges. The alleged couple faced a possible $200 fine and up to six months in jail. Dasso theorized that Peter and Sabella were lovers and had surely knocked off Francesco so that they could be together. But without a body or any witnesses, Dasso could not detain these two for murder. There was no evidence that crime had even occurred.

Dasso explained in Italian that the two were under arrest and required to leave immediately for detainment in the Oak Park jail, where they could post bond. If they had no money for bond, they would remain in detention until their case was heard in front of a local magistrate.

He likely also excluded how he had shopped around for a jurisdiction sympathetic to his accusations. Both Sabella and Peter were residents of Stickney; the developing suburb bordered Berwyn and Cicero to the north and Chicago to the east. An Illinois town needed at least three thousand residents in order to have its own court system, and Stickney wasn't even halfway there. The community tended to rely on Berwyn and Cicero for legal needs, and Oak Park was three miles to the north. It was not a neighboring community, and it didn't make sense for Stickney officials to turn to Oak Park with law enforcement matters. It was more likely that Dasso had a friend on the Oak Park force willing to help him advance the arrest.

Despite Francesco's accusation and some area gossip, the adultery accusations against Sabella and Peter were weak. Exactly where and when they were supposedly having their affair was unclear. There were no known witnesses to such a love affair, and the configuration of the farm worked against the theory. Unless the pair was sneaking off to make love in the cornfields, there was no private place for them to be intimate. The front of the house was visible from the eastern road. And the interior was packed with people—both family and farmhands— which would make having an affair difficult to achieve.

Nonetheless, Dasso handcuffed Peter and Sabella and then separated them. Sabella was allowed to take her youngest daughter, Mary, with her to jail, but Filomena was left behind on the farm with Charley and Jennie. Just five years old, Filomena was a tiny, waiflike creature. Her hair had been cropped close to her head, which revealed strikingly long ears. Her oldest brother, James, was almost twenty years her senior, and she was now at his mercy as he took control of the house. James wanted the house, he wanted cash for the tools, and he wanted his mother to take the blame for the disappearance of his father. In Filomena, he thought he might have a little witness, someone he could manipulate into claiming she saw her mother attack her father. In Dasso, James knew he had an accomplice.

———————

Neither Sabella nor Peter had the money to post bond. They would have to remain in jail and wait for an administrative hearing. Dasso continued coming around the Nitti farm during this time, interrogating the children and looking for evidence to match his manufactured motive.

James brought Filomena to his own attorney's office for questioning. He plopped the girl on the attorney's desk, and the older man sat eye to eye with her, asking what she remembered from the night her father disappeared. The *Chicago Daily Tribune* later reported the little girl told the attorney she saw Sabella and Peter loading her father's dead body onto a wagon. Dasso's and James's efforts appeared successful; the prosecutor thought five-year-old Filomena's statement was enough to advance the case.

Typically, defendants would appear in a preliminary hearing, but Sabella and Peter were reported to have waived—or misunderstood—their rights. The next step was a brief appearance before a grand jury at the end of September. The grand jury was unimpressed by the prosecutor, who presented no proof that Francesco Nitti was murdered or even dead. And there were few credible witnesses. Filomena was slight and uncertain, and Charley had gone into hiding and avoided testifying. The grand jury refused to indict Sabella and Peter.

But Dasso still had Sabella and Peter on the adultery charges. The two were still in jail, waiting for a magistrate to hear the case. Dasso was creative, to say the least. He knew that it was easy to detain Sabella and Peter on the adultery charges but nearly impossible to convict them. In Illinois, the law blended the criminalization of fornication and adultery. At first glance, it seemed as though the law was meant to protect the sanctity of marriage so that a faithful partner had recourse if his or her spouse went outside the marriage. But Dasso should have known the statute was designed with a key clause—the affair must have been "open and notorious" to the community.

The open and notorious definition indicated the creators of the law were trying to block unmarried couples from living together. If a man and woman were not married and set up a house together, the affair was considered open and notorious to the community. The charges were dropped if the couple married. The law proved useful when Mormon settlers moved into the state in the late 1830s and scandalized Illinois residents by practicing bigamy. Illinois did have anti-bigamy laws on the books, but keeping the adultery and fornication statutes in the criminal code was helpful in case a man kept his wives in different homes and claimed to officials that he was unmarried to the second or third wife.

By the time Sabella and Peter were arrested, the punishment for adultery or fornication had softened almost a century prior. At worst, they would wait in jail for their hearing and then pay a fine or possibly serve a few more weeks in jail. It wasn't much, but it was all the time James needed.

7

THE WIDOW'S AWARD

October 20, 1922

ON LASALLE STREET, James Nitti walked underneath a concrete archway and into the Stock Exchange Building. He was not a tall man, nor was he broad or imposing. But he wore a hard look on his face that encouraged others to think twice before provoking him. James was handsome, with dark brown eyes and olive skin. His thick hair softly waved, and the broadness of his forehead narrowed through his jawline to his pointed chin. He did not have the exhausted, dirty look that his mother wore, nor did he mirror her raggedy clothing. James had a suit with a high neck collar and a tie, nothing that would impress the upper classes, but respectable enough to elevate himself from his mother and her carpet shoes.

He strode through the lobby, his feet sweeping over the marble mosaic floor. He paused at the elevator bay, waiting for one of the ten automatic elevators to bring him to the thirteenth floor. James, for all his bravado, was a country boy, a *contadino*. He knew nothing of skyscrapers, office buildings, or elevator rides. At twenty-four years old, he knew of farm work and long carriage rides to an open-air market. He knew of horses and plows. Broken fences and tool repair. Sometimes he knew of factory work or road repair. But he knew nothing of the financial or legal world of Chicago. He was here because his lawyer directed him to make a statement in front of a court reporter.

James stepped into a world that was too big for him. The lobby was ornate, trimmed with mahogany and oak and brightened with electric lights. Perhaps James was aware that he was stepping outside his comfort zone, and maybe he felt intimidated by the grandness of the lobby. Or perhaps the fancy space was misleading him into thinking he was powerful and capable.

The building had been designed about two decades earlier by the famous Chicago architects Dankmar Adler and Louis Sullivan. Adler spent the better part of the late nineteenth century building the most beautiful and loved buildings in Chicago. Sullivan was a mentor to the famed Frank Lloyd Wright, and part of the team who built the White City during the Columbian Exposition.

The Stock Exchange Building was one of the last designs the famed architects created together before Adler's death in 1900. Perhaps knowing the end of their partnership was near, they placed intricate touches throughout the building so their memory would live on. Other buildings settled for sliding metal elevator gates the attendant pulled open to let passengers on or off. The gates were plain steel bars that folded like an accordion, designed to keep people inside the cab while the elevator shot toward the roof or plummeted to the basement. But Adler and Sullivan had more majestic plans for the Stock Exchange Building. They created ornate gates, loops of metal twisted into beautiful geometric shapes. Each gate presented rows of circles crossed with dashes and peppered with dots. Long lines connected each circle and made the gates seem organized, even artistic. Brass designs in the shape of a *T* hung on each door, positioned in the middle and carved with detail.

The elevator attendant appeared from behind these see-through gates and let James in. It was possible this was one of the first times in James's life that he had ridden on an elevator. The Stock Exchange Building had a trading floor where traders gestured wildly at each other and watched numbers being written onto a massive chalkboard, the size of a screen at the cinema. But in addition to traders, James would likely have been surrounded by the lawyers, insurance brokers, and real estate professionals who leased space in the twelve-floor building.

Situated across the street from the courthouse, it was advertised as the ideal location for lawyers and brokers.

These professionals crowded back to the offices that Friday morning, perhaps ready for the upcoming weekend. James knew nothing of the new middle-class weekend. Saturdays on a farm were a day of labor. And Sundays for a farmer were spent at an open-air market, trying to sell crops wholesale to hoteliers, grocers, and restaurateurs. Now that his father was dead and his mother was in jail under adultery charges, James was trying to liquidate the farm. He wanted to sell the tools and the machinery and keep the money and the house for himself. Since Sabella was in jail, there was nothing she could do to stop him.

James rode the elevator to the top floor. He wandered past the communal bathrooms, and perhaps visited the men's room to feel the hot or cold water that rushed from the sinks. The building's leasing agent boasted this feature in the sales guide. The bright electric lights and the windows were another selling point.

The Nitti house was nothing more than panels of wood hammered together on a leased piece of land, but James wanted it anyway. He planned to pick the house up and move it to his own plot of land. Earlier in the week, he had gone to the probate court and petitioned to be named administrator of his father's estate. Due to his mother's incarceration, it seemed sensible to the court that James be permitted to attend to the estate. He filed the petition on October 20, and four days later it was approved in open court.

Next, James needed to testify before a court reporter for the proof of heirship. He walked down the hallway to number 1307, the suite occupied by court reporter George Burgoyne. The process was simple. He would be asked a series of questions that would serve as official testimony. Lola P. Yonkers, a stenographer from Park Ridge, would record his every word.

These were standard questions. The county demanded the affidavit state how many times the deceased had married and to whom, and the names of all living children.

"What is your name?" the court asked.

"James Nitti."

"Where do you live?"

"Stickney, Illinois."

"What relation were you to Frank Nitti?"

"A son."

"When did he die?"

"The 29th of July, 1922."

"How old was he?"

"Fifty-five," James responded, likely guessing because few Italians had birth records or even cared much about their actual birth date.

"How many times did he marry?"

"Once."

"And then to whom?"

"Isabella," James answered, failing to note that Isabella was his mother.

"Is she living?"

"Yes."

The testimony continued. Did they have other children? What were their names and ages? Michael, Charley, Filomena, and Mary. Were any other children adopted? No.

The testimony concluded the official heir list as limited to the following kin:

> Isabella Nitti, his widow;
> James Nitti, his son;
> Michael Nitti, his son;
> Charles Nitti, his son;
> Flemy [*sic*] Nitti, his daughter;
> Mary Nitti, his daughter.

The testimony was typed on a heavy white paper. The stenographer signed the transcript, as did the notary public. The transcript was wrapped in a thick, blue paper that served as a cover. "In the matter of the estate of . . ." was stamped on the front in red ink. Someone, perhaps the stenographer, wrote "Frank Nitti" on the thin line provided.

The transcript was brought to Judge Henry Horner's court for signature. Horner signed off on the document, then a clerk took a big, blue stamp and pressed the word "Filed" onto the front cover. This appeared to be it. In James's view, the court first named him as administrator and then limited the kin list to a handful of people. With his mother in jail and him being the oldest, he nominated himself sole benefactor.

———

By the time the court formally named James the administrator of the estate, he had already sold off \$235* worth of property and pocketed the cash. The rest of the estate needed to be liquidated, and James clearly had plans to take it all for himself. He started by selling the horses. There were five of them—two mares, two males, and a colt. The gray mare fetched the highest price—fifty dollars. The colt was only worth fifteen dollars. He sold two sets of harnesses and the four wagons the horses once pulled. He sold the tools—the mower, cultivators, rack, plows, seeding machines, and corder. Inside the home, he took everything that his parents ever earned for themselves in the United States and found a buyer. He sold the wash tub, sheet sets, pillow slips, comforters, and feather bed. He sold the bed frames, dining room table and chairs, sewing machine, cutlery, baby buggy, dressers, and wardrobe. He sold the wood-burning range and the icebox. He was even able to get one dollar for two kerosene cans. The home was worth fifty dollars. He had it moved to a plot of land he purchased—likely with his new funds.

While James was busy cleaning out and selling his parents' house, Sabella had hired a lawyer, Eugene A. Moran, to defend her against the adultery charges in Oak Park. Moran knew James was acting against the estate laws in Illinois. Even though he'd been appointed administrator, that didn't mean James got to claim the full estate for himself

———

* About \$3,377 in 2016.

and walk away like a winner at the racetrack. Besides, in Illinois, estates worth less than $800 were automatically turned over to the widow.

Moran came to battle by firing a warning shot at James and his attorney, W. W. Witty. A notice addressed to Witty was entered into court record:

> Please take notice that I will on Friday, the 17th of November, A.D. 1922, at 10 o'clock A.M. or as soon thereafter as counsel can be heard, appear before his Honor Judge Horner, file a petition, and ask for an order to be notified of all proceedings in said estate, and for a rule on the administrator to file inventory, appraisement, and award within three (3) days and for an order of the court to turn over all assets of said estate to Sabella Nitti, petitioner.

As threatened, Moran stood before Judge Henry Horner on Friday, November 17. The law was clear—the estate belonged to the widow, and there was no need for an administrator, particularly one who took all the funds for himself. The judge agreed and the order was issued, stamped, and entered into record. James had five days to comply with the notice, an order he promptly ignored.

Sixteen days later, the adultery charges against Peter and Sabella, who'd been in jail three months, were dropped, and she was free to return home. She had no home to return to, however; the estate had been plundered and her rented lot was empty. About a mile away, her former farmhand Michele Desant and his wife occupied a crude shanty. Michele felt obligated to take in this mother, her three youngest children, and her tagalong farmhand, Peter Crudele. Living conditions were primitive, and the adults all slept on mattresses on the kitchen floor with a little curtain separating Michele and his wife from their guests. But the situation was meant to be temporary, a safe place to stay until James returned the $800.

James had no such intentions. A week later, Moran sent another notice to Witty threatening to ask Judge Horner to hold James in contempt of court. The words in the letter were scrubbed clean of emotion, and made the process seem more civil than the reality. Away from the courts and the stark notices and orders, the Nitti family was seething with hatred for each other. Sabella had all but given up on her oldest son, and James was becoming an increasingly desperate man.

In early January, James tried a new approach. He claimed the body of his father had never been found. People were just *assuming* that Frank Nitti died. But if there was no body, then there was no evidence that his father was really dead. His dad might have just walked away from the family, similar to what James had done to his own wife the year before when he slipped up to Michigan and lived under his cousin's name. The court disagreed and in mid-January approved Sabella as a widow entitled to $800. It was over. James lost. But he did not blame himself. To him, Sabella had stolen from him. When he had the chance for vindication, he would pounce. Until then, he waited.

8

WE LAID HIM ON THE PRAIRIE

May 9, 1923

N O ONE WANTED TO get into the water. About a dozen men stood above the manhole on Ridgeland Avenue, taking turns peering into the darkness below. A dead body floated in the water. The men couldn't see much more. They didn't know who the man was or how he had ended up in the catch basin. What they knew was a road crew had started early in the morning working on street repairs. Arthur Burns, an aging bricklayer, had found the body and contacted the appropriate authorities.

It was debatable who exactly were the proper authorities to notify. The catch basin was inconveniently located on the border between two towns near the Chicago limits. Berwyn held claim to one side of the street, and Stickney the other. Officials needed to determine which municipality was responsible for the dreadful task of pulling the body out of the basin and dealing with it accordingly. Berwyn, being a larger and more established town, had more personnel to address such unfortunate events.

Stickney was a young town and its local leadership comprised volunteers who had little experience with law enforcement. The police magistrate, Louis Kral, was a restaurant owner. His previous civic involvement was serving on the good roads committee. That type of committee was tame, perhaps even dull, and the contribution the men made to the community was their willingness to handle municipal minutiae. Ordinarily, their biggest concerns were having automobiles share the roads with horse carts or prioritizing which road repair was most needed. A rotted corpse floating in a cesspool took Kral's civic duty to an entirely new level.

Kral hovered above the manhole with the other men, trading ideas on how to remove the body. It was an unseasonably cold May morning, and the men wrapped themselves tightly in their overcoats, pulled their hats down low, and milled among each other talking. David Abram, the undertaker, stood by and assessed the situation. He had been an undertaker for several decades and also studied the new science of embalming. Embalmers like Abram made incisions into various arteries and drained the body of all the blood. Then, they pumped chemicals mixed with water back into the corpse. Few people could stomach such a job, but it was Abram's trained profession and he hoped to pass it down to his son. Even Abram didn't want to lower himself into the catch basin to fish out the corpse.

The men first tested a maneuver that didn't require anyone to slide into the murky water or make contact with the body. They removed the manhole cover—an elevated grate called a "high top" that was six inches tall and allowed the rain water, but not major debris, to run into the catch basin below. The basin was about three feet wide and six feet deep. Hidden within the basin was a connection that linked to the drainage canal about a mile away. With the grate removed, the men attempted to lower a rubber blanket into the basin below and position it under the corpse. The rubber blanket had a rope attached to each of the four corners. The idea was the men would situate the blanket under the body, and then pull the bundle out of the sewer. Problematically, they were unable to secure the blanket under the body, and no one wanted to jump into the water and orchestrate the event.

Louis Roden walked up to the overwhelmed men. He was an actual city employee, not an unpaid volunteer, and he worked as an investigator and inspector for the city of Berwyn. Roden quickly proved he had little fear of what floated in the water below.

"We are in a fix," Abram said as Roden walked up. "Can't you help us out?"

"Why, I can go home and get my hip boots and get down into it," Roden said. "It's the only way I see."

The crowd waited for Roden to go home and fetch his equipment. He returned with his hip boots, the long type worn to wade into a cold river to fly-fish. Roden pulled the boots up his legs and slipped down the basin, next to the floating body. The men lowered the rubber blanket and Roden dipped his bare hands into the water to negotiate the corpse on top. With the blanket in place, Roden climbed out of the sewer and the watery exhumation began. Each of the four men pulled on their rope ends until the corpse was hauled from the depths. The men laid him on the prairie grass, stood back, and examined the body—or what was left of it. How long had this body been floating in the water?

The body of the dead man—assuming it was a man—was decayed beyond recognition. It had clearly been floating in the sewer for months, if not years. But the body didn't smell terrible. A rotting corpse typically made itself known through a fierce explosion of odor. This corpse was different. It hid subtly in the sewage, oozed its smell into the water, and waited to be found. It was possible the corpse had expelled its odor in the canal a mile way and then journeyed through the sewer system to the catch basin. It was hard to say where the body came from and how long it had been there.

This man was possibly one of their own—a local from Berwyn or Stickney. The investigators owed the community an explanation. Who was this man? When was he put in this sewer? Who did this to him? It was near impossible to find answers with the skeleton laid on the prairie.

"Is the finger in the basin?" Abram wondered. The men looked back at Roden. Perhaps he could lower himself back into the water and search for the missing body parts?

The men decided to have another city employee help Roden pass up buckets of water. The buckets were drained and any important contents collected and preserved. Roden again lowered himself into the sewer and began lifting up buckets of water, determined to drain the sewer and collect every bone fragment and clothing shred they needed to confidently identify the corpse.

The process was productive at first. Roden found the lower jaw as well as several fingers. Then, the assistant noticed Roden had cut one of his fingers and was bleeding. The process halted. Roden emerged from the sewer a second time and Abram inspected the wound. Abram quickly disinfected the wound and wrapped a bandage around Roden's finger. That had to suffice. Roden lowered himself back into the sewer with the intent to keep his finger out of the dirty water.

Roden was losing patience for the job. Hauling buckets of water to the surface was taking too long. The others wanted to accelerate the retrieval as well. With his good hand, Roden waved his fingers through the water, looking to catch bones and other fragments from the dead body. He felt a smaller bone and raised it to the rim of the manhole and rested it on the side.

"Look," the assistant called down to Roden. "There is a ring on this." The assistant took a small stick and began pushing on the metal band. He passed it back down to Roden.

Roden was unsure what he was seeing. It looked like a ring. He dipped it into the sewer water to wash it clean. Gold shone through the dirt when Roden looked again. He sensed it was a ring and a possible clue.

"Is Dave Abram around?" he called.

"No," the assistant said.

"Is the chief of police around?" Roden asked.

"No." The officials had wandered off while Roden was swimming in the sewer.

"Well," Roden said, slipping the gold band into his overall pocket. "Nobody else gets this."

Roden collected a gold band, a shoe, and half a dozen human bones from a sewer with his bare hands. His job was complete. He climbed from the sewer for the last time and back into the crisp May air. Across the street, he saw the corpse had been lifted off the prairie grass and into a wicker work basket, the type used by undertakers. The body was loaded onto a wagon and pulled away from the scene.

Abram's undertaking business was also his home. It was typical practice in the 1920s for undertakers and their families to live close to the business where dead bodies were stored and then embalmed. Psychologically, many people might view such a close arrangement as unnerving. But logistically, it made sense for undertakers to live where they worked. The nature of the business meant being woken at all hours to attend to the crisis of death.

It had been almost nine in the morning when the police came to Abram's door and told him about the body in the sewer. Most of the morning was spent watching Roden bravely splash in the water and pull out the missing pieces. Roden had done his job, and now the burden of the body was transferred to Abram. He needed to contact the coroner's office so a physician could inspect the body and determine a cause of death. And Abram needed to organize the body parts so that the physician had all the information he needed for his investigation.

Abram had been an undertaker long enough to see all kinds of bodies in various stages of postmortem. Any experienced undertaker had seen the bodies of the old, the young, the ones who looked like they were sleeping peacefully, and the ones with the gaping mouths who looked like they were pained by death. Abram knew what happened to the body in death. But this body, this bundle of remains, was memorable. It would have been hard for even an experienced undertaker to forget the condition of the body fished from the drainage ditch.

The body was placed on a worktable, and Abram stood aside, observing the decay. Above the waist, the body had disintegrated into a near skeleton. The spleen was pushing out the back of the rib cage, trying to flee its former confines. The muscles and flesh holding the organs and intestines in place had dissolved. The organs and intestines had shifted down the rib cage. Some were able to slip through the cracks between the rib bones and slide into the murky sewer water. Others had descended into the pelvis and were hiding behind the pants that hung on the corpse's waist.

From the waist up, the corpse resembled a skeleton that one might see in a medical college classroom. Starting at the head, Abram noted, the flesh and muscle had disintegrated from the body. There was no skin, no identifying marks, and only a small tuft of black hair on the back of the skull. The eyes were gone. There was no nose and no ears. The lower jaw had detached from the face and taken the lips with it. Only the bone fragment of the lower jaw was fished from the sewer. A few of the larger back and shoulder muscles still hung on the body, but the small ones had rotted off. Moving down the body, Abram noted the arms were still intact, which was to be expected. Ligaments were more durable and decomposed more slowly than muscle tissue and fat. Eventually, the ligaments holding the limbs together would decay and the body would break apart. Hands would separate from the wrists, arms from the shoulders, and legs from the pelvis. The process had started on this corpse and the left hand was gone. The right hand remained but all the fingers were missing.

Below the waist, the man wore pants and a belt, although the undergarments had disintegrated into the water or were missing. Notably, the pants preserved the body below. The man still had his urinary tract, bladder, and genitals intact. The pants stretched down to the man's ankles. There, Abram observed that the left foot wore a shoe and a sock, the right foot was bare. This was all Abram determined—the corpse was a man. Identity unknown. Age difficult to gauge.

Abram didn't have to know the intimate details about the body; his job was to prepare the corpse for burial or disposal. The details were the responsibility of Dr. Edward Hatton, a professor in Evanston serving as a Cook County coroner's physician. He was tasked with traveling twenty-five miles that morning to Abram's garage to inspect the body and decipher what information he could about the corpse.

Hatton saw a badly decomposed body that had clearly been dead for quite some time. He suspected the body had been injured before being dumped into the sewer. He saw a depression in the skull, on the left temple. The depression was a quarter of an inch deep and pushed behind the left eye. There was also a fracture that started by the ear hole and stretched several inches toward the top of the skull. Smaller cracks branched from a third fracture, radiating across the skull. Hatton believed he was looking at a badly beaten body. The nose bone was shattered. The skull cavity was filled with blood, and the mouth was missing the front teeth as well as several premolar teeth in the back.[*]

Hatton cut into the bloated, discolored flesh on the legs. He needed to examine the bones and the arteries, which at the time doctors believed could be used to determine the age of the body. To Hatton, a fully formed skeleton indicated a man was older than his midtwenties. He also believed the arteries indicated old age if plaque was present. Hatton noted that the bones were fully formed and the arteries were in good condition.

Hatton recorded his opinion: He was looking at the body of a man who once stood at five feet three inches or perhaps five feet four inches. He was likely a white man. Most of the skin had turned a bloated shade of purple and blue, but parts of the front legs were still white. This man likely weighed around 145 pounds. His bones were fully formed, so he was older than the age of twenty-five. But the condition of his arteries suggested he was younger than fifty. He was neither an old nor a young man. He died from blunt force trauma to the head, from an object that was likely shaped like an octagon though it may have been round.

---

[*] The science regarding forensic taphonomy has advanced significantly since Dr. Hatton's era. It is possible that this body did not suffer a blow to the head as Hatton would suggest. Further, Hatton found blood in the skull, which he believed was the result of head trauma. The literature now finds that pooling of blood occurs naturally in corpses that decay in water. The body floats on its stomach and the head is pulled beneath the body, thus pooling the blood. It is noted in the literature that postmortem cracks were long difficult to decipher from antemortem cracks, and only in the last few decades has the science advanced enough to provide confident determinants. Therefore, it is possible that a modern medical examiner might diagnose the cracked skull and pooled blood in the skull as part of postmortem decay, and conclude that this corpse was not attacked prior to death.

Hatton did not know Francesco Nitti, nor was it his concern that the man had been missing since July of the previous year.* The missing man was also not Abram's concern. The undertaker's responsibility was to store the body and make it available to the coroner, police, and county officials. The coroner's physician had come and gone that morning, and now the body was a police matter.

———————

Deputy Sheriff Paul Dasso had been waiting for this moment for more than six months. He arrived at the undertaker's in Berwyn with a smug sense of satisfaction. The word that sprung to his mind when he looked at this corpse and heard the coroner's physician's report was "vindication." Fueled with a sense that his suspicions were correct, Dasso set out to round up next of kin to identify the body as Francesco Nitti.

Dasso would not waste his time asking Sabella to identify the corpse. He remained convinced that she and the farmhand Peter Crudele had been having an illicit affair that motivated them to kill Francesco Nitti. In fact, Sabella and Peter had married two months earlier, in March— but later events would indicate that the mismatched couple likely did so only to avoid another round of adultery charges.

The two remained his prime suspects, although Dasso now believed Charley was also involved. Dasso wanted to move quickly to arrest all three. The suspects had already slipped out of his grasp once. Finding the dead body gave him the grip he needed. While the first step was confirming whether the body was actually Francesco Nitti, Dasso learned

———————

* The current literature on forensic taphonomy finds that water can have a varying effect on a body. The salt content, movement, and other organisms can either accelerate or retard the decay. Additionally, the body may be a food source for maggots, other insects, birds, or animals. Without knowing the environmental conditions of the sewer, it is difficult to determine whether the body had been in there since the previous July. It is possible the body was that of Francesco Nitti and it did enter the sewer nine months earlier. It is also possible the body had been preserved by the conditions of the water and was far older than nine months, or that the conditions of the sewer supported rapid decay and the body was only a few months if not a few weeks old.

that the foul corpse was in such a state of decay that it was impossible for anyone to identify it. But the corpse was wearing pants and there had also been a pair of shoes collected from the drain. And that gold band found on the dismembered finger—that was something Dasso could work with. He needed to move strategically. There were deep fractures, however, in the Nitti family that would guide him along. Dasso sent for the oldest son, James.

It was late afternoon near the Nitti farm, about 4 PM, and James Nitti called on his mother at Desant's shanty. It was amazing the young man was allowed to visit. The shanty was packed with people, and James was to blame. He was living in the house he'd stolen from his family, and he still owed his mother the $800 the courts determined belonged to her as a widow's award.

James had come by on occasion in the past few months. During these past visits, Sabella told him about her plan to open a store with the money from the widow's award, once she received it. She wanted everyone to be involved—even James. It was her plan to pull the family from poverty and the exhausting unpredictability of farming. James agreed and acted as though he was interested in the store. But he wasn't visiting that evening to talk about the store or chat with his mother. He was there to watch the show.

James had just come from the undertaker's. Sabella did not know that only hours earlier James had identified the corpse as his father's. So had the Volpes, Francesco's friends from Bari. James and the other witnesses had looked at the skeleton laid out on the table in Abram's garage, and viewed the shoes, floating in a pail of water. And they examined the gold band found on the finger bone. Then they confirmed what Dasso wanted to hear—this was the body of Francesco Nitti.

While Dasso prepared the charges and secured an arrest warrant, James invited himself over to his mother's house with the sole purpose of watching her arrest. His sisters were unsuspecting that soon they would be ripped from their sobbing mother's arms. Trauma loomed, but their emotions were secondary, and James's anger was priority. Besides—his sisters would be fine. The Volpes had agreed to take in the girls and allow them to sleep on their kitchen floor alongside the family dogs.

The show was about to start. Charley stood at the front window of the shanty and saw Dasso and another officer approaching, revolvers pulled and ready.

"Dasso is here!" Charley announced.

"What do they want?" Sabella called from the kitchen.

Dasso entered the shanty. Everyone stood around, waiting for an explanation. Dasso explained—in a dialect of Italian that Sabella did not understand—how a body had been found earlier that morning in a drainage ditch and then identified as Francesco Nitti. The coroner's physician determined the body was beaten to death and Peter Crudele, Sabella Nitti, and Charley Nitti were under arrest for the murder of Francesco Nitti.

Sabella knew something was wrong and she burst into sobs when she sensed she was being arrested again. She collapsed on her bed, holding her young daughters. Mary clung to her mother and Sabella kissed the top of her daughter's head. "Now I will be away for another long time," Sabella sobbed.

Dasso had never seen such a hysterical reaction during an arrest. Not that Sabella's sobbing fazed him. To Dasso, she was not a poor, unfortunate woman who was being separated from her two young daughters. She was a murderer, and she should have thought about the consequences before she killed her husband.

Sabella tried to speak through her sobs. She wanted to explain the situation to Mary and Filomena, but she was consumed by grief and fear. Last time these men took her away, she was incarcerated for three needless months. When she returned, everything she owned was gone and her son James was now her enemy in court. How long would she be gone? Who would turn on her this time?

Sabella needed Mary and Filomena to understand she was being forced to leave them, and she had trouble to face. "I have a lot of trouble," she said between sobs.

Part III

TO SHIELD AND PROTECT

9

UNRAVELING THE SAFETY NETS

May 25, 1923

HARLOW A. VARNEY WAS a man who commanded respect, and his fellow members of the grand jury acquiesced by making him the foreman. Varney was tall and heavily built. He had blue-gray eyes and light brown hair, a contrast to the small, scared Italians he quietly judged from across the room. Varney likely did not know that this was the second time Sabella, Peter, and Charley faced a grand jury for the murder of Francesco Nitti. The other jury the previous September had refused to advance the case. But now there was a corpse with a crushed skull for the jury to consider.

Varney was a busy man, and being called to serve on a grand jury was an interruption to his work. At forty-six, Varney was a company president in the heavy machinery manufacturing industry, and he had enjoyed an executive status for years. He was the type of man who directed others and made serious, decisive directives on a daily basis. A man like Varney knew how to refuse someone; it was the nature of business. In order to protect the well-being of the company, he had to sometimes tolerate sad faces crumpled with disappointment or voices quieted by hurt feelings.

Now Varney's work paused while he made a decision of greater consequence. Along with the other men in the grand jury, he was tasked with evaluating the evidence in the case of Francesco Nitti's murder.

The grand jury considered whether Deputy Dasso and the other lawmen had enough evidence to indict Peter Crudele, Sabella Nitti, and Charley Nitti.

Varney and the rest of the jury had likely read about the case during the previous weeks. Reporters for the local newspapers had raced to Stickney as soon as they heard a body was found in the catch basin. Even before their first day in front of the grand jury, Sabella, Peter, and Charley were tried in the court of public opinion and found guilty. The reporters led the persecution and plugged in questionable details from unreliable sources. This type of fabrication wasn't unique to the Nitti-Crudele case. In the 1920s, journalism norms were progressing but sensationalism was standard. A person didn't need to give a reporter an actual interview to be quoted in the newspaper. And a reporter didn't need to fact-check or even witness an event—rumors sufficed.

The day after the body was found and the three suspects were dragged from Michele Desant's shanty, the *Chicago Daily Tribune* ran a convincing story with the headline Boy Tells How "Star Boarder" Slew His Father: Near Solution of Nitti Death By Finding Body. The star boarder supposedly was Peter, who was not a "star boarder" but a laborer on their farm. The headline was a middle-class misinterpretation of how the Nitti family lived.

The report was filled with more inaccuracies, and such misstatements were a sign of the coverage to come. The worst offense was attributing a quote to Charley Nitti. The reporters never heard Charley confess to police, nor did they view any type of signed confession. Someone with the police or sheriff's department, possibly Dasso, told reporters he heard a confession, and such hearsay was accepted as fact. The daily newspapers were the first safety net that any person accused of murder might hope to land in. But the net was loose—or perhaps nonexistent—when Sabella fell, and damning details slipped through the interwoven fabric of cynicism and doubt a reporter was meant to bring to the job.

The coroner's jury had been the second safety net in place. At the time of Sabella's arrest, Cook County relied on a coroner's inquest to review the evidence related to the cause of death and determine whether foul play was involved. If a man was indeed responsible for poisoning his wife or knifing a man in the stomach, then the coroner's inquest advanced the case to a grand jury. Coroner's juries released suspects if no foul play was involved, or if self-defense was a clear motivation. None of this had made sense to Sabella when she faced a coroner's jury on May 10, the day after the corpse was discovered. The gold ring was presented as evidence, as were the shoes found on the body. James Nitti testified at the hearing, then his brother Michael, and the Volpes. No one confessed to killing Francesco Nitti.

As a safety net, the coroner's jury had also unraveled when it determined there was enough evidence of foul play to advance the case. That left Peter, Sabella, and Charley dangling above the next safety net, hoping the grand jury would break their fall. Their next court date introduced them to a new type of jury, a powerful assembly of men who had the right to question the witnesses directly and to seek contempt of court against a witness who did not supply the information they sought. Varney and the other members of the grand jury were free to interrogate the witness. Varney was in his right to stare at Dasso with his cool blue eyes and demand proof of an actual confession.

Varney was in the position to demand clarity. He could have sighed and shaken his head when the only form of identification on the corpse was a plain, nondescript gold band and a pair of shoes owned by half the men in Chicago. In the jury deliberation room, he could have scoffed at such evidence and urged his fellow jury members to see the weaknesses and biases in the case. What was the motive, he could have asked. Were there any direct witnesses?

When the grand jury reached its decision, the three defendants were indicted for murder. Another safety net had dropped and the defendants plummeted lower into the depths of a capital case. Their next and only hope was a not guilty verdict in a Cook County courtroom.

10

YOU WOULD HAVE
WANTED IT TOO

I F ANYONE ACCUSED DEFENSE attorney Eugene A. Moran of taking on
a murder case that was far above his skill level, he could have easily
shot back, "You would have wanted it too." The case guaranteed coverage in all the major newspapers, and Moran would forever be associated
with one of the biggest murder trials in Chicago. If he won, the rewards
would be phenomenal—write-ups in the legal journals, guest lectures at
law schools, or perhaps a stint as a visiting instructor.

At the time, Moran was far from any guest speaking invitations. He
had spent the previous several years as a bit player in Chicago. He had
represented Sabella in her probate case against James and sent strongly
worded cease and desist letters. That case was best described as administrative. Sending letters or getting the right stamps from the probate
court was the equivalent of running legal errands.

These tasks were not fitting for a man of Moran's pedigree. He
was one of eight children of Thomas A. Moran, a prominent Chicago
judge, attorney, and politician. During his law career, Thomas was in
the news regularly for his legal and political advancements. The elder
Moran had sent his son to Princeton University for an undergraduate
degree and then to law school at Northwestern University in Evanston.
Few men in the United States were as prestigiously educated as Eugene

Moran. Yet, he responded with a lackluster law career colored by various missteps. Perhaps because of his father's legacy, he was able to maintain some semblance of productivity. Moran kept an office in the Hartford building and was a resident at the Congress Hotel and then the Virginia Hotel. But he was unable to establish himself as a lawyer worthy of serving the Chicago elite. He found himself associated with the most desperate Chicagoans. Moran often handled divorces and domestic spats that worked their way out of the home and into the probate court.

Around the same time Moran handled Sabella's probate case, he had also defended her against the adultery charges. Those charges weren't even adjudicated in a courtroom. He had ridden out to the administrative building in Oak Park and presented the case before a local magistrate. Defending adultery charges was a bit ridiculous and embarrassing for a man with such an elite education.

Standing on the outside of Chicago's elite legal scene was the norm for most attorneys, and many likely did not care. As long as they had a decent office and a good wage, many were indifferent to their exclusion from the upper echelons of Chicago legal society. But Moran grew up in that scene. He knew what he had failed to accomplish. Not only that, the few times his name *was* in the paper for something newsworthy, it was for odd or embarrassing reasons. One time, Moran placed a help wanted advertisement for an office boy and stated the boy was required to have red hair. The ad struck people in the newsroom as bizarre and a reporter visited Moran. When asked, Moran said he had a theory that redheaded boys were more industrious.

Around the same time, the newspaper reported how Moran was arrested and charged with cashing bad checks at the Congress Hotel. On three occasions, Moran cashed a twenty-five-dollar check that the hotel clerk later learned was worthless. The checks were drawn on E. S. Penny of Colorado Springs, a man whom Moran claimed was a business partner. Moran told the *Inter Ocean* that both he and Penny were solvent men and the situation would be quickly rectified. He had been busy, he claimed. First, he was sick in the hospital. Then, he was busy with a divorce case.

The *Inter Ocean* concluded the story by noting how Moran was a member of the South Shore Country Club as well as the Princeton Alumni Club. Both were organizations that his father had likely bought his son's way inside. But Thomas Sr. couldn't buy his son's way into respectability.

Moran must have wanted more for himself. And he saw a clear opportunity for notoriety and advancement when Sabella, Peter, and Charley were arrested in May 1923 and brought before the coroner's jury and then the grand jury. He would be their lawyer, he decided, when they went into the Criminal Court Building that July to face murder charges.

What lawyer wouldn't have wanted the case? It was a capital case and he would receive news coverage fitting of his father's legacy. But there was one serious problem with Moran representing Sabella. He just showed up and claimed the case for himself. It would take months until other attorneys realized that Sabella Nitti had never actually hired Eugene A. Moran.

I OUGHT NOT TELL YOU
HOW TO TRY YOUR CASE

July 3, 1923

WHEN JUDGE DAVID WALKED into the courtroom, the sight of his black robe prompted the courtroom to stand at attention. Eugene A. Moran identified himself as the attorney for the defense, and Milton Smith and Michael Romano stated they were assistant state's attorneys appearing on behalf of the people of the state of Illinois.

Sabella sat alongside Peter and Charley at the defendants' table, next to the man who decided he was their attorney. Moran had done nothing to prepare his clients for the trial. The women's block had a special makeup cabinet that was unlocked when a woman had a court date. The female inmates were permitted to powder their noses, rouge their cheeks, line their eyelids with black liner, and look their best in front of the judge or jury. Moran did not coordinate a makeup session for Sabella. Nor did he bring her a fresh set of clothes to wear in court.

Sabella slouched in a chair positioned alongside the defendants' table, dressed in the same clothes she wore to work a corn row. Her gray-streaked black hair was piled as usual into a messy bun and secured haphazardly with pins and combs. Moran should have arranged for a hairdresser to come to the jail, cleanse Sabella's hair in the cell's small sink, and pin her wet locks. After makeup was applied, the hairdresser should have removed the pins and set Sabella's hair into fashionable finger waves.

Dolling Sabella up with cosmetics and hair styling wasn't about staging a dog and pony show. Presentation was serious strategy. Sabella needed to look familiar to the middle-class men of the jury. It was vital that she appeared recognizable, not foreign. Her darker complexion already distanced her from the twelve white men selected to judge her. Her strangeness was further compounded by her disheveled appearance. The middle-class jury was accustomed to women who enhanced their appearance and hid their flaws with makeup. Cosmetics were no longer just for the daring, and even the most conservative women were apt to beautify with a powder puff or vanishing cream.

But Moran never thought about how Sabella should be presented to the jury. Nor did he coach her on how to behave in court. When the court was called to order, Sabella sat slumped in her chair, resting her chin in her hand. The jury soaked it all in. The haggard middle-aged woman next to her curiously young husband and her notably small teenage son. They knew no one like these outsiders.

———

The state called Mike Travaglio, Sabella's nephew, as the first witness. Illinois assistant state's attorney Milton Smith stood and walked from behind the table where he sat with his co-counsel, Michael Romano. Smith was a tall and broad man, the type whose confidence was bolstered by his size and the knowledge that he was physically more powerful than others around him.

Smith began the direct examination with a series of simple questions, and he asked for precision in the answers. Such a line of questions was pure strategy. Smith was going to bury important insinuations and damning assumptions in a line of mundane questions. An astute attorney could have caught a problematic question and raised his voice in objection. Moran let it all slip.

"What is your name?" Smith began.

"Mike Travaglio."

"And where do you live?"

"456 North May Street."

"In Chicago?" Smith clarified.

"Yes, Chicago."

"What is your business?"

"Laborer."

"Who do you work for?"

"Crane Company."

"How old are you?"

"Twenty-five years old."

"Did you know Francesco Nitti when he was alive?"

"Yes, I knew him."

Moran stayed silent. He did not argue how there was no proof that Francesco Nitti was even dead. Perhaps the judge would have overruled the objection, but it might have planted an important seed of doubt in the jury's mind.

Smith sensed he could push further. He repeated the same question, reinforcing to the jury that Francesco indeed was a dead man. "Did you know Frank Nitti in his lifetime?"

"Yes, sir."

"Directing your attention to the 29th day of July, 1922, when was the last time before that day you saw Frank Nitti?"

It was a clever question. Smith brought up the date Francesco went missing and added the assumption the man was dead, murdered on the date in question.

"I saw Frank Nitti from six to seven o'clock in the morning on the 29th of July, Saturday morning."

Smith repeated the answer in the format of a question, as if to ensure every detail of testimony was precisely accurate. He further checked the year of the last sighting as well as the exact streets where Mike claimed he saw Francesco selling the vegetables at a farmer's market on Randolph.

"And what were you doing there?" Smith asked.

"I went over there because I worked down—I had been working at the candy factory at the time at 412 Orleans Street, so I passed through there and I wanted to go see him, see."

"What was his physical condition at the time?"

"He was pretty good."

Mike was on track, saying everything the state needed to hear. Smith continued to ask a series of questions about the previous time Mike visited the Nitti family farm. It was an uninteresting set of questions, and the minutiae of the exchange slowed the pace of the testimony. Smith gradually confirmed Mike knew each member of the Nitti family as well as Peter Crudele. But Smith's next question should have propelled Moran from his seat.

"When was the next time after Saturday, July 29, 1923, that you again saw Frank Nitti?"

"I saw him when he was dead."

It was crucial for Moran to object to every implication that Francesco Nitti was indeed the corpse found in the sewer. The corpse was decayed beyond identification, and Moran should have forced the court to always maintain the possibility the corpse was not Francesco Nitti. But Smith had lulled the courtroom into a slow, unsuspecting pace, and Moran had yet to object.

"And what was his general physical condition there?" Smith asked.

Again Moran's hand should have shot to the ceiling, hollering for an objection and reminding the judge there was no proof the body was indeed Francesco Nitti. Instead, Judge David attempted to clarify what Smith meant.

"His physical condition?" Judge David asked.

"He was dead," Mike answered.

"I want to know the condition of his body," Smith told the judge.

Moran finally piped up. "That is not the way to get it."

Smith plowed in a new direction. He retrieved a paper parcel from the state's attorney's desk and unwrapped the paper. He held up a pair of men's leather shoes, brown with tan laces.

"I show you state's exhibit 1 for identification," Smith said.

They were the shoes found in the catch basin with the corpse. The prosecution claimed they were a positive form of identification of the body because Mike testified he had once worn the shoes for two whole days. The shoes were supposedly a gift from his Uncle Francesco, but they were too large for Mike's feet and he had given them back. The same exact pair of shoes, Smith claimed, were seen on the decayed corpse at the undertaker's and served as undeniable proof the body was Francesco Nitti.

It was a questionable story. Why would an impoverished man buy his wife's nephew a pair of shoes? Especially when the nephew had a decent job and a comfortable life in the city? Moran sensed the testimony was contrived, but he wasn't sure how to proceed, and he randomly interrupted.

"Now, Your Honor, I move these shoes be wrapped up again and taken out of evidence. They have nothing to do with the case," Moran argued.

"Overruled," the judge answered bluntly.

"Exception," Moran shot back, and in so doing preserved the testimony for future appeal.*

Moran sat down, momentarily quiet as Smith went back and forth with the witness about the exact dates the shoes were worn. After Smith asked a few more questions of no consequence, he turned the questioning over to the defense. "Cross-examine," Smith announced.

It was the moment Moran had waited for since he claimed Sabella's case as his own. All eyes on the courtroom focused on him. Would he start by asking what proof the witness had that he ever borrowed or owned the shoes? Or ask the witness to describe how the corpse was decayed beyond recognition? Or fire off a series of questions that proved it was highly unlikely Mike took note of what his uncle wore to the farmer's market?

---

* At the time, Illinois courts required attorneys to say "exception" in order to have the testimony eligible for review during appeal. The laws later changed so that all testimony is eligible for review, not select parts highlighted by stating "exception."

"And with whom have you talked about this case?" Moran asked the witness.

It was a useless question. The witness was free to answer in any manner he pleased, and Moran had no evidence to prove otherwise. Still, Mike hesitated in his answer. Moran tried four times to rephrase the question, as if Mike hadn't understood. The judge eventually intervened and Mike answered with a curt, "Nobody."

From the start, Moran demonstrated a lack of control. At times, he fumbled and failed to get a straight answer from the witness. In other moments, Moran allowed Mike to ignore questions he didn't want to answer. When Moran was met with silence after he asked Mike where James and Michael Nitti lived, he demurred to the witness and asked a new question.

"Have you got any interest in this case?"

"Yes," Mike answered.

"What interest have you got?"

"Because that was a good man and what they kill him for."

"Who killed him?" Moran asked.

"The way I heard that—"

Moran interrupted. "The way you heard, who told you?"

"Charley told me," Mike said. "Charley told."

It was another damning question and response. Hearsay evidence was rarely admissible in court. In theory, Mike was only allowed to testify as to what he *saw*. Repeating a statement that someone made to him was not proper evidence. Judge David was obligated to intervene and stop Moran from harming his own client.

"Unless counsel insists the evidence will stand, I will strike it out and instruct the jury to disregard it."

Both attorneys agreed. "The court will strike it out," Judge David announced for the benefit of the jury. "I am not letting this man pass upon the question as to who killed anybody, if there was anyone killed."

The moment was primed for Moran to push for the shoes to be excluded from evidence, as well as the gold band found on the dismembered finger. Instead, Moran launched into a series of irrelevant questions as to whether July 29 was a Saturday or a Sunday. The jury sat through ten of these mundane questions, all asking the same thing in a different way. Moran was trying to trip up the witness on a small detail, as if failing to remember a date would somehow render all the testimony invalid. When the technique failed, Moran insisted Mike try on the shoes in front of the court to see if they were indeed not the proper size as he'd claimed.

It was a disgusting thing to ask the young man to do. The shoes had been found on a corpse that had decayed for weeks, if not months or years. The spectators must have shuddered at the idea of Mike touching the shoes with his hands and then putting them on his stocking feet. Judge David seemed more concerned than disgusted. He had not yet made a ruling as to whether the shoes were admissible in court. Yet Moran insisted the shoes be further examined, and he risked proving Mike right.

Mike pulled the shoes onto his feet, but whether the shoes were indeed too large was not closely examined. Instead, Moran waited as the witness paraded past the jury box, turned, and strode back to the witness stand.

"Have you ever seen any shoes like that before?" Moran asked.

"Where they found Nitti," Mike answered.

"No," Moran snapped, as if there was only one correct answer.

Judge David stepped in to help. "You mean in their present condition?"

"Yes sir."

"When they found Nitti," Mike tried again.

Moran was frustrated. "Now, will you please answer my question?"

"What is it you're after?" the judge demanded.

Moran was flustered and didn't know how to discredit the shoes as evidence. He admitted his strategy was to force the witness to admit the shoes were standard stock shoes owned by most Chicago men.

"You are asking him now," Judge David reminded.

"I am asking him if he saw shoes like that before and I want an answer now. I cannot make it any plainer."

After two more clarifying questions from the court, Mike relented and agreed that practically everybody wore shoes like the ones found on the corpse. Moran seemed content with the answer and moved on. For the next two hours, the courtroom idled as Moran went through unrelated sets of questions.

A new battle of wills ensued when Smith asked the court to enter the gold band into evidence and allow the jury to inspect it. Mike stayed firm as Moran spent the better part of the next hour pounding him with questions. Where did Francesco Nitti wear this band? When? What finger? When did he last see the man wearing the ring? Moran asked these questions in three different ways and always received the same answer.

Moran was flustered, and in his confusion, he asked a question that suggested the corpse was indeed Francesco Nitti. "What condition was the ring when Frank Nitti had it?" Moran asked.

"The first time I saw it?" Mike confirmed.

"Where did Frank Nitti get the ring?" Moran bumbled, not receiving a response to his previous question.

"From James Nitti," the witness answered.

"How do you know that?"

"Because I knew James Nitti, the stone came off, he throwed it away, the father examined it on his finger."

"You saw the father do it?" Moran pressed.

"I don't know he did it, he told me," Mike said.

The witness's answer was the definition of hearsay. A skilled attorney would have demanded the testimony be stricken from the record. If no one *saw* Francesco pick up the discarded ring, then it could not be discussed in court. Mike had no authority to discuss the origins of the ring.

"He told you?" Moran pushed.

"Yes."

"When did he tell you?" Moran asked, his agitated voice raising.

"I don't know what date it was, I say."

"I object," Smith called from across the room.

Judge David interrupted. "No necessity in raising your voice at the witness," he criticized.

"Well, I am having trouble with this," Moran defended.

"I say there is no necessity for you in raising your voice. Go on."

There was a pause, an awkward break among heated players. Mike needed the question read back by the court reporter. This gave him ample time to think of a response.

"When it was on his finger," Mike said. "I examined this and he wore it on his finger."

"You don't know if James gave him that ring or not, do you?" Moran challenged.

"Yes, I know that James gave it to him."

"How do you know that?"

"He told me.

"He told you that?"

"Yes, sir, Frank Nitti told me that."

Judge David squirmed in his seat. The testimony was increasingly painful to watch.

"The same finger James wore it on, did he?" Moran asked.

"Same finger as James."

"It was all flattened out?"

"All flattened out, the way it was now."

That was enough. Judge David quieted the courtroom. He summoned Moran to approach him and instructed the court reporter to follow. They stepped outside the room so that the jury, the witness, and the gallery of spectators could not hear Judge David reprimand the attorney.

"You are asking a lot of questions here that are highly improper and detrimental to your clients that are not competent," the judge warned, "and I must insist, unless there is any rule or reason that—you ask the man and he brings out the answer, he told you. You must stop calling for hearsay testimony unless you insist on doing it, because such evidence is detrimental to your client and you ought not to bring it out. I ought not tell you how to try your case."

Moran was undeterred. Or perhaps oblivious. "Your Honor, I have got my case pretty well in hand," he answered.

"The court cannot stand by and allow you to constantly ask questions that are detrimental to your clients. You must stop it."

Moran thought the discussion with the judge was an opportunity to further his line of questioning. "Because the dead man there, somebody gave him the ring?"

"But you should not ask those questions."

"Your Honor," Moran protested. "I have something else in view, I will show how this ring was built up and I will discredit the statement of the witnesses just on the shoes."

Judge David again urged the attorney to stop harming his clients' case. "If you are going to insist that you are going to bring out evidence of this kind, I shall have to ask some lawyer to step in here and assist you in the defense. Now, I am telling you because the court will not stand by and allow a person where a life is at stake—"

Moran, possibly insulted, interrupted the judge. "Your Honor, I think I have practiced law long enough to know how to try a case and—"

Judge David interrupted Moran. This was his courtroom and no attorney had the right to speak over a presiding judge. "You are insisting here on bringing out evidence that is not competent."

"I am making it competent to bring out testimony of other witnesses and the whole case will break down . . . Your Honor, I practiced law here for some years."

"You may have practiced law for a dozen years or a thousand years, but it is not proper for you to bring out answers that are detrimental to your clients," the judge warned.

Moran refused to defer to the judge. He was above feigning deference. "Your Honor practiced law yourself and you had your own theory," Moran said.

With that, Judge David gave up. "You want to bring that answer out, do you?"

"Yes," Moran insisted.

"All right," Judge David relented. "I will not interfere again."

The courtroom snapped back to attention as Moran, the judge, and the court reporter returned to their places and Moran asked his final few questions.

"Did you see this ring on July 29?"

"About six or seven o'clock in the morning."

"Was it all hammered up then?"

"No, sir."

"That is all."

12

YOU DON'T KNOW WHAT BURDENS I AM CARRYING

THE PEOPLE OF THE STATE OF ILLINOIS called James Nitti as the next witness. James was barely seated when Judge David eyed the black band he wore high upon his arm.

"Who are you in mourning for, your father?" Judge David demanded.

"Yes."

"Take it off," the judge ordered. "Go outside and take it off. The jury will pay no attention to it."

Smith defended his witness. "He always had it on, Judge."

"That doesn't make any difference," Judge David shot back. "He has no business to bring it into the courtroom, I want it understood. One of the issues, I understand, is being raised in this case as to whether the body was found was the body of the deceased, is that it?"

Smith conceded. "Yes."

James exited the courtroom momentarily to remove the armband. Once the witness settled back into place, Smith began the direct examination by establishing basic facts. James Nitti was twenty-five years old, an immigrant from Bari who lived in the city of Chicago. Smith slowly verified all the members of the family and asked the witness to confirm the identities of the three defendants.

"What was the last time before July 29, 1922, that you saw your father, Frank Nitti, alive?"

"The first part of August, 1921."

Smith orchestrated a series of questions in which James testified that the next time he saw his father, the man was dead. Moran remained silent. Judge David allowed it.

Smith began a series of questions about the gold band found on the corpse. James delivered every answer consistent with his cousin's testimony. The ring was gold and a red stone had once been set upon high prongs. Moran protested as soon as James suggested the prongs were flattened down. In Moran's opinion, the gold ring found on the corpse did not have flattened prongs.

"Now, wait a minute," Moran objected. "There is nothing to show that these prongs were flattened down."

Smith conceded. "All right, I will withdraw it."

Moran continued. "There is nothing to show . . . that there is a prong."

Smith withdrew his question. But then he circled around and instantly revisited the issue of the prongs. Moran swiftly objected, and the jury listened as the two attorneys bickered over what constituted a prong. To Moran, prongs were clustered together to elevate an object such as a gem. He argued the ring had *lines*, not actual *prongs*. Judge David quickly ruled that the word *prong* was admissible.

A more strategic defense attorney would have waited and addressed the ring during the cross-examination. There was no evidence that a red stone was ever worn in this ring, and a clever attorney would have pushed the witness to admit the stone on this particular ring might have been blue, black, or clear. There was simply no way of knowing whether this was Francesco Nitti's ring or if the corpse in the catch basin was even Francesco Nitti. A skilled defense attorney would also have questioned whether James had any proof that Francesco Nitti ever wore such a ring. Perhaps a receipt? Or a photograph that showed his hand? Without additional confirmation, the attorney could have argued, the jury should not assume that Francesco Nitti ever wore a ring.

But Moran was overwhelmed by the pace of the testimony and outwitted by Smith's strategic questions. Moran didn't know how to proceed when rulings were not in his favor. His responses during Mike's testimony had been temperamental, but many litigators had an ornery demeanor, so that wasn't particularly alarming. His mental state, however, became questionable during James's direct examination. Moran was disorientated, as if he didn't know which side he was representing, and he mistakenly defended Smith from Judge David's rulings.

The defense of the prosecuting attorney first occurred when Smith asked James to describe the "pieces of metal" on the ring. "They were sticking up just like this one here," James answered.

"I object," Moran said.

"Strike out 'like this one here,'" the judge ruled. "The answer may stand."

Moran had received the ruling he needed. But he was confused and he attempted to defend Smith from his own objection. "Let him describe the ring he gave to his father," Moran blurted.

"Go on with the question, he may answer the question," Judge David sided with Moran in his defense of the prosecution.

James responded, "I broke the stone and I throwed away the ring."

"Then, what happened?" Smith encouraged.

Moran interrupted. His objection was nonsensical. "I object to that," he said. "That is not answering the question."

Judge David overruled. The same cycle replayed three times before Smith launched into a series of harmless questions that appeared to be based on fact finding. He confirmed where Sabella and Peter lived, and pushed for locations and dates about the undertaker's residence, where the body was identified. He even tried to casually bring up James's time in Michigan, and it was clear Smith wanted to give the witness enough soft questions to enable him to justify why he had left his wife and lived in Michigan under an assumed name. Moran objected to the testimony and Judge David stopped the prosecutor from discussing James's marital problems.

Smith knew when to move on. He redirected his attention to the days leading up to the arrest of Peter and Sabella. He believed there was a comment—a potential confession—that Sabella had made to her oldest son just a few days before the corpse was found. According to James, Sabella had gestured toward the window of Desant's shanty and said, "If you want to see your father, go in the cornfield."

Before this testimony could be heard by the court, the two attorneys bickered back and forth about the legality of the testimony. Did the statement qualify as hearsay? Then it was inadmissible in court. If Sabella said the cornfield comment as a confession, then James could potentially testify about it in court. But was it just an offhanded comment? Was Sabella merely gesturing to the outside world and her belief that her husband had left her? Or was she suggesting her son Michael had attacked his father and left him for dead among the crops?

Smith again outmaneuvered Moran, and Judge David allowed the cornfield comment. James was allowed to testify what he'd heard in Desant's shanty. James also said his mother told him she planned to purchase a flat for everyone to live in, even him, and together they would open a wholesale business for the family to run. James presented Sabella's invitation to live and work with the family as somehow suspicious.

Up to this point, James had succeeded in confirming all of his cousin Mike's claims about the ring and introducing hearsay evidence through the cornfield comment. But there were a few more items Smith needed from the witness. There was further hearsay evidence—Sabella had supposedly said something damning when Deputy Sheriff Dasso arrested her on May 9, and Smith wanted the jury to hear it.

At the time of the arrest, Sabella had begun crying hysterically—everyone agreed on that. But then, it was alleged, she said something both the deputy sheriff and James believed was incriminating. Sabella held her young daughter and sobbed, saying something to the effect that she would go away again for a very long time.

Moran was unable to communicate with Sabella. He never interviewed her to learn whether she did indeed say something to that effect and if so, what was meant by it. His basis for the objection was that

Sabella made the comment in Barese. A translation changed the meaning, he argued. The jury sat, possibly bleary eyed, as the court asked James to repeat the comment in Barese so that the attorneys, none of whom spoke Barese, could debate whether it meant the same thing.

Smith knew that even if something wasn't admissible, it could still prejudice a jury. Even if he had to let this one piece go, he had at least succeeded in establishing that Sabella made an incriminating comment. "What else was said there to Peter Crudele, did Peter Crudele say anything?" Smith asked.

"He didn't say nothing," James answered.

Smith asked a leading question, knowing full well the answer. "Then, what happened after that?"

". . . Pete Crudele, he was trying to skip."

Moran objected. "I move that be stricken out."

Judge David faced the jury. "No, no," he agreed with Moran. "Don't pay any attention to it, gentlemen."

"If the court please, won't you consider the witness. He doesn't know," Smith swore.

"Yes he does," Judge David countered.

"I submit he don't," Smith said, and then he cleverly restated the damning information in his protest to the judge. "I says 'what happened,' and he said, 'Peter Crudele skipped.'"

Judge David was not convinced. "Now, don't put any more questions what happened. Don't put such questions, then we won't have this or those kind of answers."

Smith disregarded the judge's ruling by rephrasing the question and trying again. James quickly followed the attorney's lead and announced to the court that Peter Crudele tried to escape. Judge David instantly shut down the line of questioning.

Smith moved on. He had far more damning hearsay to introduce. He began by coaxing the witness into recalling a meeting at the state's attorney's office the previous autumn. Francesco Nitti had been missing for almost two months, and the entire family was interviewed by the authorities. At the time, Sabella and Peter were detained at

Cook County Jail, waiting for a magistrate to hear the fornication and adultery charges, but were taken from the jail to the meeting. Smith thought there was a key moment during the interview that might work to his advantage—Charley was attributed with making an incriminating comment.

Smith painstakingly detailed each person present at the interview. Was Charley there? Sabella? How about assistant state's attorney Mr. Romano? Was Deputy Sheriff Dasso there? These questions went on as Smith tried to build up to the conversation that took place. But he couldn't get close enough to the comment and knew the wrong step would alert either Moran or Judge David to his intentions. He orbited around the questions he wanted to ask, looking for a clear path. After a while, Smith must have decided he was best to wait and he called for the cross-examination. If the defense's cross-examination was anything like the last witness, then Smith could count on Moran to inadvertently help the prosecution.

Judge David didn't allow it. Clearly, Smith was in the middle of getting at something and he needed to finish the job. Judge David ordered Smith to finish questioning the witness. Smith returned to his spot by the witness box and thought for a moment. His problem was the comment Charley made was just that—a comment. There was technically no confession uttered by Charley, his mother, or Peter Crudele. The comment was hearsay, and Moran might object or Judge David might ruin it all.

Smith began stumbling through the questions, and as soon as Moran understood the prosecutor's intentions, the defense began resisting. The jury watched as the two attorneys battled each other and the judge about the details of something that had yet to be said. Moran argued that whatever the witness had to say about the meeting in the state's attorney's office was not admissible because it was said in another language and the meaning changed when translated into English. Moran failed to argue that the comment made in the state's attorney's office was not a confession and should be treated as inadmissible, hearsay evidence.

Instead, he pushed the English-Italian-Barese communication issues, which was a relevant but weaker argument.

The two attorneys argued at length until the judge ordered Smith to proceed. James was allowed to recall the meeting in the state's attorney's office and tell the jury what he overheard.

"As near as you remember," Judge David encouraged the witness.

"Mr. Romano questioning Charley, he said, 'who killed your father,'" James began.

"I object to this, Your Honor," Moran protested.

"Overruled."

"It is hearsay," Moran argued. "It is not confronting the defendant with the living witness as the Constitution requires."

James picked up where he was interrupted. Back at the state's attorney's office, Romano had asked Charley who killed his father. Charley supposedly blamed his mother and Peter Crudele. Then, James testified that Romano had confirmed the allegation with Sabella. "Mr. Romano asked my mother, he said, 'Did you kill your husband?' And she says, 'Whatever Charley said, that is true.'"

Smith was getting somewhere. "What else did Charley say, go ahead and tell us what Charley said, everything that happened."

"And Charley said that, 'We killed him,' he says that, 'My mother, Pete and that they threatened me to help them to do the killing.'"

"Go ahead?"

"And Charley helped to put the old man on the wagon."

Judge David paused the testimony. "Now wait a minute."

Smith was one step ahead of Judge David. He called for cross-examination, and there was nothing more for the witness to add. It was late in the day and time for court to adjourn. Smith's timing was impeccable. Not only did he procure another layer of incriminating comments, but he also did so in a way that the jury would leave for the evening with James's damning testimony ringing in their ears.

The jury waited to leave the courtroom. The next day was the Fourth of July and the court would not convene. Judge David dismissed the jury, ordering them back on July 5 at 9 AM.

"Your Honor, would it be possible for us to go home tomorrow?" one of the jurors asked hopefully.

"No, sir, gentlemen, you cannot go home tomorrow. This is one of the things I cannot help. The bailiff will try to make it as comfortable as he can for you and take you to such a place in the open air as you contemplate going."

The jury filed out, their holiday plans ruined by a murder trial. Judge David waited until he was alone with the two attorneys to drill into them.

"Now, gentlemen, the effect of what you are introducing is the confession. No motion has been made to exclude the jury, none."

Moran started blathering. "I object to it on Constitutional rights for another reason."

Judge David was horrified. What was this confused attorney talking about? "Your grounds are ridiculous, Mr. Moran, you don't know what you are talking about. Now, listen, if you don't know how to protect the rights of parties, I will protect them."

"Now, Your Honor, you said that once before."

"I will say it again."

"That is only Your Honor's opinion."

Judge David plowed ahead with what he needed to tell the man. Smith had introduced a confession that Judge David felt was "involuntary," meaning Sabella was a Barese speaker who did not understand Italian. Her deference in stating, "Whatever Charley said, that is true," did not qualify as a confession.

"Mr. Moran," the judge lectured. "If you don't understand, let me tell you the rule, nothing new, it is as old as the hills, when a pretended confession is offered in evidence, it is the business of counsel to object to it and ask for the exclusion of the jury. You did not ask. Your objection as to objecting to the unconstitutional rights, is meaningless, whatever you said. I'm sorry if you take offense to the court, I say, you are not in the judgment of the court, properly protecting the rights of these parties."

Moran was offended. In his opinion, he was an officer of the court and a practicing attorney. He reminded the judge that his father, Judge Thomas Moran, was also a lawyer, and he took "violent exception" to any insinuation that he was not properly trying the case. "You don't know what burdens I am carrying," he told the judge.

Judge David did little to regard Moran's claim of hurt feelings. Instead, he proceeded to explain that Moran had not motioned for the state to disregard the supposed confession or even demanded for the court to tell the jury the confession was involuntary.

"You cut me off," Moran defended. "Your Honor shut me off."

After a bit of complaining, Moran pushed the judge to allow him to articulate a motion that the testimony be excluded. Judge David was then required to walk the defense attorney through the process of making such a motion.

"Do you wish to offer any evidence in order to claim that the alleged confession is involuntary?"

"Yes, I do."

"Then, proceed to offer it. Now the fact that they were in the state's attorney's office and the fact that they were under arrest, and the fact that they were being interrogated, does not establish anything at all."

"I will call Charles Nitti."

Perhaps Judge David cringed. Or perhaps he resigned to the reality that the defendants would likely be found guilty. Since it was a capital case, the Supreme Court of Illinois was obligated to review it prior to the execution. The judge made mention of this fact and warned he would expect the state's attorney's office at that point to make a record of this supposed confession and supply the defendants with a copy.

Judge David continued to explain to Moran that there was technically no confession. Charley had stated his mother and Peter killed Francesco Nitti, which meant Charley had confessed to nothing. He blamed other people and exonerated himself. Sabella was never directly asked in Barese whether she killed her husband, therefore her agreement with "whatever Charley said" was also not a confession. A comment was made in that office, not a confession, and the rules of hearsay limited the witness testimony regarding what other people merely said.

But Moran just didn't get it. The judge was showing him a clear path on how to knock such an incriminating comment out of testimony. Moran clung to the notion that he was capable of proving to the court that a confession was made under duress. This might have been true—Charley might have been beaten or intimidated by the Chicago police, or perhaps he was coerced by his brothers into uttering that comment. But Judge David's path to knocking out the testimony meant the comment couldn't be labeled a confession. It was either a comment that was inadmissible because it was hearsay, or it was an involuntary confession. Moran couldn't have it both ways.

Moran was relentless about proving it was an involuntary confession. Judge David again attempted to review procedure with him, how confessions worked, and what qualified as a confession. But the more Moran persisted, the more the judge must have realized the attorney before him was incompetent. Moran was finding meaning in unrelated events. He harped on about how Sabella and Peter had been pulled from their jail cells to the meeting in the state's attorney's office. The judge assured Moran that such an action was not illegal, but Moran was convinced that the act implied police abuse.

The judge reminded Moran how suspects were allowed to speak or remain silent during a police interview. At the core of the judge's remedial reminder was a hint that the contents of the interview were not a confession and that arguing a coerced confession occurred was detrimental. If the comment was indeed labeled a confession, witnesses could testify about it.

The judge must have marveled over why Moran was tangled up in this testimony. The interview was clearly inconsequential, and the grand jury hadn't indicted Sabella or Peter. It wasn't until after the corpse was found in the catch basin that charges were brought. Naturally, the prosecution wanted to expose the jury to every incriminating factor possible. And Moran, in his confusion, seemed to be helping Smith and Romano shape their case.

"Mr. Moran, you have been charged by the court insinuating you do not know how to try your case, you are objecting to evidence because it is involuntary and yet you want the jury to hear it," the judge warned.

The warning officially entered into record Judge David's opinion that Moran was incompetent and unable to try the case. Moran did not acknowledge the criticism. Instead, he persisted the jury must hear about the coerced confession. He had a plan, he told the judge, that James Nitti would repeat his testimony in Barese. Then, Moran assured, everyone would hear the words *cerello* and *prepro*, and it would all come together.

Neither word, unfortunately, had any meaning.

———————

Moran was unraveling and Judge David knew it. The defense attorney was confused, counterproductive, and sometimes paranoid. He admitted that he was carrying a great "burden" and looked flustered as he sat alongside his clients at the defendants' table. His arguments during sidebar discussions were incoherent. Judge David voiced his doubts on the record on several occasions; still, it would have been impossible for anyone in the courtroom to predict what the next few years would bring to the fragile defense attorney. What no one realized—least of all Sabella and Peter—was that Moran was on the verge of being institutionalized.

At the time of trial, Moran was a drowning man. But he wasn't sinking silently or swiftly; he was grasping at his life, trying to remain in control. Anyone who came too close risked being pulled down with him. Moran had grabbed onto Sabella and Peter when he claimed their case, and his incompetence was leading them to a guilty verdict. Anyone who could detach from Moran was wise to do so. Judge David distanced himself by making his doubts clear. And at home, Moran's wife, Connie, also sought space. Moran's marriage was ending, and the dissolution was likely the result of his increasingly erratic behavior.

Connie Oehler was about twenty years younger than her husband, Eugene, and they had known each other for just a few months when they married in 1919. She was a Wisconsin native who moved to Chicago for a two-year art program. They met when she moved into the Gold Coast building where Eugene lived. One of her friends remembered Eugene quickly wooed Connie, and the couple rushed to the courthouse for a civil wedding ceremony. They married under the portrait of Eugene's father, still on display. It was the first of three wedding ceremonies. Connie's parents insisted on a church wedding in Wisconsin and the couple obliged. Then, Eugene's sisters wanted a blessing at the Catholic Church on Superior Street, and the pair again acquiesced.

Despite their age difference, Connie and her "Gene" were a cute couple. Connie was a small woman with dark hair, a soft jawline, and wide cheeks. She had an easy smile that spread quickly across her face and showed all her teeth. Eugene Moran was not a tall man, but he was a full head taller than his bride. When she stood next to him, she made him look stronger and more powerful than he was. Perhaps that was how he presented himself to her earlier in the relationship—strong, powerful, from the finest stock of Chicago elite.

Connie was an artist who created and delivered art for advertising agencies. Advertising during the 1920s was undergoing a paradigm shift. The previous style was practical and informative. Advertisements were text heavy and described the utility of the product. But the ad men quickly realized that images better tapped into the growing cultural desire for glamour, wealth, and relief from the anxieties of life. Connie was part of this change, and she supplied illustrations for print advertisements. Her work created the illusion of an alternate, better reality that consumers hoped to construct for themselves by purchasing the right products. Perhaps in Eugene, she saw a better version than reality, especially at first.

Eugene's better version of himself dissolved quickly. The couple lived together only a few years before Connie felt compelled to leave. It was unknown whether he was violent and she was forced to leave, or if he refused help for his sinking mental state and she felt sick watching him slip deeper. Either way, in the late 1920s, Connie left for France without her husband. She kept her and Eugene's problems to herself. One friend described her letters as "delightful trivia with practically no actual news." "It's nobody's business how I feel," she told the friend.

Connie returned to the United States in 1929 and lived on her own. Around the same time, Moran moved into the Milwaukee Sanitarium* for long-term care. The sanitarium treated patients with water therapies, special exercises, jolts of electricity, and extended sedation. If deemed appropriate, some patients received sedatives that made them comatose for up to two weeks. None of this was free, of course, and the wealthy Moran family paid as much as ten dollars a week to treat their son.

When Moran was released from the sanitarium sometime before 1940, he went into the care of his two older sisters. He was still legally married to Connie, and she lived just half a mile from him, but their lives were separate. When Moran died in 1941 from heart disease, his obituary described him as a bachelor.

---

* The Milwaukee Sanitarium was not to be confused with the Milwaukee Sanatorium for Tuberculosis. The sanitarium was for behavioral and nerve disorders and exists today as a mental health treatment facility. The sanatorium, fortunately, closed as vaccinations made tuberculosis rare in the United States.

13

THE WHITE WIDOW

TUESDAY EVENING AFTER COURT Judge David had some thinking to do. He also had some cooling off to do. Moran was infuriating, and it was hard for the judge to watch the defense attorney all but drag his clients to the gallows. What was Moran talking about with the confession and the Constitution? The man had been nonsensical. And how did he not know basic procedures?

Moran wasn't the only attorney whom the judge felt compelled to correct. Judge David was known as one of the most energetic judges in the county. He regularly interjected when he felt a case wasn't handled correctly. He demanded attorneys properly introduce evidence and follow courtroom procedures. If that involved a bit of a lesson, then so be it. Years before, Judge David had lectured at the law school at Loyola University. Educating the uninformed came naturally to him.

Judge David worked tirelessly. He came to the courthouse on his birthdays, read cases, and wrote opinions. He had a relentless stamina that exhausted others. He was always moving forward, and he expected others to keep pace. Defendants were guaranteed a speedy trial, and any attorney appearing before him for the first time quickly learned that requests for continuances or delays would be denied.

The judge's industrious nature combined with his fidelity to the law made him popular with many in the legal community. These supporters considered him one of the best legal minds in the country. But others faulted him for interjecting himself into cases. He was too involved, his critics disapproved, and he inserted himself too deeply into a trial's proceedings. Other judges would have also managed the problems arising between Moran and Smith, but they wouldn't have gone as far as Judge David to send the jury out, issue warnings, lecture the attorneys on procedure, and suggest new ways for approaching the case.

Judge David was passionate, a surprising feature for a man who looked so mundane. He had fading brown hair, pale skin, thin lips, and drooping cheeks. His ruffled judge's robe overwhelmed him and seemed too large for his body, making him appear meek. But Judge David was a fervent, energetic man who felt he knew the order of things and shouted at attorneys who fumbled before him.

This particular day's fumbles likely played on his mind as he commuted to the Hyde Park home he shared with his wife, Emma. The case was troubling. There was little evidence—the body was identified only by a nondescript gold band and a pair of leather shoes worn by most men in the area. Judge David had yet to rule whether he wanted these items to be considered by the jury. Nonetheless, the defense attorney plowed ahead and treated these items with merit. And then, there was the business of the supposed confession. Judge David had tried to outline a path for the hapless Moran to follow. He recommended the attorney *not* argue the confession was coerced. Argue instead that the confession never happened. Charley couldn't confess for his mother, and the boy never admitted guilt.

It was odd, though, what Moran claimed about the Barese-Italian translation issues. Moran attempted to argue that Sabella Nitti did not speak Italian. Yet her sons did? It made no sense. As Judge David rolled into the elite enclave of Hyde Park, he began applying his experiences to his questions about the trial. His doubts about the translation issues were likely clouded by memories of his parents. They were German immigrants who learned English in the United States. They were literate and progressive, and they sent their children to school, including their daughters. In his world, women mattered. Few worked outside the home, of course, and a successful wife supported her husband's career and stretched his professional and social networks. It was even expected for a woman calling on an acquaintance to drop her husband's business card in a designated tray in the foyer. A socially skilled woman received invites from prominent women, knew how to charm without being a toady, and made helpful introductions.

The women in Judge David's world lived comfortable lives assisted by all the modern conveniences. They didn't feel their way in the dark each night to the outhouse. Nor did they sleep on mattresses stuffed with hay. They expected light switches, running water, bath soap, and feather pillows. They were well-versed in tea and biscuits, classic novels, operas, and poetry. It was a different world, and Judge David couldn't fathom the way Sabella Nitti lived. No wonder his doubts were surfacing—he knew nothing of the white widows.

At the turn of the twentieth century, many women in Southern Italy left a plate on the table each night for their absent husbands. The place at the table was superstition, a type of assurance for his safe return from abroad. Hardship in Italy drove these men to work the most dangerous, demeaning, and risky jobs Americans had to offer. They sent money home to their wives in envelopes along with letters describing their long days in an unwelcoming land. These women were the white widows— left for years at a time to manage alone. If someone threatened or flirted with a white widow, her husband was not there to protect her. If she became ill, he could not nurse her. And if she was scared or miserable, he could not comfort her. It was as if he had died.

Sabella was a white widow for most of her marriage to Francesco. She raised her boys alone in Triggiano without even the comfort of correspondence. Both Sabella and Francesco were illiterate, and she was unable to open a letter and see the assuring familiarity of her husband's penmanship. Any money or stories sent home had to be carried by a trusted friend.

Francesco had little other choice in leaving his family. The foreign powers that had ruled Southern Italy for centuries left behind an underdeveloped region with oppressive poverty. Southern Italy was stunningly behind the rest of Europe in terms of industrialization, technology, and education. The region was also centuries behind in the treatment of women.

Most Southern Italian women, like Sabella, married before the age of sixteen to a man who was at least a decade older. The marriage was akin to a property transfer, shuttling the girl from her father's to her new husband's possession. Although many women found husbands whom they loved, too many others lived with domestic violence or general disregard. Sabella lived with both, and even her sons, as they aged, felt they had a higher authority.

Many of the white widows' husbands eventually returned to Italy. For these men, their primary goal was to earn enough money to live a better life in Italy. But in the first two decades of the twentieth century, Italian migrant workers increasingly remained abroad. They sent for the wives they had not seen in years, and the white widows once again became wives.

Sabella was one of these women. She managed on her own for years in Triggiano, and then suddenly she was on a ship with two of her sons, crossing the ocean in steerage. In Stickney, she was reunited with a man she barely knew but who had the power to control every aspect of her life. When she woke up in the morning, what she ate, the time she went to bed, the hours she worked—the husband commanded all. Perhaps some women had periods of relief because their husbands were employed as laborers and left the home for the majority of the day. Sabella had no such respite. The family tended their small farm and she worked alongside her husband.

The farm in Stickney was the extent of Sabella's world, and like other Southern Italian women, she was bound by the invisible shackles of female virtue. The dominant cultural belief was that a virtuous woman stayed at home, and many Southern Italian women lived their lives behind closed doors. There were a few reasons, such as church, for a woman to venture into her neighborhood. But these outings were generally within the ethnic enclave. Many of the Italian immigrant women never knew the greater world around them, and they never learned to speak English.

Judge David didn't know the ways of the white widow. He didn't know that Sabella had lived without her husband in Bari. Or how in the United States, she had lived for years on the Nitti family farm with only other Baresi for company. Of course she didn't speak Italian. When would she have learned? She had lived her short time in the States on a remote plot of land. Her sons, as males, had the freedom to run around Chicagoland. They learned English from the Americans, and they learned Italian from the other immigrants. Sabella, in contrast, was confined to the truck garden farm. Her small world was limited to her corner of Stickney, just as it had been restricted to her pocket of Triggiano.

Judge David didn't know what he didn't know. The oppression of the Southern Italian women did not exist in his world. He didn't know whom he was looking at when he peered down from his bench and considered Sabella Nitti, hunched over the defendants' table.

On Thursday morning at 9 AM he opened the day with another warning to Smith and Moran on how to proceed. The contents of the state's attorney's interview were admissible in court, he said, but both men were urged to proceed with caution.

14

DO YOU LOVE YOUR MOTHER?

July 5, 1923

M ILTON SMITH DIDN'T WASTE ANY TIME, and perhaps Judge David
appreciated the prosecuting attorney's efficiency. With the jury
back in the courtroom on Thursday morning and the spectators hushed,
Smith began the second day of the trial by continuing the direct examination of James Nitti. One might have expected the day to begin with
Moran's cross-examination; after all, Smith had ended the first day by
strategically calling for the cross. But Judge David felt the issue of the
confession needed to be addressed, and James was directed back on
the stand.

Smith and James worked well as a team. It was an easy partnership; they wanted the same thing—to see Sabella hang. They swiftly
flowed through the testimony, and the only interruptions came from
the judge, who wanted to clarify who James meant when he called his
mother "the old lady."

In his testimony, James claimed Charley had told the state's attorneys
that he saw his father sleeping underneath a wagon the previous July. In
this story, Peter Crudele held a hammer in his hand and walked toward
Francesco Nitti, raising his arms and preparing to swing. Charley supposedly knocked the hammer from Peter's arms, and Sabella scrambled
to pick it off the ground and hand it back to Peter. Peter then swung
twice at Francesco, hitting him in the head and then the back. Sabella

worked to pull the body into the wagon for disposal, and demanded that Charley help.

When Moran was tasked with cross-examining the witness, he seemed unsure how to address the hearsay testimony. He focused instead on when James left for Michigan and pushed for precise answers without revealing why such information mattered. Moran then switched gears and pushed James to state who else was present at the coroner's inquisition. Judge David, for some reason, did not allow the line of questioning. Forced to change directions, Moran turned to a question that was potentially harmful.

"James, do you love your mother?"

"Objected to," Smith opposed.

"I have a right to know," Moran argued.

"Wait . . ." the judge ordered. "I will pass on the question."

"I will withdraw the objection."

"Answer," Judge David ordered.

"You ask me if I love her? I do not."

"Why not?" Moran asked.

"Objected to," Smith called out. Then, he thought better of the situation. "I will withdraw the objection."

"I won't love her," James repeated.

"Why?"

"Because she killed my own father, that is why."

"You don't know that of your own knowledge?" Moran challenged.

"Yes sir, absolutely."

"How do you know it is absolutely?"

"Charley will testify, and that is enough."

Judge David was forced to stop the line of questioning. Moran was oblivious to how he had allowed the witness to successfully claim his client was a murderer. The next series of questions were equally unhelpful. Moran tried to push James to admit he retained a lawyer for his own protection. Moran also hinted at how James and Anna Volpe financed James's legal fees and helped him take up a collection by asking patrons at a bar to chip in. It should have been a productive set of questions for the defense. If James had nothing to do with his father's disappearance, then why did he need to pay an attorney $700?* But Moran never fully fleshed out the answers and the jury members likely did not connect the pieces of the story. And there was so much to the story—violence between father and sons. Alcohol abuse. Constant combat. The jury would never fully sense what life was like in the Nitti family home unless Moran gave them a vivid image. He tried, but the representation was blurry at best.

"You don't know anything about the trouble that Michael had with your father, do you James?" Moran tried.

"No."

"And did you hear anything about it?"

"No, sir."

"Did you inquire anything about it?"

"No, sir."

"Your father drank quite a bit, didn't he?"

Smith objected. "What is the point?" the judge asked.

"The point is that I have a right to let them know what sort of man Mr. Nitti was, if he was a drunkard, and if he drank to excess . . ."

"You want them to know if the man that was dead was a drinking man?" Judge David asked, forgetting there was a question as to whether Francesco Nitti was even dead.

"Yes."

"Objection sustained. That might be competent at some other time."

"I have my theory, Your Honor," Moran pushed.

"Sustained."

"Exception."

Nothing was accomplished. Moran concluded the cross-examination, and Smith took another round of questioning.

"Now, your father's funeral expenses, are they paid or unpaid?" Smith asked.

---

* About $10,059 in 2016.

"They are unpaid," James admitted. This revelation may have surprised the state.

"Do you know what they were?"

"$260."

Smith backed off. "That is all," he said. The issue of the unpaid funeral expenses would crop up again in the future.

The jury watched as James was escorted from the courtroom. A new witness strode confidently past the rows of spectators, through the space separating the defendants from the prosecutors, and up to the witness stand.

15

JUST THE BARE SKULL

D R. EDWARD HATTON WAS tall and authoritative. He raised his right hand and coolly swore to testify to the truth.

It was a confidence that many reporters in the room doubted Hatton was entitled to emit. Only three years prior, the Chicago newspapers had accused the Cook County coroner's office of incompetence and negligence. Hatton was one of the six physicians serving Coroner Peter Hoffman. Several of the physicians were also university professors, and all were overwhelmed by the workload. Something had to give, and the corpses weren't in a position to complain. Most received a quick evaluation that ignored procedures and spared the doctors from troubling themselves.

As Hatton took the stand that July afternoon, he might have sensed his time with the coroner's office was coming to an end. He had been with the office for seven years and would be dismissed before the end of 1923. Following his termination, either bitterness or remorse would push him to reveal the office's inadequacies. He would speak at conferences and prepare official reports detailing the office's grave failures. There were full years, he would allege, that not one complete autopsy was performed. At times, the physicians merely glanced at a body and guessed the cause of death.

One young man died of gunshot wounds to the head and chest. According to Hatton's scathing report, the physician assigned to the case did not bother to examine his skull. The physician failed to remove the bullets and compare whether they came from the same gun. He did not precisely determine whether the bullet entered from the right or the left. And he merely wrote in the report that the victim had died of hemorrhage and shock associated with a gunshot wound.

Another physician was assigned to investigate the body of a fifty-year-old man who lived alone and died in his apartment. The man was dead for four days before anyone noticed. The physician, perhaps unmotivated without family or friends to press for answers, assumed the man died of a brain hemorrhage. But how did he know if he didn't examine the brain?

The list continued. If a victim was suspected to have drunk poison, then the physicians only opened up her torso to examine the contents of her stomach, spleen, and liver. They did not bother with the rest of the body. If a victim was stabbed, then only the areas affected by the injury were examined. The heads and necks of victims were rarely touched. And even though they were expected to remove organs and carefully transport them back to the laboratory for further testing, few physicians took the time.

When organs were harvested and brought to the lab, Hatton would admit in his report, little care was taken. The organs were wrapped up as though the doctor was leaving the butcher's shop with meat for his Saturday evening meal. Sometimes the organs were placed in containers with lids that did not properly close. The cleanliness was questionable and organs were exposed to contamination. But the most concerning confession would be Hatton's admission that victims' organs were improperly labeled and possibly confused.

Contaminated organs wrapped up like beefsteak or confused with other corpses' specimens were met with an attitude of "that's too bad." The physicians didn't mean to be sloppy, but they felt they were past capacity, and more than half the staff added to their own workloads by maintaining university affiliations. Their superior, Coroner Hoffman, allowed their side jobs. He wasn't a physician or trained medical expert, and his reelection was his primary concern. The physicians' incessant pursuit to publish journal articles or lecture at the university added an air of expertise to the office and helped Hoffman appear innovative.

The press was less impressed. In 1919, the physicians in the coroner's office beat their own record for articles published in medical journals. But the soaring rate of unsolved murders had reporters questioning the physicians' competency. It was a fair question. The physicians were pathologists who were not trained extensively in forensic science. Several, including Hatton, had only been licensed for a few years when they joined the coroner's office. It was arguable they hadn't practiced medicine long enough or seen enough death to serve in the role.

Hatton was a trained pathologist, but his university affiliation was actually with the dental school at Northwestern University. He was a relatively new physician, and had taught high school before starting a medical career at the age of thirty-six. When he examined the corpse found in the catch basin, he had little more than a decade of experience behind him. He admitted, years later, that the physicians covered their lack of experience and expertise by writing short reports with little room for attorneys to find fault during testimony.

It would have been hard for the jury to suspect that Hatton was perhaps unqualified to give the testimony he was about to deliver. Hatton's cool gray eyes and distinguished silver hair made him appear as a seasoned expert in front of the jury. He was tall and trim, and wore rounded glasses that contributed to his neat appearance.

Smith began the direct examination, using the same formula he perfected with the first two witnesses. He asked the doctor to verify mundane details about his name, address, title, and years serving the coroner's office. Then, he asked a potentially damaging question.

"Doctor, did you make a postmortem examination upon the body of Francesco—"

"I object," Moran shot out.

"No, no," the judge reprimanded. He turned to Smith. "Now, you must not ask that kind of a question, that won't do. One of the questions that is raised in this case, I understand, is the identity of a particular body. You must not ask that question, unless the person himself knew the deceased in his lifetime, I suppose you did not."

"I did not, Your Honor," Hatton confirmed.

Smith corrected his question. "Did you make a regular examination of a body in Berwyn, Illinois, on the 9th day of May, 1923?"

Hatton began describing the condition of the body, as asked. Smith focused on the clothing found on the body. The lower extremities were well preserved and it was in Smith's best interest to present the body as more intact and identifiable than it was. But Hatton had no allegiance to the prosecution and he transitioned, without prompting, from the condition of the clothing to the skull.

"And the cloth of the pants, of the lower part of the body in good condition. In the left side of this skull there was a depressed place in the temple. This was approximately at the apex of the triangle, equilateral triangle, which would extend from the mouth and to the ear, to the region in the temple where the injury was located. This depression in the left side of the skull was deepest at two places and these places were each about one quarter of an inch in diameter, one just back of the left eye, at the apex of the triangle, and which I have described, there was a huge fracture."

Judge David had to interrupt. "A what?"

"A fracture—a huge fracture of the skull of this side which extended back from this place."

The testimony was in the prosecution's favor, and Smith did not push Hatton to describe how he examined—or failed to examine—the skull. Hatton did not remove the remains and return to the laboratory for further examination. He viewed the external appearance of the corpse, made a few cuts in select places, and then reached a swift conclusion. So quickly, in fact, that arrests were made later in the afternoon.

Smith didn't push for more details. Hatton's report was helpful because it was consistent with the confession from the state's attorney's office. James testified Charley had said Peter Crudele bashed his father in the head with a hammer and then again in the back. Hatton then described the depression in the head as well as the accumulation of blood inside the cavity of the head. This worked for Smith—the jury didn't need to know that a further physical examination wasn't conducted.

All Hatton had was a list of the observations he made that morning at the undertaker's, and he continued to share his insight with the jury. The front teeth were missing, but there were no other bone fractures observed in the body. In life, the man was expected to have been between five feet three and five feet four inches tall. He was likely around 140 to 145 pounds.

Smith ignored Hatton's statement that there were no other bone fractures observed in the body. James testified there were two hits, and the coroner's physician did not note broken back or neck bones. There was also no damage to the spine. Smith discarded these facts as they were not helpful to his case. He instead focused on the head fracture and manipulatively used the plural when asking the doctor to describe "the fractures."

"At that time, Doctor, did you have an opinion as to whether or not these fractures were antemortem or postmortem fractures?"

"I did."

"What was that opinion?"

"In my opinion, they are antemortem."

Judge David interrupted to clarify. "That is, before death?"

"Before death," the doctor confirmed. "Fractures which occurred before the man died."

"Doctor," Smith asked. "At that time, did you have an opinion as to what caused the death of the subject that you made an examination upon?"

"Yes, I did."

"Tell the court and jury what that opinion was."

"My opinion of that was due to shock and injuries to the skull and brain which I have described."

"Did you have an opinion, at that time, Doctor, as to what was the cause of the injuries?"

Moran objected. He didn't like the way the question was phrased. The attorneys picked at each other and the wording of the question until the judge ruled the question was proper.

"The injuries, in my opinion, which I have described, were produced by the contact, the forcible contact of some firm or hard substance with a comparatively flat place about 1.25 inches in diameter, either round, or more or less octagonal. I believe, more or less octagonal, because of the shape of the depressions which I have described."

Smith collected all the pieces he needed, and skillfully avoided the parts he did not. He called for cross-examination. But before Moran could open his mouth to form a question, Judge David interjected and asked a question that provided a clear path as to how the defense should proceed.

"Let me ask you, Doctor," Judge David interrupted. "Was there anything in the body's face, that is, was there any mark of any kind on the face?"

"The skin and flesh were entirely gone and there was nothing but the bones and the skull left, Your Honor."

"So there is no way of identifying the face?" the judge asked.

"No, sir."

Moran picked up where the judge left off. "No ears, Doctor?"

"No, sir, no way to identify the face."

"I say, there was no ears?"

"No, sir."

"Just the bare skull?"

"Just the bare skull."

The condition of the skull was the one area Smith had strategically overlooked. Moran could have played with a few more questions about how the body was unidentifiable due to the decomposition of the face, or he could have strategically ended the cross-examination. Instead, he picked over small details that obscured the key facts Judge David had just helped him establish. Moran asked about the condition of the toes, whether the shoe was worn on the left or the right foot, and if the bones were still jointed together.

Then, he asked a question that was quite helpful to his case.

"Were there any injuries to the back of the skeleton?"

"No, sir."

"The shoulder blades?"

"No, sir."

"Or the neck bones?"

"No, sir."

"No fractures in them?"

"No, sir."

But his next question reversed his progress. "Now, as I understood you to say, the whole upper part of the body, the abdomen as we call it, there was just the frame of the body there?"

"The frame."

"The heart was gone?"

"The heart was decomposed."

"So far as anybody can tell, this man might have been stabbed through the heart, there would be no way to tell whether he was or not?" Moran asked hopefully.

"In that case, there might not be injuries to the sternum, that is the breast bone which covers the front of the heart which would lie over that part, and if such had been the case, there would have been no hemorrhage into the cavity of the skull* or about the skull bone which I have described."

Moran should have backed off, in the same way that Smith had avoided eliciting testimony that would be detrimental to his argument. But Moran dove right in. "Now, there was blood in the skull?"

"Yes, sir."

"Was this dry blood?"

"It was dry [clotted] blood."†

"The skull is a pretty hard thing, isn't it, Doctor?"

---

* Hatton did not know that a body submerged in water typically floats with the head down, which causes the blood to pool in the skull and typically fracture.

† The blood was never tested in the laboratory. It was not truly known whether the substance was blood or debris from the sewer.

"Yes it is."

Judge David interjected. The defense attorney was continuing to miss important points. "What is the name of that man," Judge David asked, ". . . [they] discovered a few years ago, that Wells speaks of in the history, of 500,000 years ago?"

"The Neanderthal man?" Moran offered.

"Antedating him. There is no way you know in medical science that a skull might last for thousands of years?"

"It has lasted for thousands and thousands of years," Hatton agreed.

"And some say for a million years?" Judge David prompted.

"Yes, sir."

"And might go to the end of time?"

"Yes, Your Honor."

Moran did not see how the judge was helping him. The questions must have seemed like meddling, and Moran interrupted the judge as he started asking whether there was any way to measure how long a body had been deceased. Moran spoke over the judge and asked a question about the broken bones. Judge David allowed eight repetitive questions about the broken bones, or lack thereof, and then again interjected about further identifying the body.

"Doctor," Judge David asked. "Is there any way known to medical science by which age . . . this body was, can be determined?"

"It depends largely upon the condition that might be found related to the arteries, to the teeth or the frame of the bones, Your Honor."

"Were you able to form any opinion as to the age of his body?"

"Certainly it was a fully developed man that his bones were completely formed, there was none of the developed part of the bones present so that he must have been over 23 to 24 years old, he must have been older than that. Furthermore, the condition of the arteries that were left in the legs and the condition of the molar teeth were such that he could not have been an aged man, that is, he must have been a man somewhere between old age or youth, that is as far as I could say as to his age."

"Between what ages would you say?"

"I should say, between 23 or 24 on one side and 50 on the other."*

Francesco Nitti was at least fifty-six at the time he disappeared.† He was also about three inches taller than the corpse found in the catch basin. Moran didn't push to make these details known, and Smith did not want to give him the chance. The defense had no more questions for this witness, and the prosecution let Hatton step down before Judge David helped Moran identify other damaging details.

––––––––––

The second day of the trial brought a constant parade of men on the witness stand. Hatton stepped down, and then a Chicago attorney was briefly questioned as to whether he could serve as an interpreter for the Bari dialect. He was eager to serve and tried to refuse the ten-dollar fee the court offered to pay. His enthusiasm was likely dimmed after Judge David dismissed him until the next day—the remainder of the day's witnesses were all expected to be English speaking.

Undertaker David Abram was the next witness. Smith began the direct examination in his predictable format, asking Abram about his address and years in the undertaking business. Then once again, he insinuated Francesco Nitti was dead.

"Did you know Frank Nitti in his lifetime?"

"No, sir," Abram answered.

"I object to that," Moran argued. "There is no testimony here that Frank Nitti is dead."

––––––––––

* Modern forensic science continues to rely on bones and teeth to determine age. Dr. Hatton's quick assessment, however, would no longer be admissible in court. Forensic scientists now use scans to learn more about the skeletal traits. Additionally, forensic scientists now look at the pubic symphyseal face and sternal ends of the ribs to determine age. Some scientists favor a chemical analysis of tooth dentin which is said to narrow the age range to as few as six years. Dr. Hatton's assessment was potentially wrong.

† His Cook County death certificate lists 1867 as his year of birth. In official records, Francesco Nitti's actual birthdate was fluid. On a return trip to the United States in 1907, Francesco was forty years old but told officials he was thirty-five. The five-year difference may have been to increase his chances of passing the medical exam and finding work as a laborer.

Judge David ignored Moran. "Proceed," he instructed Smith.

Smith proceeded to pepper the witness with twelve questions about the location of the catch basin in Stickney. The questions were confusing and risked blurring any image the jury had in their minds as to where the body was found.

"We seen this form in a catch basin," Abram said.

"Saw what?" Judge David clarified.

"This form."

"You saw a form?" Smith repeated.

"A form," Abram confirmed.

The cycle repeated itself. "You saw a form?"

"Yes, a form, so I immediately got my rubber plank out and we tried to push it under the body, then Mr. Leo Roden come along, he is working for the city of Berwyn."

"Roden?"

"Yes. He had a pair of boots on. I said, 'Leo, do you think you could slip in there?' He said, 'I think I could if you will wait until I go to the house and get my hip boots.' So Mr. Roden went into the catch basin, slipped the plank right under and we lifted the body right out of the catch basin."

"Just tell the court and jury what you saw when the body was lifted out of the catch basin," Smith advised the witness. "What did you observe, what was it you took out of the catch basin?"

"We took the body of a man out of there."

"What did it look like, describe it?"

"Well, from the waist up, it was just a skeleton, it looked like the spleen and the liver was laying toward the back bone, so we just took it right out and put it up on the prairie, then I said to the other—"

"Never mind what you told him," Judge David scolded.

Abram was not an experienced witness. Twice more he tried to explain what he said or heard, likely because he didn't know how else to communicate what he experienced. Daily life allowed people to retell what someone said, but courts forbade it. Smith wasn't gaining ground, and he rerouted the testimony toward the gold band. After Abram confirmed he saw the gold band on the detached finger found in the catch basin, Smith moved to enter it officially into evidence.

"I offer this into evidence, if the court please."

"You offer it in evidence?" Judge David needed to correct the counselor. "You mean you offer it as an exhibit to be shown to the jury."

Smith stood corrected. "We will offer this as an exhibit at this time."

"Is there any objection?" Judge David asked, fully knowing the answer.

"Yes, sir," Moran said.

Judge David outlined the options for the defense attorney. "Any grounds for objection? Do you wish to urge any or just a general objection?"

"General objection."

"Overruled."

Smith led Abram into describing the other elements pulled from the catch basin, and it was likely that he was steering the witness into bringing up the pair of men's shoes. When Abram followed his lead, the moment was right for Smith to enter the shoes into exhibit. Moran objected once again, but Judge David issued the same decision as before.

The items entered into evidence were stacking up against Moran during day two of the trial. The supposed confession was officially now a factor, and the gold band and shoes were exhibits the jury was free to touch and examine. Moran continued to be challenged by Smith's direct testimony, and the prosecution launched into a series of questions as to where the Nitti family farm was in relation to the catch basin.

The farm was actually about a mile from the catch basin, but Abram spoke without knowledge and put the distance at a few blocks. Moran should have objected to these questions on the grounds that Smith was drawing a conclusion based on the location. Smith was assuming the catch basin was in close enough proximity for the defendants to slip into the night, dump the body, and return home undetected. But the defense remained quiet until it was his turn to speak.

There was opportunity in the cross-examination for Moran to turn the case back into his favor. He should have asked Abram which finger the gold band was found on. The middle finger? The index? Was it a pinkie ring? Moran could also have pushed the undertaker to further describe the other items found in the catch basin, specifically the coat fragments. Francesco Nitti disappeared on a late July evening. The day's high had been seventy-nine degrees, and the low was in the sixties. The supposed confession claimed Francesco was sleeping under the wagon because it was too hot to sleep indoors. If it was so warm, why was the corpse that went missing wearing a coat? The prosecution couldn't have it both ways. They couldn't have Francesco Nitti sleeping outside because of the unbearable heat while also wearing long pants, a shirt, and a coat. The inconsistencies were glaring at Moran, begging to be illuminated.

Instead, Moran tried to establish how the catch basin functioned. It was indeed an important point to make. The manhole cover and the curb gate weren't the only two entry points into the catch basin. There was a large pipe that connected to a drainage canal. The pipe was large enough that a corpse could slip through. The manhole, in contrast, had a heavy cover that required special tools to remove, and the grate was far too small for a man's body to squeeze through. The problem was that Abram was not the right witness to help Moran prove his point. Moran needed to call an engineer, sewer system expert, or someone from the municipality who knew how that specific system functioned. Abram was an undertaker, not an engineer. All he knew about the sewer system was that when he ran a bath or flushed the toilet, the water went somewhere.

Moran eventually gave up on the sewer and asked a bizarre set of questions that Abram seemed hesitant to answer. "Did you ever know the Italian people around in that neighborhood that were in the truck gardening business?"

"No, sir, not personally."

"There is kind of a colony of them out there, isn't there?"

"Objected to," Smith shot out.

"Overruled," Judge David responded.

"You say there is quite a colony of Italians out there?" Moran pushed.

"Objected to as not proper cross-examination," Smith tried again.

"Overruled."

"Is there a colony of Italians out there?" Moran repeated.

"I don't think there is," the witness answered.

"No other Italians out there?" Moran tried.

"There may be one or two, but not a colony."

Moran hoped to establish there were other Italians in the area, and he wanted to know what Abram knew of the surrounding suburbs. The answers were unsatisfying. Moran didn't know what he needed from this witness, and he again ran through a lengthy set of questions that reiterated everything established in the direct examination. The jury heard for a second time which dismembered body parts were found in the water, which foot wore the shoe, and whether the socks were found on the feet or in the water. Moran eventually relented.

Neither attorney knew what to do with the next witness, which was surprising given that he was the Stickney chief of police and Sabella had knocked on his door just hours after her husband went missing. Charles Eisele was sworn in and barely had an opportunity to warm the seat before he was excused. Smith merely wanted to confirm that Eisele saw Roden in the catch basin, pulling out the corpse. Moran tried to introduce firearms that were confiscated from the Nitti family farm. The firearms were subpoenaed, and Eisele was meant to have brought them to court. Eisele reported to court empty handed, and Judge David ordered the witness to turn the firearms in the next day. He was then allowed to step down.

Eisele knew things that no one asked him about. He knew Sabella and her sons were badly beaten by her husband. It was Eisele who called for Francesco's arrest after Sabella and Charley came to him battered and helpless. He also knew that Sabella was quick to report her husband had disappeared. She sensed something was wrong and wept uncontrollably. When the police returned several weeks later to tell her they were at a loss, it was almost disturbing to Eisele how her agony was so physical. She had no sense of composure or self-consciousness. It was almost as if she had no pride. She pulled at her own hair and collapsed into tears. Eisele wasn't used to such hysterics, and he remembered the incident vividly. But no one asked him about it.

16

HE TOOK THE BODY
ON HIS BACK

DEPUTY SHERIFF PAUL DASSO moved through the courtroom to the witness stand. Dasso was a heavy-set man whose buttons strained from his girth. He wore a bow tie, a thick moustache, and an occasional scowl. The moment was important to him. Dasso claimed he had extracted three confessions from Charley Nitti. None were on the record, of course. The jury would have to take his word for it.

Dasso set the scene in part. Led by Smith, he told how in the late summer of 1922, he took a wagon ride with Charley and Peter Crudele toward the drainage canal. In his story, a guilt-ridden Charley confessed they were traveling the same route as the night of July 29. Dasso testified that Charley revealed his father was dead in the back of the wagon, killed by a blow to his head and then his back.

"Tell us what he said?" Smith encouraged.

"He said his father was lying in the wagon with his head towards the seat and the seat towards the horse and when we got to the destination, in the prairie, where he couldn't drive further with the horse and wagon, he said he took the body on his back," Dasso testified.

"He said he took the body on his back?"

"That Peter Crudele took the body on his back with the head hanging over his back and the legs in front and carried him, and we walked south, the same distance to where the bridge was, and Charley and I walked together and Pete Crudele in front of me."

"And did he say anything else?"

"And he said, 'That is where we fell with him.' He pointed out a place on a hill, an incline and said, 'This is where we fell down with it.'"

Moran, possibly defeated by the day's earlier events, did not object. He was restrained during Dasso's testimony, almost as if he was listening in on a conversation and had no right to interrupt. It was hearsay testimony, however, and Moran needed to object. Charley could not confess for his mother and Peter, and this statement did not occur within the context of an official police interview that was documented and witnessed. Both Moran and Judge David allowed it.

"Did Peter Crudele say anything?" Smith asked.

"Yes, he did."

"What did he say?"

"He said, 'Bullshit.'"

Judge David had a question. "In Italian or English?"

"English."

"Outside of that, Mr. Dasso, did the defendant Crudele say anything?"

"No, sir."

Dasso claimed the group headed back to the farm. One of the wheels on the wagon broke and the ride was jittery and uncomfortable. Dasso complained he had to climb from the wagon and walk the rest of the journey. Smith allowed his witness to finish his gripe. Then he asked, "Did Charley say whether or not Peter had any conversation with him or not at the time he placed this body in the wagon?"

"Yes, he did."

"What did he say, if anything?"

"He said, 'You keep quiet, or I will do the same thing to you.' Or words possibly along that line."

Moran found his voice. Perhaps he was going to object to the witness giving hearsay testimony? Or remind the court that Dasso did not speak Barese and could not understand the conversation between the two defendants? Moran ignored the hearsay problems. He was more concerned with the imprecision of "words along that line." He wanted it stricken. Judge David ignored the defense attorney.

It was exhausting to piece together what was said, by whom, and in what language. Judge David saved the confusion for the next day. The jury was dismissed and instructed to return the following morning at 9 AM. The judge had no words this time for the counselors. The first day ended with a stern warning from the judge. The second day ended without a warning, but with a clear indication how the trial was going to proceed. Hearsay testimony was permitted. The gold band and shoes were allowed. Unsworn confessions were included. Smith and Romano were going to try this case on circumstantial evidence and Judge David was going to allow it.

Friday morning began with Smith recalling Abram, the undertaker. The corpse was buried at Mount Carmel Cemetery in Hillside, the burial spot of choice for most Italians in the Chicago area. But the shoes and other items found on the corpse remained at the undertaker's, where Abram had buried them behind his garage. At Smith's request, Abram dug up the clothing and brought the new evidence to court.

Smith started with the trousers. He marked the pants pulled off the corpse as item number five. "Ever seen those before?"

"Yes," Abram confirmed.

"When was the first time you ever saw them before?"

"On the body of Nitti."

Moran remained silent. Judge David also failed to interrupt and remind the jury there was still a question as to whether the body was indeed Francesco Nitti.

Smith pushed forward. "Where was the body of Nitti when you first saw them?"

"In the sewer."

"What did you do with those trousers after you took them from the body of Nitti, if you did take them from the body?"

"I buried them right behind my garage."

"And have they been there ever since?"

"Yes."

Moran objected when Abram said the trousers were buried in the ground. He missed the three times Smith called the corpse Francesco Nitti. But the notion that the trousers were buried in the ground struck him as detrimental. Judge David paid the defense attorney no mind. And Smith was done anyway. He had what he needed from the witness.

Moran used his cross-examination to talk about the corpse's underpants. Abram testified that he and Hatton had removed the corpse's pants, but he had no memory of whether the body was wearing any underwear. This was very interesting to Moran, and he tried four times to clarify whether the corpse was indeed not wearing underwear or if it was simply misplaced. The missing garment bothered him—far more than the idea of a man wearing a coat on a warm summer evening. Judge David had to force Moran to leave the question.

There was something about the cross-examination that jolted Judge David. He had ruled the day before that Charley's hearsay confessions were allowed in court. Then, it appeared he was hit with another wave of doubt. He pulled the attorneys from the courtroom and asked the court reporter to follow. He wanted his offer on record. If Moran chose, Judge David would strike out James's testimony about Charley's supposed confession in the state's attorney's office.

Moran didn't accept the offer. But he didn't refuse. He claimed he hadn't much time in his preparations and he needed to think more about the matter. Perhaps, Moran suggested, after the completion of Dasso's direct examination, he could recall James for further questioning? Judge David agreed.

Judge David listened with a sharp ear as Dasso was recalled to the stand. Dasso had more to add to the story from the day before. He let Smith know there were parts missing, and he was eager to start again from the beginning and repeat the full story. Judge David heard Dasso describe Charley's supposed confession, which was said to have occurred in front of Peter, but not Sabella.

"Let me ask you. Just a minute," Judge David interrupted. "This time was the woman defendant there?"

"No, she was not."

"[This] is not admissible . . . against the other defendant, the woman. And you will disregard it, so far as she is concerned."

Smith was undeterred. He turned his attention toward the hammer that was alleged to have been used in the attack. He labeled it as exhibit 6 and asked the court to offer it into evidence. As with the other five exhibits, Moran objected and Judge David overruled.

Smith wanted to return to the interview in the state's attorney's office. He reviewed, for the benefit of the jury, all the people present. Dasso attended. The three defendants were there, and a few reporters as well. Smith confirmed Romano served as the interpreter, but did not enlighten the jury as to whether the assistant prosecuting attorney was truly qualified to translate.

Romano's parents were from Laurenzana, a town in the province of Potenza, located in the Basilicata region. Romano likely spoke the dialect he learned from his family, not standard Italian and certainly not Barese. Dasso also knew nothing of the intricacies of either dialect. He was the son and brother of Liguri immigrants, and his dialect was Genovese.

Moran interjected. He didn't know the linguistic differences between the different dialects, but he sensed something was incompatible. He wasn't fully able to articulate the concerns, and Judge David overruled his objection.

Just to be sure, Judge David quizzed Dasso on his understanding. "Did you understand all the questions that you are speaking of now?"

"I did," Dasso answered.

"And did you understand the answers?"

"I did."

"If any of the defendants made any answers, did you understand them?"

"I did."

"You may go on," the judge ruled.

Dasso continued. It was the same story of Charley's supposed confession in the state's attorney's office. Dasso added on that Charley claimed he heard a splash when Peter Crudele dumped the body into the canal. He also mentioned that Sabella was so distraught during the interview that she was crying and moaning.

But Dasso neglected to tell the courtroom that he couldn't possibly have understood a word Sabella said. Her dialect, Barese, was profoundly different from Genovese. Even if a word had the same meaning between the two dialects, the pronunciation was utterly different. Their language barrier was akin to an English speaker trying to converse with a Dutch speaker.

Romano's dialect was no more helpful. True, his family was from Southern Italy, in a region not too far from Sabella's home. But Potentino was actually a Northern dialect, imported south during the Middle Ages. Dasso and Romano had a greater potential of understanding each other, especially if they knew the standard Italian dialect. Standard Italian was technically the Toscano dialect. Italians who learned to read or write were more apt to have exposure to standard Italian in school. But Sabella was illiterate. She likely understood Standard Italian as well as she understood Genovese or Potentino. And that was not at all.

At worst, Dasso was being untruthful and purposefully hiding the fact that he did not understand Sabella Nitti, and she understood neither him nor Romano. At best, Dasso was being arrogant and assumed he understood more than he did. No one caught his mistake.

17

OH, DOUGH

JUDGE DAVID TOLD THE STENOGRAPHER to stay put. He wanted no record of what he had to say to Smith and Moran. He motioned for the attorneys to follow him to his chambers. A sense of secrecy followed the men out of the room.

The men soon walked briskly back into the courtroom. Judge David ordered Deputy Dasso to step down and leave the room while James Nitti was recalled to the witness stand. With no explanation to the jury, Moran was permitted to return to his cross-examination of Sabella's oldest son. James answered a few easy questions for the defense, testifying that his father was about fifty-five years old when he disappeared.

Moran changed direction. He pushed James to remember a time the year before when he drove with his brother Michael to pick up Charley in the city. Michael was speeding and he was pulled over by a Cicero police officer. Rather than calmly accepting the ticket, Michael told the policeman to go to hell. He was promptly arrested and fined fifty dollars.

"And who paid the fine?" Moran asked.

"Pete paid it," James admitted.

It was an interesting piece of evidence. James—who was so convinced in court that his mother and Peter killed his father—had actually turned to Peter and Sabella for help when money was needed. And Peter obliged, despite the fact that James at the time was sitting on the

$800 widow's award. Moran left the story untold, and moved on as if the information didn't matter.

Moran began to visibly struggle. He should have asked the judge to go ahead and strike the supposed confession from the state's attorney's office off the record. But he didn't have the wherewithal to do so. Instead, he tried to compare testimony from what James said on record at the Oak Park adultery trial with other statements he made. It was an attempt to impeach the witness, and a more skilled attorney could have successfully picked at the inconsistencies and persuaded the judge to disregard James's credibility. But Moran floundered and he looked for slight inconsistencies that seemed ridiculous. The cross-examination dragged as Moran tried to compare testimonies, but the statements were too vague and Judge David allowed James to justify himself.

James fumbled as he justified his earlier statements. At one point, he even revealed to the jury a conversation in which his mother complained his father had left the family. "When I got the first day out to the farm," James testified, "I asked Charley . . . 'Where is Ma?' And he said, 'She is out in the field.' . . . And she saw me and she started crying and I didn't see no tears in her eyes and she said to me, 'See, how your father don't come back? . . . He takes $300 with him, and he don't come back.' And I said, 'What he don't come back for, with the $300, we don't know where he is? If he went away on his own will, then he will come back of his own like.'"

The opportunity flew past Moran. He didn't question James any further about the possibility that his father had left his family. Instead, James was ordered to step down and Dasso returned to the witness stand.

During Moran's cross-examination of Dasso, the attorney's combative tone betrayed his frustration. He was argumentative and wanted to know why Dasso had not allowed Sabella, Peter, and Charley to have an attorney present during the interview in the state's attorney's office. Dasso knew full well, Moran pushed, that Sabella and Peter had counsel. They were represented by Moran in the adultery case, and the authorities should have reached out to Moran before the interview in question. Moran was agitated, and his argument came across as an

Sabella Nitti holds her youngest daughter, Mary, while incarcerated.

LEFT: Peter Crudele was about twenty-four years old when he was accused of having an affair with Sabella and murdering her husband.

RIGHT: Truck garden farmers lined up their trucks as early as 2 AM, seven days a week, to sell to wholesalers.

LEFT: The Cook County Courthouse and jail, where Sabella was held and tried. *Library of Congress*

RIGHT: Sabella's oldest son, James Nitti, watches as his younger sister Filomena is interrogated by his attorney W. W. Witty.

LEFT: In 1922, Sabella's youngest son, Charley, posed in the state's attorney's office with deputy sheriffs Paul Dasso (standing) and Harry C. W. Laubenheimer (seated). *DN-0075052, Chicago Daily News negatives collection, Chicago History Museum (cropped)*

RIGHT: Charley Nitti with the hammer allegedly used to kill his father. *DN-00750751, Chicago Daily News negatives collection, Chicago History Museum (cropped)*

LEFT: Defense attorney Eugene Moran and his wife, Connie. The two were briefly married in the early 1920s. The attorney's spiraling health might have contributed to the couple's separation.

RIGHT: Prosecuting attorney Michael Romano in his law school photo. *1921 Northwestern Syllabus yearbook, Students Publishing Co., Evanston, IL*

Portrait of State's Attorneys Milton Smith (left) and Samuel M. Hamilton (right) sitting in chairs in a room in Chicago, Illinois. Smith led the prosecution against Sabella; Hamilton tried the case against Belva Gaertner. *DN-0075486, Chicago Daily News negatives collection, Chicago History Museum (cropped)*

Judge Joseph David of the Superior Court of Cook County. Judge David initially tried to protect Sabella from her incompetent attorney. The judge later announced justice was served and refused a new trial. *DN-0072995, Chicago Daily News negatives collection, Chicago History Museum (cropped)*

Warden Wesley Westbrook hesitated to tell Sabella the verdict. In this picture, he teaches a self-defense course to two policewomen, Mrs. Marion Wrightman and Miss Clara Olsen, on how to take a revolver from a suspect. *DN-0062319, Chicago Daily News negatives collection, Chicago History Museum (cropped)*

Left: Young attorney Helen Cirese was beautiful, female, and Italian. Excluded from the Chicago law community, she set up her own practice. *Helen Cirese Papers, 1915–1974, HCP_0002_0012_001, University of Illinois at Chicago Library, Special Collections (cropped)*

Center: Frank Allegretti was one of six Italian American attorneys who defended Sabella on appeal. He was elected a municipal court judge in 1924, despite bias against Italians in Chicago's legal community. *From The Italians in Chicago: A study in Americanization by Giovanni Schiavo (1928)*

Right: Albert N. Gualano was one of the Italian American attorneys who defended Sabella on appeal. He was elected a municipal court judge in 1922 and was the first Italian to serve as a judge. *From The Italians in Chicago: A study in Americanization by Giovanni Schiavo (1928)*

Attorney Helen Cirese was one of the founding members of the Justinian Society. In this 1928 photo of their annual gala, she is the only woman. Defense attorney Rocco DeStefano stands to her left. *From The Italians in Chicago: A study in Americanization by Giovanni Schiavo (1928)*

Katherine Walters Baluk, also known as Kitty Malm, holds her young daughter in a courtroom. *DN-0076739, Chicago Daily News negatives collection, Chicago History Museum (cropped)*

LEFT: Before she became Belva Gaertner, Belva was a showgirl who went by the name "Belle Brown."

RIGHT: Belva's 1917 divorce to William Gaertner attracted headlines, including this photo, which ran in the *Chicago Daily Tribune* along with a story about her demands for alimony.

Belva Gaertner in court, looking at her attorney Thomas D. Nash.
*DN-0077649, Chicago Daily News negatives collection, Chicago
History Museum (cropped)*

Beulah Annan on the evening of her arrest,
still in a state of undress, mugs for the
camera. *DN-0076798, Chicago Daily News
negatives collection, Chicago History Museum
(cropped)*

WHY DID FIVE CHICAGO WOMEN COMMIT MURDER?

MRS. MALM

MRS NITTI-CRUDELL

MRS. KAVANAGH

MRS. ANNAN

MRS. GAERTNER

Newspapers typically portrayed Sabella as ugly and gnarled, a contrast to beautiful killers such as Belva and Beulah.

me love my babies and hope I go home soon. Sabella Nitti

Sabella learned to speak English, read, and write in jail. She also received a makeover. Here she holds up an example of her new skills.

attorney's hurt feelings for being excluded, not a fundamental violation of constitutional rights.

Moran was getting accusatory. "Now, Dasso, this whole case is worked up on one of your theories," Moran pushed.

Judge David intervened. "The jury are trying this case not on theories, but on evidence," he said.

Moran did not relent. He wanted the lawman's hearsay testimony to remain, and he had more he wanted to extract from the witness. In early statements, Dasso had said one of the children—it apparently didn't matter which one, he didn't specify—claimed her father was murdered and thrown in the river. Moran read Dasso's statement for the benefit of the jury: "In my unconcerned way, I asked, 'Where is the old man?' And this little child, understanding the English better than the older one, says that they killed him and threw him in the river."

Judge David interrupted. "Do you want this in the case?" he asked Moran, seemingly horrified by the attorney's choices.

"I want it in, Your Honor. I have a reason."

"Well, the court does not regard it as competent, but if you insist upon having it in, it may go in."

"Later I can have it stricken out," Moran said optimistically.

"No, no we will stop. The court rules that evidence that somebody told him something is not proper, but if you insist upon it, it will remain in."

"I have asked Dasso if this case was not being tried through this theory."

"Do you wish that?"

"Yes, I do."

Dasso did have his theories. A little after 11 AM, he admitted to the court that he had felt "vindicated" when the grand jury advanced the charges. The animosity between Dasso and Moran increased as the morning progressed. The men clearly did not like each other, and both were taking the case personally. Moran pushed Dasso to admit he couldn't understand Barese, and Dasso held strong that although he couldn't understand every word, he could understand most if they just went slow.

"Have you any prejudice, Mr. Dasso, against Italian peasants?"

"I object to that," Smith called out.

"Objection overruled. Answer."

"Do you look down upon them?"

"What is the question?" Dasso asked.

"Do you have any prejudice against Italian peasants?" the judge clarified.

"No, sir," Dasso answered.

"Do you look down upon this poor, unfortunate woman?" Moran asked.

"Oh, no."

"I object to that," Smith shot out, clearly annoyed with the use of "unfortunate" to describe Sabella.

Sabella sat in silence as the men discussed her. She understood nothing. The confusion in the courtroom intensified. Moran was nonsensical, and Dasso's testimony mixed the chronology of events and offered mere pieces of information. After Dasso stepped down, Smith called an Illinois judge to confirm that he had married Sabella and Peter earlier in the year. The purpose of the testimony seemed unclear, particularly since the marriage was entered into official county record and there was no question as to whether the mismatched couple had indeed married. The judge was released from the witness stand, and a sense of unprofessionalism hung in the air.

The amateurism continued. Anna Volpe, friend to the Nitti family, was called to the witness stand. Anna was also an immigrant from Bari and was in the same social community as the Nitti family. She was the godmother of one of Sabella's daughters, a choice Francesco apparently made without Sabella's blessing. Sabella did not care for Anna. The woman was a troublemaker, Sabella thought, always trying to initiate conflict for her own entertainment.

Anna had an interest in the case. She supported James in his quest to take the family's estate for himself. But she had little to add in terms of evidence. And so, the testimony flowed in every direction, trying to uncover whatever information might lead the defendants to the gallows.

At times, the interpreter couldn't catch everything Volpe said. An attorney by the name of Chiesesi[*] was tasked with trying to understand Anna. There was a story about Peter sitting under the tree. And perhaps had he been dismissed from employment? And something about five dollars? And then Sabella confided in Anna how she no longer wanted Francesco?

"I don't want the husband, I don't want to see him anymore," the translator repeated.

"Who is that?" Judge David asked, confused.

"Mrs. Nitti."

Romano needed them to back up. "Translate the rest of it, what she said?"

The translator jumped ahead. "She said, 'I do not want to see him anymore.'"

"Go on," Judge David encouraged.

"Then why do you send your husband away. She says, 'My husband stinks around, don't want him.'"

The translation was terrible. "What?" Judge David asked.

"My husband stinks," the interpreter repeated.

"Smells," Smith offered.

"I don't quite understand," the interpreter admitted. "The boy getting stones on the farm?"

"Don't know," Romano agreed.

The interpreter tried again, then he admitted he was lost. "There are some words in the dialect, they only speak in a certain locality, and of course, they are not—those words are not very intelligible, that is the whole thing."

Smith wasn't willing to give up on the struggling witness. "Now, Your Honor, here is an interpreter who speaks their own dialect. Will you let him interpret?"

---

[*] The translator was most likely Vincent Chisesi, an Italian American attorney and member of the Justinian Society (see chapter 23).

"I am not calling upon him," the judge refused.

It was impossible to proceed. Court adjourned until 1 PM.

————————

After lunch, the new interpreter was late. Judge David did not want to waste the court's time and another witness was called while they waited for an interpreter. Louis Roden, the Berwyn city employee who had climbed into the catch basin and retrieved the body, took the stand. He was a thorough witness and had a strong memory of the day he touched a decayed corpse with his bare hands. He was articulate and the testimony moved quickly. But he didn't have much to add. It was the same cycle of questions asked of Hatton and the undertaker Abram. Then, more talk about the gold band and the shoes.

Roden stepped down, and the court still had to address the issue of the interpreter. They needed someone now, and there was a possibility that Michele Desant, the farmhand who lived in the back shanty, could translate. Desant was present and he could fill the need. The court agreed, but Judge David was clear that Desant was not permitted to talk about how he was afraid of Michael Nitti.

Romano stood at the prosecution's table. He had a list of questions he and Smith had prepared for the witness. Smith had dominated the examination for the past two days, but the attorneys sensed Anna would respond better to another Italian, and Romano was tasked with the direct examination. Anna indeed saw an ally in Romano and tried to speak directly to him.

Judge David stopped them.

"May I ask her in Italian, or talk to her in Italian, just a minute?" Romano requested.

"I'm not going to waste any time on that," Judge David refused. The process had already been established. Romano was to question the witness in English. Desant was to translate the question into Barese. After Anna answered in Barese, Desant was to repeat the answer in English. The witness was not to address the court in English, and Romano was not allowed to ask questions in Potentino, or whatever dialect he thought was comprehensible.

Desant translated swiftly. Anna claimed Sabella was angry because Peter was dismissed from his job as a farmhand. Sabella supposedly confided in Anna that she and Peter were prepared to kill Francesco if necessary. Then, she announced she was off to have sex with Peter and flounced away.

It was hearsay testimony. Judge David allowed it.

Romano finished and Moran stepped up to question Anna. "Are you on friendly terms with Sabella Nitti now?" the defense attorney asked.

The answer was clearly no, but Anna refused to answer. She told Desant she could not understand him. Judge David focused on the inefficiency stalling his courtroom and did not comment how it was odd that Anna had understood Desant perfectly well until the defense stood up for cross-examination. Suddenly, the arrangement no longer worked?

Judge David was infuriated. He scolded both sides for not coming to court prepared with a qualified interpreter. "We are doing the best we can," Smith complained.

"No, you are not," the judge shamed.

Desant was dismissed without a thank you or the suggestion that he should receive the same ten-dollar pay offered to Chiesesi. A third interpreter was presented. Frank Allegretti, another attorney, was brought to the front of the room and asked to assist. Allegretti was from Trivigno, which was relatively close to the town where Romano's family came from. He likely did not speak Barese, and it was probable he did not understand much of what Anna had to say. But he was terribly dashing, and Anna appeared agreeable at first.

Allegretti had a full head of dark hair, pale skin, and deep brown eyes. He had a strong, masculine jaw, and medium build. Anna suddenly understood the handsome lawyer—who spoke a different dialect—better than she did Desant, a Barese speaker. It was likely that Anna knew more English than she let on. It was possible she understood the questions being asked in English and then chose words she knew Allegretti would understand.

The questioning resumed. Moran wanted to know if Anna considered herself friendly with Sabella.

"We have always been friends," she answered.

"Do you consider yourself her friend now?"

"I have always been good to her and I always wished her well now."

The courtroom was too noisy. Judge David stopped the testimony. There were Italians in the gallery who were speaking among themselves. It was possible they were catching the sudden changes in the witness's dialect, and were trading criticism about her. But Judge David took it as disrespect and hushed the gallery with a harsh warning.

The questioning proceeded, or at least attempted to continue. Anna was a hostile witness to Moran. She gave incomplete answers, reversed what she had said in earlier statements, and pretended not to understand the translator whenever it suited her needs.

Judge David might have suspected that Anna was purposefully being uncooperative. But he allowed the examination to continue. The witness perked up when given the opportunity to testify that Sabella claimed she and Peter plotted to kill Francesco if he refused to rehire Peter. She was equally successful in retelling the 'My husband stinks' story and the announcement that Sabella ended a conversation with a proclamation that she was off to have sex with Peter.

Moran did not ask any questions to refute the woman's testimony. Instead he asked, "Who have you talked with about this case?"

"With Sabella Nitti," Anna answered.

"Have you talked with anyone else?"

Anna gave a revealing answer that the court chalked up to her misunderstanding. "The children are pushing this case, I have nothing to do with it."

The answer was stricken out upon Smith's insistence.

For a woman who claimed to not have any investment in the case, Anna was consistent with James Nitti and Mike Travaglio's testimony. She described the gold band in tune with their testimony and claimed she recognized the body when she was called to the undertaker's by

Dasso. She even had more to add to the story, and she freely told Romano during the redirect.

"Have you ever seen that ring before?"

"For two years he wore it always on the third finger of the left hand."

"When you say 'he,' who do you mean?" Romano clarified.

"Frank Nitti."

"Look close," she offered, pointing at the ring. "And you will see there is dough in there he used to knead his own bread."

The point was important to Anna. She switched to English. "Look, dry bread. Look, see see."

Moran conceded. "That is dry bread."

Saturday morning at 9:30 AM, court resumed but did not progress. The first order of business was to recall Dasso to the witness stand. Both sides questioned the deputy sheriff, and the jury heard old testimony framed through new questions. But the repetition was not for nothing. Dasso was the most prominent voice, and he was called to the stand five times during the trial. The jury heard more from the deputy sheriff than any other witness. The defendants would only take the stand for a few minutes each, and the defense had only one other witness to call. Dasso was the foremost witness, and his testimony shaped the case.

Moran had other concerns. He asked the judge to remove the jury so that he might make a motion. Judge David acquiesced, and when the jury returned, they watched as Moran entered six exhibits into evidence—all relating to the probate case between James and his mother. Smith dutifully objected to each exhibit, but Judge David allowed them, even though Moran failed to bring certified copies. With the papers submitted as evidence, the defense was ready to call the first witness, Peter Crudele.

The testimony began with Moran asking questions in English and Allegretti translating, which confused Peter at times. He understood the questions being asked of him, and he was tempted to answer in

English. It took a few questions until he adjusted to the odd structure of a middleman.

"Petro," Moran asked, likely meaning Pietro. "How long did you work in Stickney, Illinois?"

"Nine months."

"When did you start to work there?"

Peter came at the end of October in 1921, but was dismissed the following May. He was back by July 1922. Moran should have paused to ask why Sabella and her husband took the young man back after he was fired. The truth was that his help was desperately needed. James and Michael barely helped. Charley disappeared for days at a time. And Francesco assigned himself the lighter duties. Someone other than Sabella needed to perform the heavy labor, and Peter was amenable to the task.

Moran tried to establish the facts surrounding the vicious fight between Francesco and Michael. It had occurred within weeks before Francesco went missing, and Michael succeeded in battering his father. It was important to the case. But Smith stepped in front of every attempt Moran made to lead the witness into the story about the fight.

"What was the occasion of [Michael] leaving his father's farm?" Moran asked.

"I object," Smith called. Judge David sided with the prosecution.

"Exception," Moran responded. "Here, Your Honor, the state is trying to show a certain motive for Petro to have killed Francisco." The missing man was actually named Francesco. No one noticed the mistake.

"I object to the speech."

"Sustain the objection to that question. Put another one."

Moran refused to yield. "I certainly have a right to say, Your Honor, what my purpose is in putting the question to a witness."

"I have sustained the objection."

"Exception."

Moran tried again. "Do you know of any trouble that Michael had with Francisco?"

"That is objected to."

"Objection sustained."

Moran made a third attempt. "What occurred on July 22, 1922, at the farm, that you know?"

"I object to it."

"Objection sustained."

"Exception."

Moran gave up. The judge had tolerated Anna testifying how she heard Sabella brag she was moments away from having sex with Peter. He had allowed Dasso to tell stories that came from words he could not understand. And he had permitted James and Mike to enter passing comments into testimony. But the judge would not permit the defense to introduce to the jury the beating Francesco received from Michael shortly before his disappearance.

"Where were you on July 29, 1922, Petro?"

"At the farm."

"What were you doing on the farm?"

"I was working."

Moran detailed the responsibilities that Peter had on the farm. He cleaned the horses. He cut the oats in the machine. He harvested the vegetables, prepared them for market, and loaded them on the truck. He went to the city to purchase fertilizer, manure, and other supplies. The day Francesco disappeared was like any other. It was a Saturday, and Peter finished his work at 6:30 PM and went to the house for his dinner.

"How long did it take you to *mongari* that night?" Moran asked, mispronouncing the Italian verb meaning "to eat."

"Are you talking Italian?" Judge David accused.

"I just did then."

"Don't use it," Judge David scolded.

Peter switched between English and Barese. Judge David listened to the witness and determined it would be fine if he answered in English. Peter's words were heavily accented and he spoke in short sentences. But it was easier for the court than dealing with the translator.

Peter explained that it took them all an hour to eat. Then, he had more chores in the barn. Three other workers including Desant were with him. After he finished his work, he went to bed and slept through the night until 6:30 AM.

"What did you do at half-past six?" Moran asked.

"Went to fix doors."

"And went about the chores on the place."

"Yes."

"Petro, did you ever see this hammer before?"

"No."

"Was that ever on the Nitti family farm while you were there?"

"No, sir; I never see it."

Moran tried to start a line of questioning about the adultery and fornication charges. He wanted to address the testimony Peter gave before the magistrate at the end of October 1922. "Before Judge McKee, in Oak Park, didn't you *testimonia?*"

The word meant nothing. "Who, me?" Peter asked, confused.

"Yes."

"I don't remember."

"Did you *testimonia?*" Moran repeated.

"No, don't you use the Italian, you use the English," Judge David ordered.

Moran moved on. "Did you give testimony before the Coroner on May 9, 1923 in Berwyn?"

"There was James Volpe and his wife."

Peter didn't understand. Moran asked a series of questions that failed to receive a proper answer. Instead of trying to clarify the answer, he moved on to a new question and received an equally confusing answer. In his frustration, he inched closer to his client. Judge David ordered him back.

Moran stepped back. "Did you on July 29, hit Frank Nitti on the head with a hammer?"

"No, sir."

"Wait a moment and then carry his body in the drainage canal and throw it in the drainage canal?"

"Never."

"Never," Moran repeated. He turned toward Smith with a challenge. "Take the witness."

Smith refused. He wanted a translator. Judge David ordered Peter to continue testifying in English, and Smith refused to participate. There was no cross-examination. Peter had said all he was permitted to share with the jury. He stepped down and returned to his seat at the table. Charley was called next.

Charley had grown his hair long and it made him look older. The year before, when all the troubles started, he shaved his hair down to the skull and it made him resemble a young boy barely past ten. Now sixteen, his face still did not require a razor. His Adam's apple did not yet bulge from his neck and he looked closer to thirteen. Smith looked at the boy as he walked up to the witness stand. Charley was notably small, and it was possible the jury would feel sympathetic.

Moran began questioning the witness in English. Charley was intimidated. He spoke quietly as he answered that he didn't know his exact birthday but he knew he would be seventeen the following May.

"Charley, talk up right to me here, make me hear, so these gentlemen over here can hear," Moran encouraged.

Charley spoke up. He established the last time he saw his father was the morning of July 29, 1922.

"You have heard certain witnesses make certain statements that you said certain things," Moran asked.

"Yes."

"Did you say certain things?"

"I object," Smith interrupted.

"Objection sustained," Judge David ruled. It was a concerning decision. Why wasn't a witness allowed to testify as to whether he made the statements others accused him of making?

Moran tried a different approach. "Under what circumstances Charley, did you say such things?"

"I object," Smith blurted.

"Objection sustained."

"Exception," Moran said, defeated.

"Do you know where your father is now, Charley?"

"No, sir; I do not."

"That is all."

Smith started the cross-examination and quickly learned he had to be careful. Charley was highly intimidated. He spoke softly and Judge David had to ask the boy to speak up. Smith established that Charley saw his father throughout the day on July 29 but then he disappeared after dinner. He did not ask the young man any questions regarding the statements others made. Perhaps he didn't want to hear him deny all wrongdoing. Or maybe he didn't want the jury to think this young man was too small and vulnerable to hurt anyone or be an accessory to murder.

"No further cross-examination," Smith said.

18

SABELLA ON THE STAND

Moran motioned for Sabella to stand. Her eyes were almost always diverted to the floor and her quiet presence made it seem as though the trial was happening without her. Now on the last day of testimony, the burden of the defendants' rebuttal fell on Sabella.

Moran addressed the court. "Now, this witness does not even speak pidgin English, she does not even understand me, so I will have to call on the interpreter."

He paused. "What is your name?"

Sabella's Barese voice filled the courtroom. Then the interpreter spoke. "Sabella Nitti."

"Where do you live?"

"On the farm."

"Where are you living now?"

"I used to live in Cicero, but my house has been taken down by the bum of my son."

"I object to the latter part," Smith said, predictably.

"That may stand," Judge David allowed.

"Where do you live?"

"In jail."

"Were you living on the farm on July 29, 1922?"

"Yes."

"Sabella, were you ever in jail before?"

"I object to that," Smith called out. Judge David initially agreed, but then he allowed the witness to answer.

"I was in jail the 14th of September . . . I was under suspicion."

Sabella was allowed to explain how she had been in jail for almost three months, along with her youngest daughter. When she was released, she boarded with Michele Desant. Sabella referred to Desant as "Mike," and Moran failed to clarify for the jury that she was not living with her son, Michael Nitti.

Moran was permitted to lead Sabella into remembering the meeting in the state's attorney's office. "What was being done, or what was being said there?"

"They want to take up in separate places or separate houses, and they wanted to beat us, and I had a baby in my arms."

Smith interrupted with an objection. Chicago police were notorious at the time for beating suspects, and the legal community had a high tolerance for inmate abuse. But Judge David did not want to hear any insinuation that the defendants were harmed in custody. The jury was ordered to disregard Sabella's testimony.

Sabella tried to repeat the answer; her memory of the incident was strong and she wanted to be heard.

"Did somebody talk to you in Italian?"

"The young man said, don't go, don't go, they will kill you."

"Oh," Smith said. He didn't even bother to object. "If the court please."

Judge David agreed with Smith. Sabella had no right, in his opinion, to tell the court that she believed she was going to be beaten. It was hearsay evidence, and Judge David was not going to allow it.

Moran forged ahead. "At that time, Mrs. Nitti, did you say that whatever Charley said was right?"

"No, no, no."

Moran was distracted. Another attorney was whispering from the gallery, trying to help him. Judge David stopped the proceedings and asked if Moran wanted the counselor to be moved to the defendants' table. Moran declined, and Judge David used the break to remind Moran that he was still getting too close to the witness box. He had been warned before to stay on his side of the courtroom. Moran retreated near the defendants' table.

"Sabella, have you ever seen this hammer before? Look at it."

Sabella pointed at Anna in the gallery. "At the house of James Volpe."

"When?"

"About a year, I don't go to her house."

"Was that hammer on the farm, July 29, 1922?"

"It was never at my house. I know all the tools at my farm."

"When did you last see your husband, Frank Nitti?"

"On the 29th of July."

"What time?"

"Nine or ten o'clock, I didn't have a watch."

Sabella confirmed Peter's testimony, but when Moran asked her if she knew where her husband was, the question was lost in translation. Moran seemingly wanted Sabella to provide an answer that suggested Francesco was not dead. Instead, Sabella remained focused on the night Francesco went missing, and explained how he sent her to bed.

"All right," Moran gave up.

"I object to it," Smith shot out. "There is no question."

Judge David overruled. Sabella was allowed to repeat her answer.

"He said, you go to bed, I am going out to the oats and see that somebody does not put a match to it and burn it up."

"Did you and Peter Crudele hit Frank Nitti on the head with this hammer and kill him on July 29, 1922?"

Sabella was adamant. "If I had seen Pete Crudele strike my husband on the head with that hammer, I would have killed Pete Crudele before he would have killed my husband."

Smith objected. It was a yes or no question, not a declaration. Moran was asked to read the question again.

"No," Sabella answered simply.

Smith stepped in Moran's way again. When the defense tried to bring up the animosity Anna and James Volpe felt toward Sabella, Smith blocked the question. Moran pivoted and tried to bring up Anna and James's role in the probate case. Smith moved swiftly and blocked again.

Moran gave up. "That is all. Take the witness."

Smith charged at Sabella. He wanted to know her name. When she answered, Sabella Nitti, he challenged her.

"Are you a married lady now?"

"Sure."

"What is your name?"

"Crudele."

"When did you become Crudele?"

"Ninth of March."

"What year?"

"Three months ago."

"1923?"

"Yes."

Smith pushed Sabella to say that she didn't know whether her husband was dead or alive when she married Peter.

"I waited nine months," Sabella defended.

Smith asked an easy question, a buffer before the much harder one that hid behind it.

"How many children have you?"

"Five."

"How many?"

"Five."

"And you were in love with Peter Crudele weren't you?"

Sabella caught the insinuation Smith threw at her. "I don't know. I know Peter Crudele since the 9th of March."

Smith didn't understand what Sabella meant by "I don't know." She meant that she and Peter were not intimate until after the wedding. Smith took the answer literally. "Didn't you know Peter while he worked on the farm?"

"Yes, I knew Pete, I was the supervisor of the force on the farm."

"And you slept with him while he worked on the farm, didn't you?"

"I didn't know him."

Smith tried the question twice more. Both Moran and the judge had to inform him that it was a figure of speech. The question was asked and answered.

"And what did you mean when you told Anna Volpe that your husband stinked?"

"Anna Volpe has always been the troublemaker in my house," Sabella shot back.

"Anna Volpe was a good friend of yours, wasn't she?"

"She was always a troublemaker."

Smith pushed Sabella to admit that Anna was godmother to one of her daughters, and that both her daughters were placed in her care while she was incarcerated. Sabella reminded Smith that her sons were bums who were all over Chicago.

Smith didn't like the answer but Judge David allowed it. Smith tried the question again.

"Anna Volpe has taken care of your children ever since you have been in this trouble, hasn't she?"

"Nobody asked her to, I said to take them to the Sisters," Sabella said, meaning the order of Catholic nuns who ran orphanages.

Smith dropped the questions about Anna. He returned to the evening that Francesco went missing and reviewed who was present on the farm. "Now, what did you do when they were all there?" he asked.

"I used to work night and day, and my children, my bum children were bumming."

Smith ignored the insults. He believed the farmer's market was closed on Sundays and he wanted Sabella to admit to the court that her husband did not send her to bed in order for everyone to be up early for the farmer's market. He tried five times but Sabella never gave him the answer he wanted.

Smith's assumption that the market was closed on Sunday showed how little he knew about the case or the people involved. Since the 1880s, the market on Randolph Street was the place where truck garden farmers sold their crops wholesale. This was not some fresh air market that closed on Sundays because the clientele were housewives or maids who had church to attend or family to visit. No, the clients were hotels, restaurants, grocers, and other institutions with a business to run every day of the week. The farmers came as early as 2 AM to find a parking spot on Randolph, set up their displays, and if necessary, pay their fee to the market master. They came every day, even Sunday.

If Moran had been taking notes, he might have caught an inconsistency and an opportunity to impeach Mike Travaglio. Sabella's nephew testified that in July 1922, he worked at a candy company located on the 400 block of Orleans. He lived about a mile away from the factory on the 400 block of North May Street. He claimed during his testimony that he went through the Randolph Market the Saturday Francesco went missing.

The market was more than half a mile away from the factory where Mike Travaglio worked. It was not on his route home, and the market wasn't open to the public. The Randolph Market was for wholesalers, and not a shopping spot for individual consumers. Just north of the vegetable market was the meat market, also a wholesaler. Mike had no business in either spot, and it's plausible that he never walked through the market that Saturday morning to see his uncle. Even if he did, it was likely that their encounter would have been brief. Mike claimed he walked through the market around 6 or 7 AM. Francesco would have been busy selling his merchandise to buyers.

Smith's insinuation that Francesco did not leave at 2 AM on a Sunday morning for the market was dangerously unjust. Moran missed it. Sabella held firm, and Smith moved off the question, although he possibly implanted another seed of doubt in the jury's mind. Would they believe the market was closed on Sunday? Would they assume that her story was just a cover-up?

Smith pushed on to Dasso's claim that Francesco was asleep under the wagon. "After you got through with your supper, your husband went over and lay under the wagon, is that not right?"

"My husband always used to sleep with me. He never did have no reason to go away and sleep under the wagon."

"After you had your supper that night, it was a hot night, wasn't it?"

"Yes, in July," Sabella agreed, even though the temperature never hit 80 degrees that day.

Smith moved on to confirm who was in the home and where they slept. Sabella couldn't remember whether Charley was home that evening. He left the farm for days at a time to go into the city and was often unaccounted for. "I don't remember well," Sabella said. "Charley would always go like that night, he was never in day or night."

"Was Charley a bad boy?" Smith asked.

"Wait a minute, I object," Moran contested.

"Objection sustained," Judge David agreed.

Moran's moment of lucidity passed. "He must be bad," he announced to the court. "When he is indicted for murder!"

Judge David hushed the defense attorney. Smith waited and then resumed. "Now, when you woke up the next morning, did you see your husband?"

Sabella told her story about waking to find her husband missing. Her second son, Michael, she added, also didn't come home for a week. Smith was unprepared for her response and he tangled in her answer. "Who didn't come home for a week?" he asked, not realizing the answer was problematic.

"My son Mike didn't come home for a week."

Smith backed off the damaging fact that the night Francesco disappeared, two of his sons were missing. He instead confirmed that she went to the police to ask for help in finding her husband. But he dropped the topic when he realized her rapid plea for help was also not a helpful element to his case.

"Isn't it a fact that you hate your husband?" Smith asked aggressively.

"He was always my husband, I lived twenty-five years with him, and he never disturbed me," Sabella said.

"Did you like him?"

"You bet. If I didn't like him, I would not go walking around," Sabella answered, meaning her visit to the chief of police to ask for help.

"Didn't you try to have him arrested a short time before he disappeared?"

"Yes."

Moran interrupted. He didn't want the jury to know that Sabella was a battered woman who had turned to the police for help. Judge David permitted the testimony, but by then both Sabella and the translator had forgotten the question and needed it repeated. This irritated Smith. He felt the witness talked too much. "In answer to every question she is giving a lecture," he complained to the judge.

Judge David reminded Smith that the witness had the right to give a whole answer. Sabella was permitted to speak and she launched into the memory of the time Francesco began beating Charley and then turned his fists on her. They thought that visiting the police and asking for help would "quiet him down."

"Is that the time that Charley took a shotgun and was going to kill your husband?" Smith asked.

"I think we are going close to the line," Judge David warned.

Sabella held back her answer. Moran spoke up. "They are blowing hot and cold now," he said, nonsensically.

Judge David looked at the defense attorney. The man was ridiculous. "Do you object to it?"

"Yes."

"Well, why don't you do it? You didn't?"

"I am now," Moran scowled.

"Objection sustained."

Sabella continued to irritate Smith. He wanted to pin down the dates on which Peter was fired from the farm. Sabella didn't understand the word "fired" and the question had to be repeated with "discharged." She also didn't remember the dates or the details very much. It wasn't of consequence to her.

"Your husband discharged Peter in May because of his intimate relations with you, wasn't that right?"

"No, no," Sabella denied. "My husband was insulted from [James] Volpe, when he told him I had something to do with Crudele. I asked my husband, and I told my husband to put out Peter Crudele because I cannot stand it. I am Sabella Nitti, and I couldn't stand it."

Smith was incredulous. "You asked your husband to discharge Peter?"

"I told my husband, he is a good man. I told my husband, Peter is a good man. He is a good worker and he helps around the farm, but my sons are bums. One of them is a bum for two years in Chicago."

"Did you ever tell your husband to discharge Peter?"

"Yes, if you have a bad head or a bad temper, put him out."

"What did you mean by that?" Smith clarified.

"My husband was insulted by Anna Volpe, and he always used to pick on me, and I said if you have—"

Judge David interrupted. "Now, let's get along."

"I object to that," Smith said, seemingly offended. "And move that it be stricken out." He paused. "Everybody in the neighborhood knew that you were sleeping with Peter?"

It was Moran's turn to be offended. "I object."

Judge David chastised the prosecution. "Objection sustained. You should not ask that kind of question. It is not the legal way to prove anything."

"It's not fair, either," Moran chimed.

"The jury will disregard it. The question is improper."

Smith moved on to the hammer. Sabella denied it was her husband's and said it belonged to James and Anna. "And how do you know it is [James] and Anna Volpe's?" Smith challenged.

"I went over to the house one time and I took it in my hands and split wood."

The questioning paused. The tension between Smith and Moran had degraded into bickering. Moran felt Smith stood too close to the witness and it wasn't fair. After all, when it was his turn, he wasn't allowed to stand near the witness. Judge David warned the two attorneys to stop talking back and forth to each other. The next attorney who did so would face punishment from the court.

The two men fumed, but the jury was unlikely to know the undercurrent of hostility was indicative of a greater problem. It was natural for litigators to show some emotion in court. Some even used emotion strategically and gave forceful or angry performances to compel the jury to feel outraged. But it was also natural for such litigators to turn off such emotion and not take rulings personally. Attorneys who battled in the courtroom often chatted pleasantly in the lobby at the end of the day. There was an ease to these conversations as they asked about each other's families or upcoming holiday plans. It was based in professional courtesy, but also the knowledge that the legal community in Chicago was quite small. Exchanging pleasantries was mandatory for getting along and getting ahead. A lawyer never knew which former rival might advance to a judge position. Opposing counsel might one day serve on a hiring or nominating committee. But decorum on the part of Moran and Smith was lost that week in Judge David's courtroom.

Judge David ordered calm. Smith put the hammer down and stepped back from the witness. "When did you see that hammer at Anna Volpe's house?"

"I don't remember, it was one time when I took it in my hands, I know, because it was split and I had a splinter in my face one time from splitting wood," Sabella explained.

Smith took the gold band, held it up to Sabella, and asked if she had ever seen it before. "That is not my husband's ring, he never wore it," she said.

"Is that your husband's ring?"

"No, no."

"Did you ever see it in your life?"

"No, no."

"That is all," Smith concluded.

"That is all," Moran agreed.

Both sides rested. For a moment, it appeared that Sabella would be the last witness to testify. This might have been helpful to the defense. She had denied everything, introduced glimpses of life on the Nitti family farm, and suggested that this life was not as Smith had presented. Perhaps her strong testimony was what caused the state to introduce a new witness in rebuttal. James Volpe, the husband of Anna, was sworn in as a witness for the state.

The man did not have much to offer. Smith questioned him only briefly. All he did was confirm that he knew Francesco in his lifetime and the hammer in question belonged to the Nitti family farm. "He had more of them, he had two like that," James said through the translator.

"That is all, cross-examine," Smith rested.

Moran stood up to question the witness. The hammer had been in the state's possession since the autumn of 1922 when Sabella was held under fornication and adultery charges while Dasso tried to push the murder charges. The hammer in all likelihood came from the Volpes' farm. A shrewd attorney would have pushed James to admit as much. But Moran was more interested in telling the jury how James had a wife and children in Italy whom he had abandoned when he moved to the United States and started anew with Anna.

Smith objected as Moran pushed the witness to admit he was a bigamist. Judge David quickly shut down the line of questioning. Moran changed direction and tried to push the witness to admit the hammer was a common object used by workmen around the city, and there was nothing distinct about the hammer to suggest it was owned by the Nitti family or used as a murder weapon. James refused to cooperate, and he claimed they did not use any hammers at his job at Crane Company, a manufacturer of heavy industrial products. Nor did he think blacksmiths in the area used such hammers. He told the jury the hammer was unique to the Nitti family farm.

Moran didn't know how to cut through Volpe's claims. He was frustrated and defeated.

"That is all," he told the courtroom.

19

DON'T THINK OF HER
AS A WOMAN

THE JURY WAS LED OUT OF THE COURTROOM. Before the closing arguments began, Judge David wanted to address the case against Charley Nitti. There was not enough evidence against the boy, and the judge didn't want the case to proceed to the jury. Judge David called the attorneys to the bench. "There is no legal evidence," Judge David began, "that would justify the State's Attorney as asking for a decision against the defendant Charles Nitti."

Smith began to protest. "The state at this time also feels—"

"I don't care how you feel," Judge David interrupted. "You haven't any legal evidence."

"The statement as to what Charles did. He helped take away the body," Smith said.

Judge David scoffed. "That has nothing to do with the murder."

"He is an accessory after the fact."

"He is not indicted as such." Judge David shot him down.

"Or accessory before the fact," Smith tried.

"He is not."

Smith was getting desperate. "He knew that the father was going to be killed, and he stood there, and he saw him killed, and he acquiesced to the killing."

"I think the attitude is absurd," Judge David said bluntly. "And if necessary, I will instruct the jury . . . that notwithstanding the suggestion the state's attorney refused to acquiesce in this."

Smith was backed into a corner. He could either give up the case against Charley, or the judge would tell the jury to disregard any evidence against the young defendant. Smith had to consider how each option might weaken his case against the two adult defendants.

The judge reminded Smith of the flaws in the case against Charley. "I said in the judgment of opinion of the court, you have no case against this boy. He is only a boy, he was not then sixteen. And the evidence would tend to show that he did not go in there under coercion. He didn't strike the blow, he didn't strike nobody; he didn't do anything."

"The old lady didn't strike anybody," Smith argued.

"She didn't have to," Judge David fired back. "You have evidence that she handed the hammer to him. Your evidence is sufficient as to the other defendants, as far as going to the jury is concerned."

Smith tried to barter. If the judge kept the charges against Charley, perhaps the verdict could be set aside? The judge refused. Moran tried the same with a verdict against Sabella or Peter. Could that too be set aside? Judge David again refused and pushed each attorney to estimate how long they needed for the closing arguments. Smith guessed at least two hours. The state planned for both Romano and Smith to address the jury. Moran really couldn't say; he expected to respond accordingly to the prosecution's arguments. Judge David thought for a moment. It was already 11:30 AM on a Saturday, pushing lunchtime. The closing arguments would take all afternoon and then the jury would deliberate. As much as he disliked sequestering the jury for another day, it was necessary. The court adjourned until Monday at 9 AM. Judge David made it clear—he wanted the case to end on Monday. Closing statements, deliberation, and verdict would need to happen before the close of court.

Romano awoke Monday morning in the home he shared with his mother. He dressed in his crisp white shirt, pulled on his trousers, tightened his tie, and buttoned his vest. He looked in the mirror and held a comb to his thick, wavy hair. When he was in law school just two years earlier, he wore his hair parted in the middle. Now the fashion was to smooth it with pomade and comb it straight back. Pomade was practical; it never dried and always had a shiny, wet appearance. And it lasted much longer than other hair products. Romano could go for days without washing his hair or adding more product.

Romano pulled on his suit jacket and stepped into the morning sun. It was an unusually cool day for July and the temperature was still in the upper sixties. This was helpful for a man about to address a jury. He did not want to appear sweaty or nervous. It was crucial that he exude confidence and convince the jury the prosecution was competent.

Romano looked young in his suit. His face was soft, with smooth cheeks and a cleft in his chin. But his towering height gave him a commanding presence. And he possessed the certainty that one would expect from a young man so prone to success. He was not yet twenty-six and his life had been a string of achievements. First he graduated St. Ignatius high school, one of the most prestigious in Chicago. Then, he matriculated to the University of Illinois for his undergraduate education, and on to Northwestern University for his law degree. He was an officer of his law school class, and the state's attorney's office was quick to hire the rising legal star. Romano stood in front of the jury, confident in himself and what he had to say.

"May it please Your Honor and the Gentlemen of the Jury," Romano began. "After a week's listening and attention to the different witnesses who have testified in this case, gentlemen, we approach the very last lap of the journey. We approach the stage of the proceedings where the responsibilities are lifted gradually from the shoulders of the state's prosecutors—who have done their best to give you all the evidence in this case—to your shoulders."

It was a typical introduction. Romano urged the jury to "sit in judgment" of the two defendants, whom he argued were guilty of their crimes. Then, he turned his attention to the defense attorney. Mr. Moran, he assured the jury, was actually a very mild-mannered and courteous man outside the courtroom. Moran's behavior in the courtroom, Romano presumed, was based on his desperation to help his clients cheat the rope. He scoffed at Moran's attempt to push the blame onto Michael or James Nitti.

Romano began to review the evidence with the jury, starting with a summary of Mike Travaglio's testimony. Romano reminded the jury how Sabella's nephew said he received a pair of shoes as a gift from his uncle Francesco. The shoes were too big and the witness returned them. He saw those shoes on his uncle the day he went missing, and then he saw them again on the corpse at the undertaker's.

Romano moved on to the ring. Mike had identified it, and James had agreed the ring once belonged to him and then his father. Anna had identified fine bits of dough in the prongs. "If this fails to satisfy you," Romano continued, "you have the added testimony of Dr. Hatton." Romano recalled Hatton's testimony but misquoted the doctor and claimed Hatton said a blow from a blunt object killed Francesco.

Romano was smooth and convincing. He never reversed himself. He didn't pause or stutter. He spoke to the jury with the utmost confidence that he and Smith had fairly tried this case and brought justice to Francesco. He was so assured that he gracefully worked his way around the glaring problem that the corpse could not be positively identified as Francesco. The principle of corpus delicti required that a crime must be proven to have occurred, and there was no proof that Francesco was even dead. Not only might the corpse in the catch basin not have been Francesco, but that corpse might not have been murdered. But Smith and Romano had a plan for working around corpus delicti. There were other cases in Illinois law in which victimization was in doubt. Guilty verdicts were rendered nonetheless, and Romano intended to share such case law and assure the jury the precedent was firmly established.

Romano began by detailing *People v. Sapp*, a case from 1917 in western Illinois in which Bert Sapp was convicted of murdering Emma Larkins and leaving her body on a railroad track. The evidence was circumstantial. Emma was in town only to work at a fairground, and few people knew her well enough to identify her. She was identified by the jewelry witnesses testified they saw her wearing. The only known interaction she had with the defendant was that she was once seen sitting in the horse stall he was using as a makeshift bedroom. The defense tried to claim that it wasn't known whether the victim was in fact Emma, or whether the person found on the track was even murdered. She had wounds on her head, as if she had been in a fight, but no one could truly say whether they were the cause of her death.

Emma battled a morphine addiction and was previously institutionalized for treatment that was not deemed successful. Near the time of the alleged murder, she was seen with hypodermic scars and marks on her arms. The defense unsuccessfully tried to argue other possibilities for her death. A woman with such a troubled history could have injured herself. And it was not known whether she was truly dead—jewelry wasn't a positive identification. But the jury was unmoved and the defendant received a twenty-two-year sentence.

Romano read from the case law as if he was giving the jury a lecture at the law school. He moved on to *People v. Campbell*, a case from 1917 in which a young, unmarried couple was accused of murdering their illegitimate newborn. The father was found guilty of infanticide and sentenced to fourteen years. Romano had several more examples. He spared the jury the details of each case and instead read from the rulings how the judges were satisfied that corpus delicti was proven. "It may be proved by circumstantial evidence," Romano quoted, "if it is strong and cogent, and leaves no room for reasonable doubt."

Romano described another case, one with which he was certain the jury was familiar. It involved a husband charged with giving his wife arsenic injections. The defense challenged the cause of death, and even suggested the amount of arsenic found in her system was not enough to kill her. Romano read from the case law, and included the section and page numbers as appropriate. He went on for the better part of an hour, lecturing the jury on verdicts that had nothing to do with the case he had just tried.

Romano eventually closed the law books and worked his way back to the case against Sabella and Peter. There was no money motive, he promised the jury, for Michael or James Nitti to frame their mother for murder. "The money eked out of that estate by the careful administration, and counsel of Mr. Witte, the lawyer in that case, was used to give the father an honest, decent burial. That could not have been the motive."

Moran objected. "I object to that. That is not so. The estate of the probate court has not been distributed, it is pending on appeal, and there is no evidence here that Mr. Witte paid for funeral expenses out of the estate. The testimony is that James Nitti said he still owed $260 when the funeral bills were filed."

"Go, on, Mr. Romano," Judge David ruled.

Romano was unflinching. "Suppose I say the bills have not been distributed, suppose we say the amount in the probate court does not exceed $350. Can you think of a son of such depravity of mind that would kill his own father for $350? Can you fasten the commission of this crime upon any other motive other than the motive that these two people were found in their illicit relations by the husband himself?"

"Just a moment. I object to that," Moran called out. "There is no proof of that before this jury."

"Objection overruled."

Moran tried again. "Objection to, there is no proof of that in the record."

"I have ruled."

Moran was correct. Sabella and Peter had been brought before the magistrate on charges of adultery and fornication. The magistrate had heard the case and dismissed it. Judge David erred in allowing mentions of a charge that had been proven to have no merit.

Romano forged ahead, setting a scene, describing Francesco as a hardworking man who set up a truck garden farm with his family. Out of kindness, he hired Peter and then was unfairly rewarded by the young man taking interest in his wife.

"Everything went along for a while after the arrival of Peter Crudele, when Mrs. Nitti suddenly discovered a suppressed desire for Peter Crudele and yielded to his embracement. The illicit relations that are narrated by Charles Nitti, continued until Frank Nitti discovered them in the very act of intercourse."

Romano continued to describe how the two lovers resorted to a "diabolical plan" to "do away" with Francesco. Romano was a skilled storyteller. He gave quotes that he attributed to various witnesses, embellishing the words and editing the context. He took the jury to the day Francesco disappeared. He told of the day's work and the dinner that evening. Then, he re-created what he must have believed to have been true. Peter and his "Lady Macbeth" pounding a sleeping Francesco twice with a hammer and dragging his body to the drainage canal. But, he added a new twist to the story—the body was never dumped into the canal.

"Peter Crudele saddled that body on the wagon again and returned to the catch basin four blocks distant from the farm and threw it in there, and then returned to the farm."

"I object, that is not in the evidence," Moran said, rightly.

Perhaps Judge David was so tired of Moran's incompetence throughout the trial that he no longer listened to anything the defense attorney had to say. He allowed the statement to stand.

Romano repeated the story of the catch basin for good measure. He told the jury he was a bit disconcerted by the "ramblings"—meaning the objections—and needed to back up to where he was interrupted. Then, he launched into the adultery and fornication charges.

Romano reminded the jury that Sabella was a "lusty" woman who was impulsive like an animal. "The motive of this crime is the motive of a woman, 45 years of age, who is dissatisfied with her husband, and possibly unsatisfied as to the pleasure that go with it at bedtime. She resorts to the young, 23-year-old paramour, for the satisfaction of her lust that culminated in the murder of [Francesco Nitti]."

Romano described a scandalous scene in which a poor, hardworking man, Francesco Nitti, was emasculated by his wife. This woman before them, he promised, was a fiend. She was not the sweet tender woman that the jury men knew in their wives or mothers. She was not the virtuous woman they knew in their sisters. She was a cold-blooded killer, and it was their duty to the State of Illinois that they find her as such. He thanked the jury and returned to his seat at the prosecution's table.

Moran stood up and approached the jury. It was their duty, he began, to deliver a not guilty verdict. The state had not proven beyond a reasonable doubt that Sabella or Peter killed Francesco. Moran was lucid as he began ripping into the state's case. He attacked Anna and James Volpe as biased witnesses. He told the jury that no one ever weighed or measured the corpse—Hatton just made estimates, and those estimates didn't even match Francesco in terms of age, height, or weight. Then, he launched into the background of the probate case, detailing the time line of events.

Part of the time line included the interview in the state's attorney's office. No one had been under oath, and the contents of the interview were of no consequence. They weren't included in the testimony before the magistrate in the adultery and fornication case. "You never heard of it, and I never heard of it until we got here last week," Moran dismissed.

Then, Moran explained to the jury, Sabella and Peter were released from jail on December 6, 1922, just as Moran filed a new petition in probate court to grant Sabella the widow's award. James countered through his attorney Mr. Witte that there was no proof Francesco was dead and that his wife was a widow. "There is no proof here that this man is dead," Moran told the jury. "Now, they did that in order to keep the widow out of her estate. Now, the judge said to them, 'You cannot come in here one day and blow hot—'"

Smith interrupted. "We are here, if the court please."

Judge David looked at the prosecution. The failure to follow procedure in this trial was highly bothersome. "Wait a minute, was there some objection?"

"Yes, I objected," Smith said.

Moran defended himself. "I was relating the proceedings in the probate court."

Judge David had allowed Romano to inaccurately paraphrase witness testimony when Romano claimed Hatton identified the body as Francesco. But the judge granted the defense no such leeway.

"There is no evidence the judge said that," Judge David said, referring to the probate court judge.

"No, that was the legal effect of it," Moran replied.

"Well, you better not say that the judge said anything. Proceed."

Moran's momentum was broken. He began to stumble and then unravel as he lost his lucidity and focused on details that had no bearing on the case. He believed the witnesses did not properly report whether the shoe was on the corpse's right or left foot. That was telling, he argued, as was the fact that the corpse's underwear and belt were missing. Evidence had been destroyed.

"I don't know how in any possible way you can find these defendants guilty on the character of the evidence here presented to you. And I thank you for your attention," Moran ended abruptly.

Smith popped up from the prosecutor's table. He crossed the courtroom and approached the jury. He was a contrast to the feeble defense attorney. He was young, yet experienced and mature. He was confident, strong, and presented himself as a protector. The men of the jury could look to him as a leader, someone who would direct them to the right decision.

"'Tonight is the night we are going to kill your father,' is what they told Charley Nitti," Smith argued.

Moran did not object to the fact that there was no evidence this statement was ever said. Dasso manufactured this statement, and Smith successfully embellished it. "A clean, cold-blooded murder, gentlemen of the jury," Smith said dramatically. "They planned and waited for the chance to kill this man. And then, this is the night in question, when he is lying under the wagon asleep, they bring this weapon down on his head with one blow."

Smith raised his arm as if he held a hammer and threw it down to visualize how Peter must have looked when he pummeled the victim. "And that splits his skull open." He threw his arm down again. "And one blow in the spine."

Smith ignored the fact that the coroner's physician saw no evidence of damage to the spine. He held his hand up to his own skull and indicated how the skull fractured. "A fracture in the skull from here around to the rear, and down to here. That is how hard that blow was, gentlemen of the jury."

Smith worked to convince the jury that the varying statements Charley made did not contradict each other in the least. And Moran's claim that Dasso fabricated these stories was ridiculous. "Well, Charley was here and Moran was his lawyer. Charley was on the stand. Why didn't Charley say so? Mr. Moran, why didn't Charley say so?" Smith challenged.

"You didn't cross-examine him," Moran said combatively from his place at the defendants' table.

"He didn't say a word," Smith argued back.

"He denied he knew anything about his father, and you didn't cross-examine him."

The arguing was against courtroom procedures. Judge David stopped the two attorneys from addressing each other. Smith seemed outraged by Moran and urged the jury to be equally offended. He went through the list of witnesses whom Moran had attempted to dispute, and treated them as victims. "Moran says Dasso was a liar because he couldn't smell the stench from the body when he parked his car within 20 feet of the manhole. Was Dasso a liar because he couldn't smell that? Is Hatton a liar? Is Abram, the undertaker, a liar? The body was there, wasn't it?"

Smith continued with indignation. "He talked about Anna Volpe. I don't think there is a man on this jury that don't feel Anna Volpe is a good, clean, fine woman."

He contrasted Sabella to Anna, and called the defendant a "black-hearted wretch" and a "cold murderess" who never knew friendship. Poor Anna, Smith said. She was willing to care for Sabella's children while she was incarcerated, and Moran had the nerve to insult her credibility. "Eugene Moran, take a woman like Mrs. Volpe on the witness stand, and talk about credibility. I know you men think that she is a decent, respectable, law abiding citizen, I know you believe what she says . . ."

Smith reviewed Anna's testimony in which she claimed she saw Peter the previous year, lingering about the Nitti farm even though he had been fired. "He was in love with this woman," Smith gestured at Sabella. "And she was in love with him. As ugly as she is, he was in love with her, gentlemen of the jury. That is something we cannot understand."

The way Smith presented it, Sabella was a wicked woman who swept through people's lives and left trails of destruction. Poor James, Smith sympathized—that young man only had the finest intentions in caring for his father's estate.

As his argument drew to a close, Smith turned to the alleged murder weapon. "A blow to the head, gentlemen of the jury, that characteristic one good, strong wallop on the head. You will have the hammer there and you can lift it, it will prove just exactly what Dr. Hatton said the condition in which he found the body when he got it out of the sewer. Big hole, cracked all the way."

Repetition was key to Smith's persuasive strategy. He reviewed the story of the supposed killing again. He asked the jury to envision it. Couldn't they see it—Sabella holding her young lover's hand while he murdered her husband?

"Can you see that woman? No. She isn't a woman, she is a fiend, she is not a woman," Smith accused. "Can you imagine why the state is asking for the death penalty for both this woman and this man? Do they deserve it? Do they deserve any consideration?"

Smith returned to the memory of the supposed deceased and encouraged the jury to feel sympathy for Francesco Nitti. "The craziest man in the world would not kill a man any worse than this man was killed. Any more fiendish—lying down and having his brains knocked out. His very own life taken from him. He had a right to live, man. He was only 54 or 55 years old. He was a hardworking citizen of the United States. He had a right to live. Nobody had a right to take his life away from him at that time."

Smith would have the last word in the closing arguments. He pointed at the defendants. "That woman and that man have forfeited their right to live, according to our law, when they killed Frank Nitti that night. Give them the extreme penalty. . . . I respectfully submit that never before in the history of this country has so horrible and fiendish a murder been committed or perpetrated upon any citizen. I ask you in the name of the people of this country, gentlemen of the jury, in the name of the state's attorney's office of this county, to not wait any time to bring the penalty that carries with it a punishment of death."

Part IV

NINETY-FIVE DAYS TO DIE

20

THE GUILT OF OTHERS

July 12, 1923

G ENEVIEVE FORBES DID NOT SEEM SORRY. She was likely embarrassed and definitely irritated by the complaint letter her *Chicago Daily Tribune* editors received the day before. But she would never apologize for how she reported the Nitti murder trial. She described Sabella in her stories as she saw her—dirty, ignorant, and crouching. Sabella Nitti was a peasant, and according to the jury's verdict, she was a cold-blooded murderer and philanderer who helped her young beau brutally murder her husband.

It had been three days since the jury announced the guilty verdict and fixed Sabella's punishment at death, and two days since the verdict was translated and Sabella fainted in fright. Sabella spent the time in her cot, recovering from her failed suicide attempt. Her head was likely pounding in pain after she rammed it against the wall. She suffered on her straw mattress, physically and mentally wounded, and the women in the cell block had never seen her so destitute.

The language barrier meant Sabella never had more than a few words to say to any of the other women. But she had earned their respect in the two months she had been incarcerated. Sabella was a serious woman. She was diligent and self-disciplined. She also had a motherly instinct the troubled women found calming. And notably, she never stole from anyone—even though she was easily the most desperate inmate in the block. Many of the inmates had family who visited and brought food to supplement the sparse jailhouse meals. Sabella had no one. Yet she never asked for a handout and never took anything that was not her own.

Sabella had endured her poor living conditions with grace and worked daily at the laundry or with housekeeping to keep the cell block sanitary. And now, this industrious woman was reduced to a moaning, bedridden casualty of the courts. It was difficult for the women in the cell block to watch, and they were jarred by her defeat.

The women began whispering to each other, trying to find something they could do to help Sabella's cause. They believed she wasn't guilty, just an unfortunate woman held up as an example to the rest of the city. They discussed the verdict across the cafeteria tables during meals. They whispered about it when they trudged through the block carrying mops and buckets of soapy water. And they shook their heads when they walked past Sabella's cell and saw her incapacitated on her cot.

Most female murder suspects in Chicago never made it past a coroner's jury. The jury usually sensed the woman acted in self-defense, dropped the charges, and stopped the case from progressing. A few cases made it before a judge, but they were typically stricken off before going to trial, especially if the defendant was pretty.

Anna McGinnis was the most recent example of Chicago juries' leniency toward attractive women. Anna was a beautiful blonde accused of shooting her husband in their home. Anna's sister and their two young boyfriends were also on trial. The sisters admitted to shooting Michael McGinnis, but they concocted a story of self-defense that the jury readily accepted.

Some of the women in the jail were incarcerated alongside Anna and her sister. The inmates suspected the sisters were guilty, and they speculated that beauty would bring Anna freedom. Anna was well-spoken and feminine, and she knew how to present herself as vulnerable to the all-male jury. As expected, less than three weeks before Sabella's verdict, Anna, her sister, and their two boyfriends were acquitted by a jury. Seeing her walk free compounded the women's sense of injustice toward the Nitti trial.

There was little the women could do for Sabella. They offered her comfort, but she blinked back at them with a stone face. Her devastation made them further question the verdict. Sabella didn't seem like a murderer to them, she seemed more like a victim. And they were angered by the way the newspapers—especially Genevieve Forbes's stories—portrayed this powerless woman. If the women could pick only one reporter to admonish publicly, then the *Chicago Daily Tribune* reporter was it. Paper and pen were supplied. One woman wrote the letter to the editor, but the message spoke for all of them. They were the "comrades of Mrs. Nitti" and they intended to blast Forbes for her mean-spirited and biased coverage. The letter also admonished the *Tribune* for its coverage of Sabella and named Forbes responsible for misrepresenting a poor, helpless immigrant as a cold-blooded killer.

The comrades were savvy women. They were in jail for theft, prostitution, and an array of other crimes that stemmed from the problems in their life. And they proved adept at ensuring the letter reached the appropriate editors. They either mailed the letter to the right person, or passed it to a reporter who disliked Forbes as much as they did. Either way, the letter found the proper contact, and Forbes was obligated to turn the women's support of Sabella into a story. She did so grudgingly and wrote a page-three piece that slightly mocked the letter, yet allowed her to establish a distance from the criticism.

Forbes described for readers how the letter seemingly came from "a gathering of matrons, sitting and sewing on their piazzas" but actually came from "a group in the shadow of a jail cell." Forbes repeatedly referred to Sabella as "Sabelle" and once called her "Senora Nitti." Forbes was either oblivious that the Italian translation was *signora*, or she intentionally used the misspelled Spanish title as a slick form of disrespect.

Forbes continued to paraphrase the letter and distance herself from the controversy. "The 'comrades' rallied to Mrs. Nitti's support because she was miserable and illiterate," Forbes wrote. "Then they blamed a representative of THE TRIBUNE for pointing out she was just that. They cried out that the cards were stacked against her because she wasn't a 'vamp,' but they wince at the adjectives 'dumb' and 'crouching' as used in *THE TRIBUNE*'s description of Sabelle."

The complaint letter praised Sabella as the cleanest woman in the cell block, who kept her cell and her personal appearance as pristine as possible: "Therefore, Mrs. Nitti cannot be classed as a 'dirty, repulsive woman,'" Forbes quoted directly from the letter. "She is the mother of two small girls and has shown her motherly spirit here with the girls always." Forbes then reminded readers that the source of these complaints was a lowly group of incarcerated women. When the women referenced Anna McGinnis's acquittal, Forbes mocked that they were as "detached as any women's club committee" analyzing the verdict. When they argued Sabella was being made an example, Forbes teased them for trying to be "psychologists."

Women's club committees in Chicago were indeed analyzing the verdict against Sabella, and like the incarcerated "comrades of Mrs. Nitti," the Chicago ladies took action. Instead of holding a lecture on Aristotle or planning next year's flower show, ladies' clubs across the city debated the case. It was the defendant's looks, most women agreed, that brought in the guilty verdict. The juries in Chicago were biased, and a beautiful woman like Anna McGinnis got away with murder, but women like Sabella got the noose. The double standard was highly threatening and unfair.

It was a time when women questioned inequity. The right to vote had been granted to women just a few years prior, and politicians were suddenly mindful of women and how progressive policies might attract them as voters. Despite the significant new freedoms many women were enjoying in the 1920s, the Nitti verdict emphasized women's vulnerabilities. Men still wrote the law, served on juries, and ruled the courtroom. Women were at their mercy. This unnerved many women in Chicago, and multiple women's clubs began taking up a collection to help Sabella with her appeal.

While the club women debated the case privately, other women made public comments about Sabella's impending execution. Winnifred Mason Huck was a former US congresswoman and a woman of privilege.

Her father had been a US congressman who died during his term, and Mason Huck won a special election to fill her father's seat for five quick months. Without a trace of irony, Mason Huck claimed the trial was an example of natural selection. Sabella was simply not strong enough to survive the trial. Other women argued differently. Florence King, a Chicago attorney, told the press that Sabella was on trial for her looks. She opposed the death penalty verdict in the case and worried it set a precedent for future cases.

Two sides emerged. One side viewed the verdict suspiciously. The scales of justice tipped by Sabella's lack of beauty. In the past—and perhaps in the future—a woman only needed fashionable attire, a powder puff, and an air of vulnerability to earn an acquittal. "Can beauty be convicted?" several newspapers questioned.

The other side embraced the verdict and saw it as a form of equal rights. If women wanted the vote, if they wanted to have jobs and compete with men, then they had to accept the same penalties men faced. Never mind that juries were devoid of women, and the law was written by men. Or that the police, coroner, and coroner's physicians were all men.

On July 14, the jailhouse matrons roused Sabella from her cot. Sabella was due to appear in court in front of Judge David for her formal sentencing. She was panicked and crying by the time she got into court, and it's likely she thought she was moments away from the gallows. The gallery was full when she was ushered to the defendants' table. Some of the audience members were the usual spectators who followed high-profile cases and pushed their way to front row seats. But many in the gallery were outraged citizens who came to speak out against the verdict and how the case was handled.

The reporters were also present, some seated as near to Sabella as possible. But a spectator didn't need to be close to the defendant to see her tremble. She swayed in her seat, unable to control her fear and the tremors it sent through her body. Peter sat next to her, and Moran took his usual place at the table.

"All rise," the bailiff instructed. Judge David appeared from a side door and walked up the steps to his raised seat. Before sentencing, he allowed the defense to make any necessary motions.

Moran promptly motioned for a new trial. He spent the next hour arguing how the prosecutor had distorted the facts. In the closing statements, he pointed out, both Smith and Romano had paraphrased the testimony from expert witnesses such as the coroner's physician and undertaker, and both attorneys had misspoken to the jury when they claimed these witnesses identified the dead body as Francesco. Moran also argued the hearsay statements James had made were not admissible in court.

Moran further argued the prosecutors had made inflammatory remarks to the jury, calling Sabella a "fiend" and a "Lady Macbeth" during the closing statement. They had described her as a "cold-blooded" killer who was filled with lust for her young love. Romano had even embarrassed himself, Moran said, by telling the jury Sabella was unhappy with Francesco Nitti in the bedroom and desperate to go outside her marriage to have her sexual needs filled.

The gallery buzzed with excitement. Many of the members had criticism and condemnation for the court. For a moment, the hearing resembled a public forum. A retired judge, McKenzie Cleland, stood from his seat in the back of the courtroom and stepped forward. It was a bold move to interrupt a courtroom, but Judge Cleland was a bold man, and he was in his element.

Judge Cleland was sixty-one years old and about half a year from his own death. He was ailing and the reporters mistook him for elderly. Despite his poor health, he still had an enormous spirit. Cleland was an earnest man who believed in people and the possibility for redemption. He was best known for spearheading the parole program in Chicago. He disdained the prison in Joliet and found it a horrifying punishment far too drastic for most petty crimes. And with men imprisoned, Judge Cleland reasoned that their families suffered.

As a judge, Cleland was compassionate, and sometimes emotional. He sat in the criminal courts of Cook County, far from the New York farm where he was raised, and heard tragic tales of defendants who lived a wretched existence and inflicted their misery upon others. At times, Cleland struggled to hide his agitation. Both attorneys and their clients knew they had pushed the judge too far when he removed his glasses and began cleaning them with a cloth. The statement that followed always revealed his waning patience.

Judge Cleland was a bony man. He had high, visible cheekbones emphasized by his pale skin. His light brown hair faded as he aged, and the crease above his lip deepened. He had a serious demeanor, and the court watched as he left his seat in the back and slowly moved up the aisle, uninvited, toward the front of the courtroom.

"May I say a word, Your Honor?" Judge Cleland asked.

Perhaps Judge David felt he had little choice but to hear from his esteemed colleague. "Yes, Judge McKenzie Cleland, I will hear from you."

"I am not here to argue on the guilt or innocence of this woman," Cleland pleaded. "But just to try and save her. Whatever the facts, she should not be hanged. She is a mother and a mother has never been hanged in the history of this country. I do not believe the honorable court here will permit a mother to hang."

Judge David was outraged and insulted. He leapt to his feet and screamed back at the ailing jurist. The reporters rushed to write down the angry judge's response. "I will not listen to suggestions from anyone as to the court's duty," Judge David yelled. "The court has taken an oath of office and will follow it. Public sentiment or even the clamor of the mob will not sway this court in doing its duty. I will not permit any outside organization to tell this court what its duty is."

Judge David's harsh response did not calm the gallery or inspire other critics to remain silent. Attorney Francis T. Sullivan rose to his feet and addressed the court. He pleaded for leniency and argued that Moran missed several key elements. He spent the next few minutes describing Moran's faults in trying the case. Sullivan's appeal was bold, especially because Moran was present and absorbing every word of the criticism. But it was no use. Judge David's mind was fixed and he denied Moran's motion for a new trial.

"The courts of our land are for the purpose of seeing that every person gets justice," Judge David said. "I feel this court has done everything in its power to give these two people a fair and impartial trial. I warned the state's attorney that he could not take advantage of a woman. The record is clear. The supreme court will pass upon the question later on. The governor will have to decide, but for me, in my minor capacity can only carry out the wishes of the jury. The motion is overruled."

Judge David took no responsibility for how the case was tried in his courtroom. He continued to reiterate to the courtroom that he oversaw a fair trial and criticisms were unwelcome. "I feel that the evidence presented at the trial proved beyond all doubt that the defendants were guilty of a most atrocious murder and the jury was justified in returning a verdict of guilty," he said.

The judge refused further discussion of the trial. The motion for the new trial was denied and the judge's last duty was to officially set the execution date. He picked October 12, Columbus Day, and repeated the same language the jury was compelled to use when announcing the verdict. "I order the sheriff to take you and each of you to a safe and secure spot between the hours of 9 AM and 6 PM on the day of October 12 and hang you by the neck until dead."

Sabella knew few English words, but "dead" was within her limited vocabulary. The word jolted her and she surged with fear. "They choke me? They choke me?" she asked, looking around the room for answers. She locked eyes with a reporter sitting nearby and her terrified face searched his. He shook his head "no," and she appeared momentarily relieved.

Court adjourned, and Sabella again did not understand the outcome of the hearing. She stood when the guards compelled her and allowed them to lead her from the courtroom. The hallway was busy with the activity of spectators, peddlers, attorneys, staff, and reporters. In the confusion, the guards escorting Peter allowed him to walk alongside Sabella.

Peter leaned down into Sabella's ear and whispered something only she heard and understood. The reporters in the hallway watched as her face transformed and the panic returned. She had misunderstood the reporter in the courtroom and thought she was safe from the gallows. Peter told her otherwise.

Sabella's frantic eyes searched the hallway and sighted an open elevator shaft. She broke free from the guards and bolted toward the open doors. The elevator shaft housed a series of pulleys and cables lined against the wall. At the bottom was a concrete floor, but uncertain death. The courthouse was only three stories high, and Sabella would have to dive headfirst into the elevator to increase her chance of dying. She tried, but she didn't get far. The guards caught her before she reached the open doors. It was their duty to keep her alive until October 12.

21

EIGHTY-NINE AND NINETY

S HERIFF PAUL DASSO CONSIDERED himself an artist. He painted oil on board, using muted colors to create nature scenes that told of no specific time, place, or season. One of his paintings depicted a placid little pond, surrounded by meadow grass and faint trees. The pond was pale as if it had been unfed, and the green meadow grass was quieted by swipes of yellow. The trees were vague and mostly bare, possibly in the process of shedding their leaves for the winter. Or perhaps beginning to sprout new buds for the spring.

Dasso's art was a hobby, a break from the aggression he needed to make an arrest, or the callousness he summoned for executions. In the span of his career, Dasso oversaw more than sixty executions. He walked the condemned through the process of death, transferring a doomed man from one holding cell to the next. He heard clergy members offering last rites and praying for eternal salvation. He saw men eat their last meals and smoke their final cigarettes.

Dasso watched as the condemned considered all the pleasures in life they would never experience. Never again would they sleep soundly through the night. Have sex. Drink a glass of beer. Sit in a warm bath. Some of the men had family members or girlfriends they loved. But they had hugged, kissed, and touched their loved ones for the last time. The only thing a condemned man expected to feel was the tightness of the rope as his hands were tied behind his back, his legs were secured at the ankles, and the noose was slipped around his neck.

Sometimes the men didn't fully accept their fate. Just a few years earlier, Dasso had attended the execution of Earl Dear, a twenty-six-year-old drug addict and auto thief. On a painfully cold January day, Dear and an accomplice watched a chauffeur, twenty-four-year-old Rudolph Wolfe, park his employer's automobile and disappear into a restaurant for a meal. Wolfe didn't see the two robbers then enter the car, but he heard the sound of the motor. He raced from the restaurant and jumped onto the running board alongside the car, trying to stop the theft. He was shot two times; one bullet tore into his stomach and the other punctured his lung. The robbers were quickly apprehended, and Wolfe was able to identify both Dear and his accomplice before dying.

No one was surprised that Dear murdered a man. He had a growing list of prior arrests and convictions. But he was seemingly immune to serious punishment. In 1916, he was arrested for auto theft and deserved several years of imprisonment. The jury fixed the value of the stolen vehicle at a shockingly low ten dollars, and Dear served only a few months. He was also favored by the head of the auto theft ring, and she produced more than $36,000 to bond him out of jail. When he was arrested for the Wolfe murder, Dear had several other cases pending.

"I'm innocent as usual," Dear boasted to reporters. He was nonchalant about the arrest, and indifferent to the life he had taken. Wolfe's infuriated employer, Dr. Philip Schuyler Doane, demanded the state push for the death penalty. At the time of the killing, Dr. Doane was in Washington, DC, serving the US military, but he returned to Chicago to ensure that justice was enforced. The auto thief met his match in Doane, and when Dear's lawyer asked prosecutors for a sentence of ninety-nine years, they told the court they wanted to see him hang.

Dear's lawyers claimed he was drunk during the robbery and unaware of his lethal actions. But a waiter at the cabaret Dear had visited earlier in the evening testified he left the place sober. And then two witnesses said they saw the entire event close up and identified Dear as the man who shot the chauffeur. Dear sat arrogantly in the courtroom, assuming he would soon slip out of trouble. His young wife, Margaret, sat primly in the gallery, looking anxious. Margaret sensed his impending doom, and she screamed with anguish when the judge read the guilty verdict and the death sentence. She had to be carried from the courtroom, and order restored only after her screams faded down the hallway.

Dear waited in jail for six months before he and three other inmates overpowered a guard and escaped. The newspapers ran photos of the four escaped convicts, and the image of Dear showed a young man with thick wavy brown hair, a broad forehead, bulging eyes, and a smirk. The story repeated his claim that he was from a wealthy Pennsylvania family and was the self-appointed "black-sheep." He also claimed to use the name of his foster parents, Adam and Margaret Dear, so as not to shame his real family. The press swarmed with speculation. Was Dear secretly a Mellon? A Heinz? A Carnegie? Reporters believed Dear, and he would take his true identity with him to the gallows. But Earl Dear was indeed the son of the Dears, and the claim to greater connections was a product of his imagination.*

When Dear faced the gallows, Dasso was tasked with watching over the doomed man for a six-hour shift while the clock ticked toward his execution. He stood by as Margaret Dear appeared at the jail, wearing a casual ensemble of a blue tailored suit, blue hat, lace stockings, and rhinestone-buckled pumps. She cried to her husband and promised he was the only one she ever loved.

"Yes," came the indifferent reply.

Margaret begged for a kiss, and Dear obliged with a quick peck through the bars. She begged him to kiss her again—like he used to— and Dear complied. The reporters lurking nearby sensed the kiss meant nothing to him. He was equally indifferent to his parents, who promised

---

* Birth and census records were not searchable to reporters in 1919, which is why they were unable to confirm that Dear was indeed the son of Adam and Margaret Dear. He was the second of three boys. His father was a skilled craftsman, and his older brother served in World War I in the army while Dear awaited execution. The black sheep part wasn't too far off.

him that he would be fine and the governor was going to send a reprieve at any minute. Dear tried to sleep through the night. When he realized the telegram from the governor was never going to arrive, he finally lost his stoic demeanor and rose from his cot and pleaded through the bars for Dasso to drug him.

"Sorry old man," Dasso consoled. "You know the orders. Will you have a cigarette?"

"Cigarette, hell!" Dear exploded. "What good will a cigarette do me?"

Dasso arranged for the reverend to come and comfort Dear. He also brought him fresh, hot coffee after Dear announced there would be no point in trying to sleep through the night. Eventually, exhaustion calmed Dear. He walked up to the gallows and saw the jailer tugging at the rope for a last-minute test. When asked, he offered no final words. Then, the trapdoor swung open and his body plunged beneath the gallows. After a while, his shoulders slumped forward and the body quietly spun in the air.

The audience beneath the swinging rope was suddenly jolted by a choking sound. The stunned spectators turned to see a gray cat hack, cough, and then casually pad across the room. "He's been at every hanging over the past five years, and he always makes that damnable choking noise when he hears the trap fall," a guard explained.

It was just after 9:30 AM when the body was lowered and a physician held his stethoscope to the chest. Dear's heart was still beating. He lived for another four minutes. There was an established procedure in place for what happened next. Under guard, the body was placed on a cart and wheeled to a waiting hearse and driven to the county morgue. The body was carefully guarded in case accomplices attempted to resuscitate the dead man.* At the morgue, Wolfe's widow and mother demanded to see the body to ensure Dear was properly dead and justice was served.

---

* Resuscitation attempts did happen. In April 1921, gangster Salvatore Cardinella arranged for his body to be claimed immediately and rushed to an ambulance ready with doctors, nurses, oxygen, and an electric battery to revive him. The guard stopped the ambulance and forced everyone to wait until Cardinella was past the point of return.

They were denied entry but permitted to view the death certificate, which Wolfe's mother deemed satisfactory.

When Dear's body was ready for burial, the state released the corpse to Dear's parents and widow. They brought it home to Pennsylvania for burial, and spared the state the expense of disposing of the body. Dasso had seen instances when no one claimed the body. He had seen men refuse to see their family members. A few denied the reverend from saying a prayer. Others clung to any sense of support or tenderness. All the executed men were distinct, with varying reactions. The only thing constant was the gallows.

The gallows that awaited Sabella were almost as old as the woman they waited to hang. They were first built to hang the labor activists convicted for the bombings at the Haymarket Riot in 1887. Four men were hanged in mid-November from nooses lined in a row. A fifth noose was added the following year to hang Zephyr Davis, a seventeen-year-old factory foreman convicted of killing his fourteen-year-old employee by hacking her to death with a hatchet.

The gallows were erected in Cook County Jail, in a room large enough for an audience of lawmakers and ticketholders to attend the event. The audience tended to have political connections that entitled them to witness the execution. These spectators' lack of any association to the condemned made the event feel exciting, as if they were attending a show. The witnesses at Davis's hanging were particularly festive as they talked, joked, and even smoked during the proceedings.

The platform to the gallows, a stage positioned seven feet in the air, was made from a wood that grayed over the years. Witnesses sat below on long wooden benches with their necks craned up to watch the hanging. The platform was ten by twenty feet, large enough to hold the condemned as well as the executioner and the county officials who crowded around the noose. It was a simple structure, but sophisticated in its design. The beams above the platform formed a half-square, which made the structure look like a doorway. The nooses hung from the middle beam, securely attached with bolts.

By the time the gallows were retired in 1927, eighty-six prisoners had walked across the gray planks and had the rope encircle their necks. Dasso had been witness to most of these executions—about 70 percent. He saw how the men reacted differently to their fate. Some reactions could best be described as hysterical, like when the wife-killer Carl Wanderer sang his way to the gallows. Others cried and expressed remorse. And some were not sorry for their crimes and expressed regret only for being convicted, or hatred toward those who carried out their sentences.

In his many trips to the gallows, Dasso observed all types of criminals. There were those who were naturally aggressive and whose crimes were unplanned. Someone or something sparked their rage and they murdered in a frenzy. Others were cold and strategic. They created a murder plan and calculated every aspect of the crime. And some were mentally ill. Dasso oversaw the executions of gang leaders, gamblers, and career criminals. But he also walked a peddler up to the platform, and a musician. There was a railway worker, a clerk, and a milliner. A horse jockey and three butchers.

Carl Wanderer was execution number 85 in the Cook County record books. Peter Crudele would be number 89, and Sabella was set to follow him as 90. She would have the distinction of being the first woman the county ever hanged. She would also be the thirteenth Italian to hang in the county. Would her death resemble that of number 39—slow and excruciating, a seventeen-minute asphyxiation? Or would the rope snap like it did for number 24? The execution of George H. Painter had been a terrible embarrassment. The rope snapped immediately after the trapdoor dropped. Painter plummeted to the concrete floor below and his head cracked open. He was already dead when the physician checked for a pulse. But the state was ordered to hang the man, not kill him with a head injury. His lifeless body was carried back up the steps and his bleeding head slipped into a second noose. The trapdoor swung open once again and Painter was officially hanged by the county.

In the early 1920s, it was likely that only a minority of Chicagoans felt sympathy for the executed. After the First World War, the cultural climate was anxious, and Americans worried that the revolutionary ideals expressed in Russia threatened the United States. Five US states that had previously abolished the death penalty reinstated it. State-sanctioned killing was deemed moral, and even necessary. Except when the condemned was female. When a woman was condemned, Americans were torn.

22

THE SURRATT EFFECT

W HEN RETIRED JUDGE McKENZIE CLELAND implored the court to grant the defendants leniency, he had urged the court to remember how Sabella was a mother, and no mother in the history of the United States had ever been executed. It was not an accurate statement. By the time Judge Cleland pleaded for Sabella's life, more than three hundred women had been executed in the United States. Many of them were mothers, which did not appear to influence juries, judges, or lynch mobs.

Colonial history was filled with examples of executions of women who were hanged, shot, or burned alive while mobs cheered. White women during these years were almost exclusively executed for witchcraft, but there were select instances of adultery or murder. Black women were typically executed for murder, arson, supporting a slave rebellion, or theft.* Age was not a cause for leniency in these executions, and the accused were as young as twelve and as old as sixty-six. But the execution of one notorious woman caused many in the justice system to question whether states were right to execute females.

Mary Surratt was about forty-two years old when she was arrested for conspiring in the assassination of President Abraham Lincoln. After a military tribunal, Surratt and three co-defendants were given the death

---

* The racial differences in capital crimes were reflective of systematic racism.

penalty. Mere months passed between the assassination and execution, and the country was wracked with grief. In the following years, public sentiment softened, and some Americans questioned whether the execution was the right choice or merely an emotional reaction.

Public sentiment also evolved to question whether Mary Surratt was even responsible. She owned the boardinghouse where John Wilkes Booth and others convened, and many wondered if that may have been the extent of her involvement. The thought of possibly having executed an innocent woman—a middle-aged mother at that—discouraged many Americans from supporting female execution.

Surratt's execution had a chilling effect in the following decades, and few women were given the death penalty at the end of the nineteenth century. In the years leading up to Sabella's death penalty verdict, only five women were executed in the United States over a twenty-five-year span.* But for those who were condemned, little had changed since Surratt's hanging. Executions still swiftly followed verdicts, with opportunities to appeal limited to a few short weeks. Sabella's execution was set for ninety-five days after the verdict was handed down. The defense had a mere three months to motion for a new trial and, if that failed, petition the Illinois Supreme Court for a writ of error.

The motions and petitions were delayed by the time needed to prepare and send the appropriate documents. Hearings were scheduled weeks in advance, which meant precious time was wasted awaiting the designated day on the court calendar. Defense attorneys truly had only a few days to prepare responses and try to save their clients. All the while, the client had weeks to agonize about his or her impending death. After her sentencing, Mary Surratt had spent the next two days listening to

---

* These figures do not include lynchings. It was estimated that more than one hundred women were lynched by mobs from 1850 to 1950, which means about 2 percent of lynching victims were female. Women were seen as passive and defenseless, and lynching a female was overwhelmingly considered immoral. Black and white women were lynched in similar numbers, but black female victims suffered a level of brutality their white counterparts were spared. See Kerry Segrave, *Lynchings of Women in the United States* (Jefferson, NC: McFarland, 2010).

the gallows being built in the courtyard of the Washington Arsenal. She heard the hammers pounding nails into position. She listened to the saws cutting the wood planks down to size. Then, in the last two hours before her execution, Surratt and the other prisoners heard the gallows being tested, the trapfloor repeatedly whipped open to identity any flaws and prevent malfunction. Sabella did not have to listen to her gallows being built, but she faced the same extended agony of knowing her death was imminent.

Moran was running to save Sabella. But in typical Moran form, he ran in circles. Day one had been spent finding a translator to tell Sabella the verdict. Days two and three had been spent preparing the motions for a new trial that Moran argued unsuccessfully on day four, at the sentencing. The next two weeks were a blur of wasted days. Moran focused his efforts on freeing Sabella's two young daughters from the custody of Anna and James Volpe. A hearing was held in late July, and the judge, Oscar Hebel, was presented with testimony from the older daughter on how the children slept on the kitchen floor with the family dogs and cats. The judge ordered the girls removed to a home run by the Catholic Church.

Meanwhile, several women's groups in Chicago banded together and hired an attorney to help Sabella. On day eighteen, attorney Leo Shankstone filed a writ of habeas corpus and argued that Sabella could not hang because the law specifically used male pronouns and therefore did not apply to a female defendant. The attempt failed miserably, and Judge Michael L. McKinley was so insulted by the attorney's petition that he walked off the bench and disappeared into his chambers. After waiting for the judge to return, Shankstone realized his defeat, collected his papers, and left the courtroom.

Others took a different approach to save Sabella. Attorney Florence King, the same outspoken voice who criticized how the law was written by men, pushed a public campaign. She started a petition to send to Illinois governor Lennington "Len" Smalls to insist he commute Sabella's sentence. While the petition circulated, others publicly announced their support for Sabella. Many clubs and professional organizations passed resolutions admonishing the verdict. Although these resolutions were mostly symbolic, they were indicative of public sentiment, and Judge David felt threatened. He warned against such resolutions and promised to silence any actions by holding their participants in contempt of court. But letters poured in to his office by the bagful, and the judge was too overwhelmed reading his mail to hold anyone in contempt of court.

By early August Sabella's execution date was seventy-three days away. Soon the Cook County officials would order two nooses—one for Peter's neck and the second for Sabella's. Soon they would test the trapdoor. Tickets would be printed and issued to people with connections.

Or could someone stop Sabella from swinging? The only one who could save Sabella at this point was a new attorney. Someone who was clever, motivated, and willing to take the case for free. Someone like Helen Cirese.

23

DUST OF THE FEET

HELEN CIRESE WAITED FOR the elevators on the eleventh floor. Her law firm, Bonelli, Quilici & Cirese, was located in the City Hall Square Building on Clark Street in Chicago's Loop. The building was a little more than a decade old and boasted steam radiators, picture windows, and quick-speed elevators. When the elevator rumbled up to the eleventh floor, Cirese stepped on and pressed the ground-level button. In less than a minute, she strode through the lobby and out onto Clark Street.

It was a brisk ten-minute walk to the Cook County Courthouse and Jail. Cirese crossed the Clark Street Bridge, glancing at the Chicago River below. At twenty-three, she was a young and capable lawyer who was struggling to prove herself. Women did not serve on juries at the time, and the typical spot for a woman in a courtroom seemed to be in the gallery or on the witness stand. Cirese had been one of five women in her 1920 graduating class at DePaul University Law School, and had delivered a compelling commencement address in which she urged her classmates to fight for peace.

Cirese had certainly found her first few years in the law profession to be peaceful—in all the wrong ways. After graduation she'd had to wait ten months, until her twenty-first birthday, to gain admission to the Illinois bar. The newspapers printed her picture and marveled at the "girl lawyer" who had almost a year until she reached the bar's minimum age requirement. The quiet continued once she passed the bar exam and found Chicago law firms unwelcoming to a young, female attorney.

Cirese had two strikes against her. She was female and she was beautiful. When her photograph appeared in the newspaper, readers saw a young woman with dark hair, olive skin, a slender nose, and full lips. One time, a newspaper ran her photograph with the headline AMBITIOUS on a society page. Next to her image was another woman, a socialite engaged to a French count, positioned under the headline BETROTHED. The editors called the socialite "vivacious" and a "belle." In contrast, Cirese was "not content" with being one of the few female attorneys and was also considering running for a magistrate position in Oak Park. The editor subtly celebrated the socialite and sneered at Cirese.

Cirese was smart, beautiful, and from a good family. Her prospects for marrying a prominent man were immense. For traditionalists, it made no sense that Cirese was ignoring such opportunities in favor of a law career. Such disapproval, subtle or overt, was nothing new. Cirese had received those criticisms when she graduated Oak Park and River Forest High School and entered a legal studies program at DePaul University. Then, she had heard them when she graduated from law school. The local newspapers had reported her graduation, calling her a "girl" attorney as if she were a child who had wandered into the courtroom wearing her mother's oversized high heels and carrying her father's giant briefcase. Other papers mocked her political and civic ambitions.

The socialite might have been vivacious, but Cirese was fearless. She was first-generation American, born in Indiana to parents from Sicily. Her family was from Termini, from the Northern Coast of Sicily. Her parents began their life together in Indiana in the 1880s and then moved to the Chicago area. They settled in north Oak Park with their nine children in an attractive foursquare.

Oak Park was evolving into an urban neighborhood, which was foreseeable because it was the first suburb to the west of the city. The wooded land had given way to a mixture of modern apartment buildings, modest bungalows, and lavish mansions. For Cirese's high school classmate, author Ernest Hemingway, the village was an extension of his oppressive mother. He craved adventure and experiences far from the village's organized, repetitive city blocks. He left after graduation, eager to never return. But for a young woman like Cirese, Oak Park was freedom. The village was less than five square miles and entirely walkable. It also connected to Chicago through the "L" train and streetcar systems. Cirese's home was about half a mile from the Lake Street "L" line, which zipped into the city faster than any horse and buggy. She stayed local after graduation and made her family's house on Cuyler Avenue her lifelong home.

Maybe it was the autonomy she enjoyed in Oak Park that made the young attorney fearless. Or perhaps it was her character to see possibilities, not obstructions. Whether it was nature or nurture, Helen Cirese sensed what she could do and plowed ahead, regardless of the limitations other people set.

Cirese also surrounded herself with ambitious people. In late 1921, several dozen Italian lawyers in the city joined forces and formed the Justinian Society of Lawyers. If they bonded together, and helped each other, they could penetrate the highest layers of civic and political life in Chicago. Cirese was a founding member. She shared an office with several other attorneys, including Rocco DeStefano and Nuncio Bonelli. DeStefano was a respected attorney in his late forties. Bonelli was in his midthirties and notably industrious. In his short career, he had worked his way up from courtroom bailiff to counselor.

Bonelli was a short man with light brown hair and blue eyes. Compassionate and ambitious, he had plans—which he would one day achieve—to become a judge in Chicago. He would serve on the bench for eighteen years, primarily in the criminal courts, staring into the eyes of angry murderers, unrepentant molesters, and dangerous bootleggers. Bonelli wasn't afraid of any of them.

Bonelli and Cirese talked about the Nitti case. They saw possibilities in overturning the verdict. There were risks, however, to taking on such a case. If all their efforts failed and Sabella swung, their names would be attached to the failure. It was a fear that prevented other attorneys in

Chicago from offering their services. But what did Cirese have to lose? The men of the Chicago legal community didn't accept her anyway.

Cirese and Bonelli dissected the discrimination they read about in Sabella's trial. Was Sabella being sent to the gallows because she was guilty? Or because she was Italian? Or because Americans perceived her as ugly? The attorneys wanted to know. There were others who wanted answers too. Frank Allegretti, the handsome attorney who served as the second failed translator, joined their growing appeals team. Albert N. Gualano, the first Italian American judge, was ready to enlist. Frank Mirabella said he would donate his time as well. And DeStefano told everyone to put his name on the line. He would stand up as the lead attorney in the appeal.

Weeks after the verdict, a new defense team was in place: six lawyers, all founding members of the Justinian Society. DeStefano was at the head, but Cirese was the foundation. The team conferred and decided it was best for Cirese to reach out to Sabella. Cirese needed to gain Sabella's trust, and then offer the team's services in taking the case on appeal. It was crucial the first meeting went well. The pages were flying off the calendar, and the team didn't have spare time to devote to proving their credibility to the defendants. Sabella and Peter needed to trust blindly in the team, and Cirese was the best representative of their good intentions.

Cirese stepped off the Clark Street Bridge and walked north to Hubbard Street. A few years earlier, the poet Carl Sandburg had written a poem about the structure. He depicted the bridge in the early hours when the dust of the feet and wheels had quieted and an emptiness dominated. He heard silver voices singing, softer than the mist and stars. Cirese's heels clicked alongside the wheels and through the dust. She was making an imprint for all to see.

———————

Cirese did not speak Barese. No one on the team of six spoke Barese. Her colleagues were largely Lucani, mostly from Potenza—the same area that Romano's family came from. Cirese and her colleagues were educated and likely spoke standard Italian as well as a regional dialect. They were capable of speaking with each other in Italian or attending a meeting for one of the local civic organizations that was conducted in Italian. They skimmed the local Italian language newspapers or followed along with the opera. But communicate with Sabella Nitti? It would be a struggle.

In the weeks following the trial, Sabella knew she was doomed. She was panicked and desperately trying to communicate with the other inmates, the reporters, and anyone who passed by her cell. She picked up basic words in English and she was beginning to string together sentences that allowed her to express her fear to others.

Several of the reporters mocked Sabella's efforts. They quoted her in the newspapers, adding on vowels to the end of her words. When Sabella asked in the courtroom if she would choke, the reporters wrote, "They choka me? They choka me?" to portray her clumsy efforts. Forbes also enjoyed mimicking Sabella's English to the *Chicago Daily Tribune* readers. In the story about the letter sent from the jail inmates, Forbes wrote how Sabella knew Anna McGinnis and the other guilty ladies were perceived differently by juries. Sabella supposedly summed up the situation by complaining the women had "nice face, swell clothes, shoot man, go home."

Sabella was trying. She was picking up vocabulary but still working on verb conjugation. Her progress was both remarkable and indicative of her acumen. Learning a new language was far more difficult for an illiterate woman who lacked the benefit of seeing how words were spelled. Sabella was unable to use visual reminders from books or vocabulary cards. She didn't have the benefit of looking at a picture of a chair or a tree and seeing the word written alongside it. Every word she heard, she filed into her memory and tried to retrieve it when the context felt right. It was doubtful her detractors could have done better.

When Cirese stood outside Sabella's cell in late July, Sabella saw a tall and slender woman smiling through the bars. Cirese was a contrast to her surroundings, and the reporters took note. Her photograph was published in the paper the next day and showed a comely young woman wearing a clean white blouse and a stylish cloche hat. Unlike some of the reporters who slinked around the jail and hunted for a story that might deliver recognition, Cirese wasn't at the jail to be noticed. She had come with a specific purpose—to convince Sabella to allow the team of six to take over her appeal. She also wanted to assure the scared woman and communicate that people were indeed on her side.

The two women likely started with a careful mixture of Italian, Sicilian, and Barese that was supplemented by hand motions, facial expressions, and long pauses to see if the intended message was correctly understood. Even if Sabella understood little of what Cirese said, the young attorney's presence was reassuring. It was the most time anyone had spent with her since she was incarcerated.

After their first meeting, Cirese made it a point to visit Sabella every week. She sat with her client and allowed her to try new words in English. At times, Cirese brought along Margaret Bonelli, the wife of attorney and defense team member Nuncio Bonelli. Sabella seemed to find Margaret comforting. Margaret was in her early thirties and the mother of a fifteen-year-old girl and a fourteen-year-old boy. She knew loss from the death of her first husband, and as a mother, she could likely imagine the pain Sabella felt in her separation from her two young daughters.

Margaret kept up with the fashions and bobbed her dark hair just below her ear. She typically wore a cloche hat and a modern skirt cut below her knees. She was curvy and soft, which made her seem approachable. She reached out to Sabella with a compassion the condemned woman had rarely experienced in her life. One time, a *Chicago Daily Tribune* reporter photographed Helen and Margaret visiting Sabella. Cirese stood slightly back from the chair where Sabella sat. She focused her gaze on her client below and kept her expression neutral. Sabella looked away from her attorney and at the comforting face of Margaret. Sabella seemed nervous and she searched Margaret's face for assurance. Margaret smiled down at Sabella and wrapped one hand around Sabella's back and placed another hand on her shoulder.

When Cirese wasn't sitting with Sabella at Cook County Jail, she helped the team of six on the appeal. The first order of business was to go to court and substitute the team for Moran. On August 4, day twenty-six, the attorneys appeared before Judge McKinley and successfully presented themselves as Sabella's and Peter's new legal counsel. They also tried to file a motion to vacate the sentence, but Judge McKinley was afraid to get involved. He referred the new defense team back to Judge David's courtroom.

On the same day, lead defense counsel Rocco DeStefano appeared before Judge David and again tried the motion to vacate the judgment. Many in the Italian community considered DeStefano to be the "dean" of the Italian community in Chicago. He was born in Chicago to parents from Southern Italy and graduated from the Lake Forest School of Law in his early twenties. Success came easy to him, and other Italian attorneys were known to avoid setting up shop in the Loop. It was too hard to compete with DeStefano.

DeStefano was almost fifty years old when he stood before Judge David. DeStefano was the most senior of the legal team. He was also notably regal. He was tall and trim, and his brown hair had faded to gray. He had deep blue eyes and sometimes wore an unconcerned look on his face, as if he had all problems under control. DeStefano's substantial experience likely told him that Judge David was problematic. The trial judge was increasingly hostile regarding the Nitti-Crudele verdict. The judge, who once reminded the jury that the identity of the corpse in the catch basin was in question, became defensive after criticisms were directed toward his decision. Every letter he received, every passing comment, seemed to set him further against the defendants.

When DeStefano presented his motion to vacate, Judge David was barely listening. He agreed to a hearing—set more than three weeks away—but warned the new defense team that their efforts would be useless. "This is a grave matter," Judge David told DeStefano. "I will consent to hear you, but there is not one chance in 100 the sentence will be vacated and a new trial granted."

At least the team of six knew what they were up against.

24

YOU'VE GOT ME

THE TEAM OF SIX was not investing hope in Judge David or the hearing on August 29. The judge had made himself clear—the hearing was a formality and there was almost no chance a motion might be granted. The team prepared for other actions, and they had to move fast. There were only five weeks until the October 12 execution date.

It was likely the team spent the first two weeks reviewing the trial, identifying key players, and chasing down witnesses who had new information. The team also had to weigh different strategies and determine the best path forward. Did they want to merely avoid execution? Or push for a new trial for Sabella? These were distinct approaches. The first approach was safer, for the attorneys at least. Public sentiment was largely against the idea of executing a woman. If the right argument was delivered, the defense might convince Judge David to reduce Sabella's sentence to a prison term. Doing so would satiate the increasingly unnerved public and relieve Judge David from admitting his court was responsible for any procedural wrongdoing. If Judge David refused, the attorneys could appeal to the Illinois Supreme Court. Assuming the execution still stood, the team of six would then focus on persuading the governor to commute the sentence. There was no guarantee, however, this approach would benefit Peter. The news-reading public was disturbed by the fate of "Mrs. Nitti." The same concern did not extend to Peter, and it was possible the team of six would have to compromise Sabella's reprieve with Peter's execution.

The second option—to push for a retrial—was far more difficult. The attorneys would have to prove the defendants were entitled to a new trial. Courts were not obligated to grant anyone a retrial, and the defense was required to demonstrate that grievous errors had been committed in the first trial. Awkwardly, this process began in the same trial judge's courtroom, and there were few judges who admitted their own faults. Predictably, the next step was to file a writ of error with the Illinois Supreme Court and demand a new trial. The second option might take the better part of the year. It would be costly, time consuming, and risky. But it was a chance the defense wanted to take.

The team needed reinforcements for such a monumental challenge. Anna Schiner, a notary public, was recruited to help interview witnesses and notarize the resulting affidavits. Thomas E. Swanson, an attorney, was asked to serve as additional counsel. Swanson helped the team by examining errors in the first trial, and Schiner was also tasked with helping uncover new evidence. The team sensed the full story had not been revealed during the trial. Major pieces were missing, which had enabled the prosecution to convincingly rewrite events.

Cirese started in Stickney. The first helpful affidavit came on August 22, day forty-four, when she connected with John Cieslak, a Stickney resident who was familiar with the Nitti family and occasionally saw them in the area. "I've known Frank Nitti for the last four years," Cieslak told Cirese. Then, he took her back to the night of July 28, 1922—the day before Francesco Nitti disappeared. It was a Friday evening, sometime between seven and eight. The sun was still in the sky, and Cieslak saw Francesco Nitti driving a horse and a loaded wagon. Francesco Nitti was heading east on Pershing Road, as if he was going into the city.

Cieslak said he looked directly at Francesco Nitti. He saw the man's face was swollen and badly bruised. One of his eyes was black and his other facial features were almost beyond recognition.

Francesco Nitti looked at Cieslak and called out, "My bum son did this."

Cieslak had nothing more to add. He signed the affidavit and Cirese stamped it with her notary seal. Back at the office on Clark Street, Cirese added it to the packet of documents they intended to file with the county. Cieslak's statement was helpful. The first trial never quite established how the Nitti household was violent. But in her investigation, Cirese was finding that a vicious fight indeed occurred between Michael Nitti and his father just two weeks before Francesco Nitti disappeared.

Other witnesses began to illuminate life inside the Nitti home. The sons were wrathful, and new evidence indicated that Sabella sensed something horrible happened to her husband on the night he disappeared. Defense team member Nuncio Bonelli sought an interview with Charles Eisele, the Stickney chief of police.

Eisele had testified only briefly during the first trial. The prosecution merely wanted the police chief to confirm how he saw Roden pull a corpse out of the catch basin. Meanwhile, Moran's questioning of Eisele had fixated on firearms that were confiscated from the Nitti family farm. The firearms were never brought to court as promised, but they were inconsequential anyway. There was no evidence that anyone was ever shot, and merely owning guns did not demonstrate that a crime occurred.

But Eisele should have been an essential witness for the defense. He had a vital fact to contribute—Sabella had knocked on his door within hours of Francesco's disappearance and begged for help. "Mrs. Nitti screamed very loud, stating that her husband, Mr. Frank Nitti, did not return home that night," Eisele told Bonelli.

Sabella's early morning visit to Eisele's home was a crucial detail that had been omitted from the first trial. During closing arguments, Smith had claimed Peter pretended to toss the body into the canal but actually stuffed it into the catch basin. The intent, Smith argued, was to hide the body so well that it would take police months, perhaps years, to find the decaying corpse. Eisele's affidavit countered Smith's fabrication. If Sabella went to the police within hours of realizing her husband was missing, this suggested she hadn't committed a crime; rather, she suspected her husband badly needed help.

Day forty-five was proving bountiful for Bonelli. In addition to Eisele's, he secured an affidavit from Louis Kral, the police magistrate for Stickney. Kral's contribution was brief but also crucial. He stated that Sabella came to his home at 3 AM on the morning of July 30, 1922, and said her husband was not home and she wanted help finding him. He directed her to Eisele, who stated she knocked on his door at 5 AM.

Both men's statements matched Sabella's testimony in court, yet such corroboration was never presented in the trial, and in just a few days, Bonelli had locked down the true order of events.

The next affidavit was the most crucial of them all. The team found Michele Desant in his new home in Cicero. Desant explained he had known the Nitti family for more than eight years and lived in a shanty about a mile behind the farm. On a typical workday, he and his wife ate with the Nitti family and then left sometime before midnight. On Saturday, July 15, 1922, at 9 PM, Desant revealed, Michael Nitti had come to the family farm.

"I heard an argument between Michael and his father in the kitchen," Desant stated. "Michael asked his father for $500. His father refused to give him the money."

Francesco Nitti was apparently offended that his son asked. He slapped his adult son, which sparked a rage inside the young man. "Michael turned on his father," Desant recalled. "He knocked him down. Kicked. Beat. Punched and bruised him about the face and body. He was almost unconscious."

Francesco Nitti clutched his stomach and began to cry. His face, nose, and lips were bleeding and swollen. A bruise surfaced on his right eye, and he appeared to be in great pain. "You've got me," he whimpered as he crawled out of the house.

Francesco Nitti was humiliated and hurt. He stayed at home for three days to physically heal, Desant revealed. Then he disappeared for four days, perhaps to emotionally heal.

Desant's testimony further proved that a fight had occurred between Michael Nitti and his father about two weeks prior to Francesco's disappearance. It was possible that Francesco left the family on the night of July 29 with the intent to never return. It was also possible that he died from internal injuries sustained during the fight. Francesco suffered extensive head injuries and was almost unconscious from the beating. He also appeared to have significant stomach trauma, which might have resulted in broken ribs or organ damage. But it was also likely that Michael Nitti returned to the Nitti family farm on July 29 with the intent to harm his father.

Desant had more valuable evidence to share. He explained in detail how the family farm had three wagons, but only one detachable shaft. That meant that only one wagon was drivable at a time. Desant's shanty was about a mile behind the farm, and he was in the practice of driving home each night. On the night that Francesco Nitti disappeared, Desant took the only shaft, attached it to a wagon, and drove himself home. Dasso's claim that Peter, Charley, and Sabella loaded the body onto a wagon and drove it to the canal was impossible. There was only one functional wagon, and Desant had it in his possession.

Desant had two more facts to share with the defense attorneys. He said it was already 11 PM when he left the Nitti family farm on the night of July 29, 1922. Francesco Nitti was still awake and outside. He stood alongside the wagon as Desant drove away and the two men wished each other a good evening. This meant Francesco Nitti went missing between the hours of 11 PM, when Desant last saw him, and 2 AM, when Sabella awoke and realized he was missing. Francesco Nitti had been missing for just three hours when Sabella sensed something was wrong and sought help.

Desant used his statement to tell the attorneys what he wasn't able to reveal during the trial: Michael Nitti had threatened him and warned him not to reveal what he knew. Desant told the lawyers he was afraid for his life. Michael was capable of killing a man with his bare hands.

––––––––

In piecing together the evidence, the defense team was discovering a new possible explanation for what happened the night of July 29. The animosity between Francesco and his sons had exploded into a raging hatred. Francesco was paranoid and worried someone would burn his crops in the middle of the night. While he kept watch, he went missing.

Sabella, meanwhile, was proving to be a credible witness. Everything she had said on the stand was now verified by public officials and key witnesses. If the defense team had more time, they might have found and interviewed more people with knowledge about the Nitti farm violence. But the team was on a deadline imposed by the court. The hearing was set for August 29, and they were required to file the affidavits with the county in advance and supply the state's attorney's office with copies. As soon as Desant's interview was complete, the papers were rushed to the courthouse and then over to the state's attorney's office.

The team drafted the motion for a new trial based on grievous errors in the first trial, and continued finding new evidence in the hope it might be permitted into testimony. Team members spread out, reaching around the city and back into Stickney. They again connected with Eisele and determined the dimensions of the catch basin where the body was supposedly stuffed. The manhole cover in the middle of the street was too heavy for a person to inconspicuously remove, and removal required special tools. The grated opening on the curb was far too small for the body to fit. They requested Eisele appear in court on August 29 to testify.

On the day of the hearing, the team collected affidavits from Sabella and Peter. It was unknown why the team waited to gather such information. Sabella and Peter were available in jail and easy to access. It's possible the defense did so as a strategic move so that the prosecution had less information to work with. Or the team might have waited in case Sabella or Peter needed to emphasize or deny specific statements.

Sabella's affidavit began by addressing Dasso and his many fabrications. She said he had pressured her to confess to the crime and promised she would avoid prison because she was a woman and a mother. Sabella had maintained her innocence and refused to confess. She also stated that she never heard—in any language—a statement in the state's attorney's office that her husband was murdered. She also noted how no one asked her this question during the trial. She was never allowed to tell the court whether she confessed to a crime. Now her affidavit made it clear—there was no confession.

Sabella also stated that she never hired Eugene A. Moran as her defense attorney. After her arrest, she was not familiar with the US court system and did not realize that an attorney was not permitted to simply claim a case for his own. She did not pay Moran for his services, and she was unable to talk to him because of their language barriers.

The statement continued and disputed other claims that were made against Sabella during the trial. Sabella clarified that she never told Anna Volpe that Francesco stank. She also never said she planned on killing her husband. And during her arrest, she never cried to her daughters or said she was leaving for a long time. She made no admission of guilt and gave no confession. She said she was innocent and asked that the judgment be vacated and a new trial ordered.

Peter's affidavit corroborated Sabella's. The same outline was used, and only a few new pieces of information were added. Peter confirmed Sabella never confessed in the state's attorney's office or agreed "Whatever Charley says is true." He declared his innocence and said that much of what he heard during the trial was untrue, but he had not been permitted during his testimony to address such falsehoods.

Both Sabella and Peter were illiterate. Helen Cirese signed on their behalf and then notarized the affidavits. She skimmed both documents, looking for possible errors. She found in Peter's affidavit a sentence that required clarification. There was no time to retype the statement, and she drew a small arrow above the line in question and handwrote in a few words. It was the best she could do. She had to get to court.

On August 29, the team of six surrounded the defendants' table, swarming around Peter and Sabella like guards. Milton A. Smith took his place at the table across the aisle, and the courtroom waited for Judge David to appear. The reporters positioned themselves in the gallery and noted the heat emanating from the six lawyers at the defendants' table. They readied themselves for a show.

Judge David entered the courtroom and saw the small army surrounding Sabella and Peter. If he didn't know it already, he was in for a fight. DeStefano, as lead council, began the motion. He was direct with the judge, leaving nothing to misinterpretation.

"If the court please," DeStefano began, "this is a motion to vacate judgment and the orders denying motion in arrest and for new trial. We are asking the court to reconsider the motion previously made for a new trial by the counsel who tried the case, on additional grounds to those already urged. The court will remember this motion was entered on July 14, within the judgment term, and Your Honor set the hearing for today. We desire to present a written motion of the additional grounds, and affidavits in support of the motion."

DeStefano was an experienced, competent attorney who knew procedure. When Judge David stated the affidavits must be filed before they were introduced as evidence, DeStefano was one step ahead of him. "The affidavits have been filed and I now offer them in evidence," DeStefano answered, using the precise terminology Judge David expected.

"Did you submit copies of them to the state's attorney?" the judge challenged.

"Yes," DeStefano confirmed. "I submitted copies of them five days ago, all of them with the exception of the affidavits of the defendants which I was able to obtain only this morning. I have handed the state's attorney a copy of these affidavits also."

"Very well," the judge conceded. "You may introduce them into evidence."

The team of six took turns presenting the new evidence. The defense attorneys argued passionately and tried to encourage outrage among the gallery. A sense of disgrace was building, and Smith did not appreciate the accusations that he, Romano, and Dasso fabricated facts. The tension in the courtroom elevated as the associated defense attorney, Swanson, argued that Smith's story about Peter disposing of the body in the catch basin was complete fiction.

Smith held firm that the dimensions of the grate were not as Police Chief Eisele described in his affidavit. The two sides went back and forth until Swanson challenged the court to seek the truth.

"Now, the chief of police . . . is here and if there is any doubt in the court's mind, I would like to call him," Swanson pushed.

"Who?" Judge David asked.

"The chief of police . . ." Swanson countered. "I would like to show the dimensions of this manhole. I would like to show the dimension of the outlet of the manhole to show—"

Judge David interrupted the defense attorney. He must have wanted to appear lenient and fair, and he was quick to show his agreeability. "You can show anything you want. I will listen to everything you have to offer."

Swanson called Eisele forward. While the police chief took his place on the witness stand, Judge David reviewed the facts with Swanson as if he was new to the case. "There was a body in the manhole," Judge David said.

"There is no question about it," Swanson said.

"There is only one place that it could get in."

"That is our contention," Swanson replied. "If the court agrees on that, I won't ask him any questions . . . about it being chucked into the manhole."

"You want to make your record?"

"Let me make my record."

Eisele was sworn in and Swanson asked a few questions to establish the witness's identity and his participation in the first trial. "Tell the Judge here the width of that manhole, the diameter, the width or diameter across?"

Eisele used his hands to measure the distance for the court. "It must be about three feet or so, three and a half, that big around."

"Circular, was it?"

"Yes sir."

"About what is the depth of it?"

"Five and a half or six feet."

"There was an outlet from the manhole, wasn't there?"

"Yes sir."

"A drain, called a drain?"

"Yes sir."

"What was the diameter of that drain?"

"Why I don't know whether it is six or seven inches."

Judge David interrupted. "Nobody claims that it came through the drain."

"That is all I want to show, that it would be impossible to come through the drain."

DeStefano spoke up. Judge David erred when he said no one claimed the body was pushed through the drain. It was precisely what the prosecution had claimed during the trial. The three-foot metal manhole cover was too difficult to remove. The curb-entry was assumed to be the spot where the body was deposited.

"The state claimed it," DeStefano called out. The judge ignored him, but DeStefano succeeded in slipping it into the record.

Judge David ended the testimony; he ruled the other details Eisele had to present were established in the trial and unnecessary to repeat. The defense took his resistance in stride and began to argue how Moran's incompetency entitled Sabella and Peter to a new trial.

"The evidence in this case justified the verdict," the judge dismissed. "The crime was most atrocious and committed deliberately and with the apparent loss of all heart and feelings. The motion is overruled. I feel that I am doing the right thing for the community and civilization by so doing."

Judge David left the courtroom, leaving the defense to calm their clients. But the judge was not yet done with this case. He still had to sign and date the typed opinion. This was a task he put off for almost two weeks. On day sixty-four, he finally signed the opinion. The team of six now had thirty-one days to stop the execution.

25

GIVEN UNDER
MY HAND AND SEAL

O<small>N</small> S<small>EPTEMBER</small> 25, almost a month after the failed hearing in Judge David's courtroom, the team of six waited anxiously in their office on Clark Street. The team had filed a writ of error with the Illinois Supreme Court, and they were awaiting a decision. If granted, the execution would be stayed until the higher court had an opportunity to review the case. If denied, the execution would proceed in just seventeen days.

The writ identified eighteen errors in the original trial. It began by addressing the unconstitutionality of the first trial. The second item argued the defendants "have been deprived" of their lives without due process of law, in violation of the Fourteenth Amendment.

The next two items were against Judge David. Item three accused the trial judge of not appointing competent counsel to assist the defense. Item four argued that Judge David erred in allowing incompetent evidence to be introduced.

Items five and six addressed the flimsy evidence and argued that corpus delicti was not proven beyond a reasonable doubt. The jury's passion and prejudice was noted in item eight. Item nine argued that such prejudice was calculated by remarks made by the prosecution. And items ten, eleven, and twelve found error in the jury instructions.

Items thirteen and fourteen tasked the court with allowing the prosecution to make improper and prejudicial remarks to the jury. When reviewing the case, the justices would likely find such prejudicial remarks in the closing statements and the description of Sabella as a "cold-blooded killer" or "Lady Macbeth." The blame shifted back to Judge David for items fifteen, sixteen, and seventeen because he had denied a new trial and refused to vacate the judgment. The last item summed up the judgments as contrary to the law and the evidence. "Wherefore, the plaintiffs in error and each of them pray that the judgments of conviction be reversed."

Cirese had signed for all six attorneys and added Swanson as "of counsel." And then they waited. The paperwork was sent down to Springfield, a distance of a little more than two hundred miles. News of the decision, however, fired back rapidly. The team's office was wired with a telephone, and a long-distance call could be routed all the way from Springfield. Before the written response made its way to Chicago, the team knew their clients were safe—for the time being.

Justice Orrin N. Carter of the Illinois Supreme Court wrote the writ allowing supersedeas: the execution for both defendants was suspended until the supreme court gave further order. Carter signed and dated the document September 25, 1923, and affixed his official seal. The supreme court still had the option to side with Judge David and allow the executions to proceed. But that possibility was pushed into the future, and the team was given what they needed—time.

———————

Cirese strode out of the elevators and onto Clark Street. She was headed to Cook County Jail to deliver the good news to her clients. Peter understood immediately when Cirese explained they had been granted a stay of execution until the supreme court reviewed the case. He began to cry with relief, and possibly a bit of hope. But Sabella, who was still developing her understanding of English, misunderstood the good news. When Cirese told her she received a stay of execution, she thought they had lost the fight. She began to sob, and her attorney had to interrupt her weeping to explain she was safe.

Sabella and Peter were under the state supreme court's protection. That was the good news. The bad news was the Illinois Supreme Court had a lengthy list of other appeals to consider. The high court did not plan on reviewing the Nitti-Crudele case until February. For Peter, the wait was excruciating. He had been in jail since May and the experience was akin to an animal living in a crate. For the winter months, he would be confined to his cell, wondering if the supreme court would save him or send him to the gallows. For Sabella, jail was more bearable. She had limited comfort but was allowed to move throughout the women's block, keep busy with work, and interact with the other women. Nonetheless, it was still time spent separated from her young daughters.

For Cirese, the wait was perfect. With the help of Margaret Bonelli, she planned to transform Sabella Nitti from a disheveled and foreign woman into a comely American mother. Sabella might not be as demure or charming as the acquitted McGinnis sisters, but now there was time to make her over.

Cirese evaluated her client. Sabella's arms were muscular from years of hard labor, and her skin was damaged and toughened from exposure to the sun and wind. Her dark hair was streaked with gray and appeared dirty, and she was painfully thin. To Americans, Sabella lay outside the standards of beauty. But Cirese saw Sabella's potential.

Cirese brought a hairdresser to the jail and shared her vision for how to make Sabella beautiful. The hairdresser fussed with Sabella's hair and then applied color to turn her graying strands into a deep, rich brown. She combed through Sabella's long locks and picked up the scissors. Sabella needed a modern haircut in order to resemble a modern woman. Her long hair was dated and reflected another era that most Americans were keen on forgetting. But long hair was easy to manage when she was working on the farm. Sabella simply combed it back and secured it high on her head.

The stylist cut Sabella's hair into a bob styled with soft waves. Around Sabella's hairline, the weak and broken hairs were turned into bangs. It was likely that Sabella was not too shocked by the change. In previous years, she had tried to fold her hair under her cap so it looked as though she had bangs and a bob. Now the look was permanent, and professionally styled.

Cirese made efforts to apply cosmetics to Sabella and clean her hardened hands. It was a transformation that Sabella readily accepted. She was aware of how juries reacted to attractive women, and she knew American men did not find her good-looking. Cirese likely made assurances along the way and told Sabella she was beautiful. It may have been decades since Sabella heard such a compliment, if she had ever heard it at all.

The newspapers took note of Sabella's makeover, and Cirese never hid her attempt to make her client more beautiful. Admitting her efforts was a smart move. It avoided any appearance that the defense was trying to be underhanded or manipulative. And it allowed critics to chastise the Cook County legal system for acquitting beautiful women while a homely but innocent woman was subjected to a trial so faulty that the Illinois Supreme Court had to intervene.

While the case waited among the backlog for the high court's review, Cirese polished her client. Although the makeover efforts were never concealed, Cirese was far more discreet about her efforts to feed and fatten her client. Cirese never admitted as much, but she was Sabella's most consistent visitor and advocate. It was likely that it was Cirese, and perhaps Margaret Bonelli, who supplied Sabella with additional food items to supplement her sparse prison meals.

Before the team of six intervened, Sabella's jailhouse meals had been limited to a bread roll and the occasional cup of soup. Because she was industrious and insisted on working throughout the day, Sabella burned more calories than she consumed. She was emaciated when she came to the jail in May 1923. Her cheeks were hollow and stretched thin, which made her large eyes seem bulged. She seemed to grow smaller, thinner, and older looking during the summer and early autumn. But in the coming months, Sabella's hard angles would soften as her weight steadily increased.

The makeover was one part of the plan. Cirese had other goals for helping Sabella appear more refined. Sabella's English progressed during the winter and she was learning American mannerisms. Grunting, for example, was not becoming of a woman. Sabella was learning to keep in the sounds that made Americans cringe but felt so natural to her. She was also advised to refrain from the rocking she had a tendency to do when she was nervous.

Sabella's polishing meant learning how to contain her physical presence. American women tucked into themselves. At times, they made themselves smaller. Sabella had been in the habit of hunching and sitting with her legs open. With Cirese's help, she was learning to squeeze her body together. Legs needed to be kept close, arms folded into the lap, and the back held straight and stiff.

The papers made mention of the "jail school," and the *Chicago Daily Tribune's* Genevieve Forbes commented on how "jail can do a lot for a woman." The comment was directed toward not only Sabella but also the other women who were beginning to doll up before court and ask for access to the cosmetics cabinet.

The makeup cabinet was about to see plenty of use. A new cohort of lady killers were headed to Cook County Jail, each one determined to woo the all-male juries with their femininity. The pressure was on the state's attorney's office to hold these women similarly accountable for murdering men. Smith and Romano didn't want to let Sabella's case slip, especially when beautiful women were hard to convict. Someone in Cook County needed to pay for their crimes, and Sabella was ugly prey the attorneys could target. They weren't giving up.

Part V

PASSING THROUGH THE FIRE

26

MONKEY MEETS A TIGER

Kitty Baluk pushed open the wood door to the police station on Hudson Avenue. She climbed a short stairwell to the first floor and walked into the lobby. She was calm and collected, and didn't quite resemble the "wolf woman" the papers were describing. "Do you want me?" she asked the sergeant on duty. "I'm Mrs. Malm. I wanted to see my baby."

Kitty wasn't really Mrs. Malm. She never married Otto Malm; she only lived with him after her marriage to Max Baluk became too violent to endure. It seemed less disgraceful if she referred to herself as Mrs. Malm, although not being married was the least of her problems.

Kitty and Otto had tried to rob a knitting factory about three weeks earlier. Maybe it wasn't their intent to kill anyone, but shots were fired when the night watchmen surprised them. Now an eighteen-year-old aspiring watchman was dead, and the owner of the security company was wounded. Otto was arrested first and claimed the deadly bullet came from Kitty's gun.

Kitty looked around the station lobby as if she might find her two-year-old daughter sitting in one of the wooden chairs. She immediately began pressing for the right to see her little girl, perhaps not realizing that she had to first satisfy questions from a slew of police, prosecutors, and reporters.

Assistant state's attorney John Sbarboro was wrapping up an interview with Otto Malm when he received word that Kitty was at the Hudson Avenue police station. The warrant for her arrest had only been issued the day before, and Kitty had the decency to respond promptly. But her surrender only complicated the case for Sbarboro. Police already had Otto Malm in custody for an unrelated robbery, and the longtime felon admitted to the knitting factory crime and named Kitty as his accomplice. But Sbarboro also had another pair in custody—Walter Bockelman, whom the victim had named as the killer before dying, and Ethel Beck, a known prostitute. Walter and Otto resembled each other, and it wasn't surprising if the victim confused the two. It was dark when the night watchmen shone their flashlights on the young couple robbing the factory and were promptly sprayed with bullets.

The past few weeks had seen a series of convoluted confessions and recanted statements. Kitty had signed a confession. Otto had confessed and then recanted. Walter maintained his innocence. And Ethel had recanted her earlier statements. She even claimed she owed Walter "a big apology." Ethel was clearly confused, and at only eighteen years old, her sad life was one of mental illness and forced prostitution. None of the police, or even the reporters, seemed too concerned about Ethel's tragic backstory. Their main concern was sorting through the two couples to determine who deserved a murder indictment.

Sbarboro sat across from Kitty and looked at the young woman. She was nineteen, still more than eight months away from her twentieth birthday. She had short hair, cropped into a dark bob just beneath her ears. Kitty had an oval face, but there wasn't a softness to her expression. She seemed hard and even a bit masculine.

Kitty looked at the unapologetic man across from her. Sbarboro was a tall man with light brown hair and gray eyes. He had a thick, sturdy build and a limited tolerance for nonsense. Kitty had no way of knowing that Sbarboro was a full-time assistant state's attorney who occasionally helped in his family's undertaking business. The business was just a few blocks from the Hudson Avenue station, and it was the preferred vendor for Chicago's most notorious mobsters. Not only did the Sbarboro family have enough intrepidity to service the mob, but they were audacious enough to demand fair payment. When "Mike" Merlo died of cancer in November 1924, the Sbarboro family served as undertakers. The next day, they oversaw Dean O'Banion's $10,000 funeral.* The parlor sent the estate an itemized invoice that was entered into the probate courts and considered against the deceased gangster's assets. The Sbarboro family was all business, and John Sbarboro conducted his interview with Kitty with a clinical approach. He didn't want to hear Kitty's backstory. He didn't want to hear about the sadness in her life. He needed to know whether she and Otto were culpable, or if the confused prostitute was to blame.

"What's your name?" Sbarboro asked.

"Katherine Walters," Kitty answered, giving the anglicized version of her maiden name.

"Are you married?"

"Yes. To Max Baluk, 1765 Clybourn Avenue."

Sbarboro's strict line of questions didn't open space for sympathy. He stuck to the facts related to the case. It didn't matter that Kitty had been only seventeen and already pregnant when she married her husband. It wasn't Sbarboro's problem that Kitty left the marriage and met Otto Malm at the cheap hotel where she was staying.

"What is your address?"

"I ain't got one just now."

"Do you know Otto Malm?"

"Yes. I married him about a month ago today in Crowne Point."

Sbarboro went straight for the prize. "Are you willing to make a statement?"

Kitty was impulsive, but she was sharp. "I'm willing if I know what it's about."

"What occurred on November fourth between 4 and 6 AM?"

"I know but I'm not telling."

"Were you out with Otto?"

---

* About $140,000 in 2015.

"I reckon I was."

"Were you on Lincoln Avenue with Otto Malm and Eric Noren?"

"I won't answer that."

Sbarboro tried a new angle. "Don't you want to tell?"

"Yes. I just came from Indianapolis on a 9:30 train. I wanted to see my baby. That's why I gave myself up," Kitty answered.

The thought of her daughter overwhelmed Kitty. She opened up and told Sbarboro how she went to the knitting factory the night of the shooting. "He said, 'Stay outside.'"

"Who said that?" Sbarboro interrupted.

"My husband. I was standing there while he opened the door and went in."

"What kind of gun did you have?"

It was a leading question, but Kitty didn't fall for it. "I didn't have any," she answered. "He had a blue steel but I don't know the difference between sizes."

Kitty kept going. She admitted how the two night watchmen surprised them as they tried to pry open the door. "He was under the stairway when I saw the flashlight the two men were carrying. They didn't say anything to me, but one said to my husband, 'What are you doing here?'"

Kitty claimed Otto fired at the night watchman. "The fellow with the watchman started to run in our direction. My husband turned and fired a shot at him. Then I got shot. That's all I know."

Sbarboro didn't quite know how to read the situation. Kitty was calm in her interview, even guarded and perhaps a little strategic. She didn't seem the violent murderess that Otto told police to expect. He even warned police that Kitty had a gun on her and was desperate enough to shoot at police. She was a "two gun woman."

Kitty's story contradicted Otto's confession, but at least she admitted she was present at the scene of the crime. Sbarboro continued the interview. "How did you leave there?"

"I told my husband, 'Honey, you shot me.' He said, 'Don't fool me.' I thought if I dropped they'd get me, so I kept going."

The back of Kitty's head had been grazed by a bullet. Her hair was cropped off when Otto attempted to tend to the wound himself. Sbarboro considered Kitty, a toughened and weathered young woman who casually mentioned being hit by a bullet during a robbery. As he processed her story, he quietly compared Kitty's version with the ones he heard from Otto, Walter, and the young prostitute. He paused, thinking he didn't quite have what he needed to make his case. It seemed Kitty and Otto were to blame, especially since Walter always held firm that he was innocent and not even at the scene of the crime. And Ethel wasn't a credible witness. She was confused and possibly delusional.

At least Kitty was honest. She told the attorney how she had avoided arrest when the police came knocking on her mother's door. She slipped her younger sister a five-dollar bill and instructed her to buy supplies for the baby. "[I] went down the back stairs while the cops came up the front," Kitty confessed.

Kitty also admitted to a string of failed burglaries. On at least four occasions, Kitty and Otto tried to break into area factories and shops. Each time, they struggled to get into the building or avoid attracting the watchman's interest. Kitty didn't seem embarrassed that she and Otto were terrible at their chosen profession.

Sbarboro was at a loss. He brought the information to his boss, who had the idea to bring the four suspects together for an interrogation. It was almost midnight when Kitty was led into a room with Otto, Walter, and Ethel. Several reporters stood in the background, eager to see a confrontation between the four suspects. Both the reporters and the police seemed to think the suspects might respond to each other, angrily blaming their counterparts for their troubles. But each of them seemed lethargic, and more focused on the police than each other.

"Stand up there!" Sbarboro instructed Walter.

Walter had been in jail for almost three weeks and felt no one was listening to him. He seemed defeated and focused his gaze on the wall. "You, Malm," Sbarboro barked at Otto. "Have you ever seen that man before?"

Otto shook his head. "No, sir."

Sbarboro asked Otto in three different ways whether he knew Walter. He answered each time that he did not.

The meeting was not progressing as Sbarboro had hoped. Kitty had asked to speak to Otto in private and pouted when refused. When the reporters evaluated the four suspects, they saw two indifferent and exhausted men, one pouting woman, and the other woman, Ethel, casually viewing the situation as if she weren't involved.

Sbarboro ordered the guards to separate the suspects and bring them back to their cells. The state's attorney ordered indictments for Kitty and Otto, and maintained the two against Walter and Ethel. But the grand jury court proceedings had to wait. The next day was Thanksgiving, and Chicagoans were preparing for a celebration.

———————

For the second time, Sabella found herself in jail on Thanksgiving Day. She was learning how Thanksgiving was a day for Americans to feast, express gratitude for all that had gone well in the past year, and project optimism for the year ahead.

Not everyone, of course, could afford a feast, and helping the needy was part of the holiday tradition. Some churches and charitable organizations supplied poor families with ingredients to make an improvised feast. Local high school students cooked and delivered a meal, smiling for the *Chicago Daily Tribune* photographers who made sure their efforts weren't anonymous.

Someone provided the needed ingredients for the jail to supply a holiday meal to the female inmates. For Sabella, it was likely that Thanksgiving meant a rare nourishing, hot meal of turkey meat, vegetables, and a sweet for dessert. Given the circumstances, Thanksgiving was a good day for her. It wasn't a tradition she celebrated, so she wasn't haunted by memories of better Thanksgivings that she might never experience again. And she was new to American culture, so she wasn't tormented by a sense that she had nothing to be grateful for.

Over at the Hudson Avenue police station, Kitty Baluk was spending her first holiday in police custody. She was learning the police were not terribly sympathetic, and neither were the reporters. That morning, the *Chicago Daily Tribune* ran two stories about Kitty on the first and second pages. The front-page story stuck to the facts about the case and highlighted the confusion Sbarboro and the state's attorney felt about the four suspects. The second-page story was written by Genevieve Forbes, to whom Kitty had unloaded the day before.

When Forbes found Kitty in her cell, she had seen a young girl who seemed both hardened and scared. Forbes wasn't the only reporter crowding around Kitty, but she was the most observant. She took note of Kitty's wrinkled mouth. At times, Kitty frowned to stop herself from crying. "Ugly wiggles," Forbes wrote in her notebook to describe Kitty's facial expressions. "Face is pretty. Well-molded."

"How come Otto confessed?" one of the reporters asked Kitty.

Kitty tried to fight the tears but couldn't. "They made him do it," she told reporters. "When I see him last night I could see it. He looked so bad; God, it got me. Men, they're brave as the devil, but they can't hold out the way a woman can. Now me, they could of beat hell out of me and I wouldn't have squealed. Say, they could have built a fire under me and I never would have squawked."

Forbes watched the girl cry and determined her tears were sincere—she wasn't crying to win sympathy for her situation. But Kitty was exhausting. Forbes took note of how Kitty seemed to fluctuate from one emotion to the next. One moment, she'd cry about her daughter, then she'd proclaim a hardness the police could never break. Forbes thought Kitty's emotions swung like a pendulum. But whichever way it swung, Kitty remained honest, and Forbes believed the girl was credible.

Forbes was interested in Kitty's backstory, and she was the first reporter to take note of the young arrestee's history. Kitty was born in the Austro-Hungarian Empire in the summer of 1904. She immigrated with her family when she was seven. By fifth grade, she had stopped attending school.

"My mother said there was no need for girls to go to high school— just spend money on them and then they get married—but fine for the boys," Kitty told Forbes. "Still, I ain't blaming my mother, for she had no money. So I went to work in a machine factory with her."

Forbes listened to Kitty and continued to jot notes in her pad. No other reporter provided as deep a character profile as Forbes. There might have been something about Forbes that made Kitty feel she was speaking with a safe source, and she began to tell the reporter about the violence that shaped her young life. The factory where Kitty worked with her mother was infested with sexual violence. Whether Kitty coded her language or Forbes did so on her behalf was unknown. But the result was a story in which Kitty told Forbes that the male workers at the factory wanted to "marry her," which was likely a coded word for unwanted sexual advances.

"Fellows, always fellows," Kitty sighed. "I didn't want to marry 'em. Then they'd try to scare me, saying they'd scar me and spoil my looks with a razor or a gun if I wouldn't marry 'em." Forbes wrote down the curse words Kitty added to the story as she described the men who threatened her at the factory. "Finally," Kitty continued, "Max Baluk, the Russian in the factory, he married me in 1921. Then I learned what rotten names a bad man can call his wife."

Forbes again jotted down the obscenities Kitty spewed. "Then, my baby came."

On the marriage license, Max claimed he was ten years older than his seventeen-year-old bride. But other records suggested Max was closer to sixteen years older than Kitty.

Max indeed appeared to be twice as old as his new wife. His thin hair had receded to expose a wide forehead that pulled tightly into his eyebrows. His nose looked as though it had been broken many times, and his hard demeanor suggested he really didn't care if it broke again.

In her interview with Forbes, Kitty began speaking about her baby, and then said something that likely melted Forbes's sympathy.

"God, I could kill a woman who'd rather have a dog than a kid."

Forbes was unmarried at the time, and although she would marry another *Chicago Daily Tribune* reporter within a few short years, she never had children. Forbes continued the interview, and Kitty explained how she left her husband because of his abusive ways and found work as a waitress. When she met Otto Malm through friends, she asked him to pose as her husband and scare off a man who was giving her trouble. They were a couple ever since.

"He was a prince," Kitty assured Forbes.

Kitty wanted to be clear with Forbes—she did not squeal on her man. "I'm for him forever. If we get out of this together, I'm with him. If I get out and he's in, there won't be no other."

Forbes had what she needed. She packed away her notepad and left the Hudson Avenue station. Back at the newsroom, she typed her story and left it for her editor. When the story hit newsstands the next day, the headline screamed a story about the SAVAGE MOTHER.

Soon, Kitty's media persona, like Sabella's, dissolved into a Forbes creation. She was a "gun girl." A "tiger woman." A savage. But she was also desperate and broken. The weight of her loss was becoming too much for the young woman to shoulder, especially when she had no one to consider a friend.

———

Kitty was desperate for contact with Otto. They were both in custody at the Hudson Avenue police station, but they were not in the same holding cell. The separation didn't stop them from discussing their troubles through the open bars. The police station was a red brick rectangle situated on the corner, and the building was taller than it was wide. That meant Kitty and Otto were separated in their jail cells, but within close enough proximity to communicate with each other.

It wasn't enough for Kitty. She wanted to be alone with Otto. She begged repeatedly for permission to speak with him in private. In the three days since her surrender, she badgered police for alone time with Otto. When she wasn't begging for a private conversation with her co-defendant, Kitty pled for a visit with her daughter.

Kitty wore out the police's patience within three short days. The day after Thanksgiving, the officers guarding the cell block reported to their supervisor that Kitty and Otto were debating their options. If a jury returned a guilty verdict along with the death penalty, then both Kitty and Otto felt suicide was preferable.

Kitty was promptly removed from her cell and transferred to the West Chicago police station. There she was greeted by Officer Agnes Whalen, one of the force's few women. A twelve-year veteran of the force, Whalen was part jail matron and part social worker.

Kitty followed the officer to her cell. Whalen was a large woman who was simultaneously strong and obese. She had a large bosom that sat above a protruding stomach, and she wore a floor-length, blue police dress with her Chicago Police Matron star positioned above her heart. Whalen was intimidating when required and comforting when needed.

Kitty asked the matron for paper and a writing implement, and Whalen obliged, not realizing that Kitty intended to write good-bye letters to her mother and Otto. Kitty began with her letter to her mother. She hinted at the sexual violence she had suffered at the factory and the marital abuse she had endured with Otto. She begged her mother to care for her younger sister and guide her from contact with "such men as I have known."

Kitty set the letter to her mother aside and began work on her message to Otto. She urged him to place all blame on her so that he might walk free and care for her daughter. "Otto, dear, you are the light of my heart," Kitty wrote. "But, Honey, they will not let me be with you and I can't live without you. I know I ought to live for the baby's sake, but what's the use if I can't have you? And, Honey, if you get out of this alright, grant me just one wish and that is always to provide for Tootsie and love her like I would want you to. Don't let anyone insult her and ruin her like they did me."

It was almost midnight when Kitty slid the sheet off the bed and tied it into a noose. She skillfully wrapped the noose around her neck and suspended herself in the air. She was slowly dying when Whalen came back around to check on her.

Whalen knew Kitty was not emotionally well, and she peered into the dark cell expecting to see Kitty's silhouette on the cot. "How are you feeling now?" Whalen asked.

Whalen focused her gaze through the darkness and saw the bed was empty.

Whalen paused. There was no response. She reached for her keys and unlocked the gate. Once inside, she flipped on the light and saw Kitty hanging. The girl's face was gray from the lack of oxygen.

Whalen cut the sheet and screamed for help. Kitty regained consciousness before the ambulance arrived and burst into hysterics. She was outraged at Whalen for interrupting her chance to die. "Why didn't you leave me alone?" she sobbed. Crumpled on the floor, she descended into body-wracking sobs. "I won't miss next time," she threatened.

Kitty was inconsolable. "It won't do you any good to save me. I'll end it the next time," she cried. "You've separated me from Otto Malm. He's the only man I ever cared for. He is good to me and my baby. And you've taken the baby away. Well, when I can't have either of them, I don't want to live. And I'll kill myself sure as hell."

Kitty's letters, meant for her mother and Otto, were instead distributed among the reporters, who printed snippets along with updates on the unfolding drama. By the time Kitty was transferred to the women's block at Cook County Jail, she had endured days of interrogation by a grand jury. She even returned to the alley where the shooting occurred and reenacted the scene for the jury members. It was a glimpse of her near future. In the next few months, she would review every detail with her attorney.

It was unknown how Sabella reached out to the young inmate; such kindness wasn't the type of story that made the papers. They didn't take notice if Sabella hugged the crying girl during her first, most painful days in jail. They never noted if Sabella helped clean Kitty's cell or showed her the way to the laundry. They did eventually observe how Kitty became the most engaged and kindest inmate toward Sabella as the older woman awaited the decision of the Illinois Supreme Court. Kitty patiently helped Sabella as she stumbled her way through English phrases. And on dark days, Kitty was known to clown around until Sabella finally smiled.

It was good for Sabella to have a friend. The winter loomed in front of her with a long wait in jail. She had no guarantees the court would find in her favor and overturn Judge David's ruling. There was a chance she might languish in jail all winter only to be told the high court agreed with Judge David and the jury. And then, she would hang.

27

MY GOD! WHAT DID THEY DO?

February 18, 1924

Kitty stood behind the bars of her cell and waited for the matron to open the door. The matron turned the key and pulled open the cell door. Kitty stepped out of her cell and into the hallway. The other women watched as she was led from the women's block toward the bridge that connected the jail to the courthouse. Her trial was beginning with the jury selection.

Kitty dressed for the occasion. She wore a seal hide cloak and a matching hat, and neatly positioned her cropped hair. Her appearance was a thoughtful response to how the press—especially Genevieve Forbes—portrayed her: a tiger girl, a wolf woman, a savage beast. In person, she wanted the jury to think of her as a young mother painfully separated from her daughter.

Her nerves intensified as she entered the courtroom. The gallery was filled with sour-looking reporters, many of whom she had seen at the police stations and the jail. Genevieve Forbes was in the gallery, ready with her notebook and pen.

The guards led Kitty to the defendants' table, around which five defendants were crowded, waiting for the judge's attention. The original suspects, Walter Bockelman and Ethel Beck, were waiting to have the charges against them dismissed. The other three were waiting for their fates to be determined.

The morning was a plea hearing for Kitty and the two co-defendants, Otto Malm and Eric Noren, the driver of the getaway car. The three partners were no longer in business together. Otto planned to plead guilty to avoid a jury trial and the possibility of the death penalty. In his plea, he would also stage an attack against Kitty, to make sure she shouldered some of the blame. Eric had the least to do with the crime. For his part, he planned to plead guilty and mitigate his involvement by saying he never left the car. There were consequences for Eric, but not as extreme as either Otto or Kitty faced.

Judge Walter P. Steffen entered the courtroom and his hulking figure commanded the room's attention. Steffen was a former football star at University of Chicago and two-time all-American quarterback. Steffen coached at Carnegie Tech in Pittsburgh on the weekends, leaving Chicago on Thursdays and arriving home on Sundays. Steffen was still young, not yet forty, and had been on the bench for less than two years. He had served as an alderman for six years, and the time he spent in the courtroom as an attorney was as a prosecutor.

Kitty's attorney knew he was facing a former prosecutor but felt confident in the case. He encouraged Kitty to plead not guilty and bring her case before a jury. She was instructed to seem confident in her chances, which made her seem cold and indifferent. Otto and Eric took more humble approaches.

"How do you plead?" Judge Steffen asked Otto.

"Guilty," Otto admitted. Then, he took a stab at Kitty's case to help his own. "There were three shots fired and I fired only one."

Otto was clear with the judge—the other two shots came from Kitty's gun. Otto looked over at Kitty as he spoke, a move that made him seem truthful, as if he had no problem meeting her gaze.

Kitty responded with a shrug and an air of indifference. "Any fool could tell it wasn't me. There was only one gun. And suppose I had a gun, would I have shot myself? Say, that's a hot one."

Her assurance seemed to grow as the morning progressed. The prosecuting attorneys had offered a plea deal—fourteen years in prison if she pled guilty. Her attorney was so confident that she'd walk free that Kitty rejected the plea and decided to take her chances in front of a jury. The prosecutors were irritated by the plea rejection and planned on asking the jury for the death penalty. It was an extreme penalty, but one they might achieve with helpful testimony from Otto and Eric. Both men awaited sentencing and wanted to appease Judge Steffen.

Kitty pled not guilty and was then set aside so the court could address the other defendants. Charges against Walter and Ethel were dropped, and the two were released after spending more than four months in jail. The defendants present at the table dwindled as each inmate's case was addressed. Kitty began to make herself comfortable as space opened up.

Forbes watched as Kitty became warm and removed her seal hide cloak. Kitty flopped the wrap over the back of her chair, revealing the purple silk lining inside. Kitty took no notice as the cloak brushed against the bailiff seated behind her. Forbes took note, scrawling in her pad how Kitty acted as though she were in a theater.

Kitty continued to make herself comfortable as the gallery watched. She removed her hat and shook out her hair. She pulled a small Bible from her pocket and began to read. The Bible was for show, and Kitty seemed quite aware that she was being watched. "I read it all," she announced to anyone who was listening. "I know it almost by heart, for I was brought up in the Catholic Church, you know, even though I am really a Lutheran."

Forbes distrusted the performance, and her cynicism heightened as Kitty rotated between several contrived roles. She bounced from being a Bible-reading member of the Lutheran church to a hard woman boastful of her problems with police. "It's always ladies' day when it comes to shoving something up before the coppers," she complained. "Men are quitters. They're long on talk, but Lord, when it comes to the show-down, they're yellow."

Kitty thought she was being tough with her talk, but it revealed her nerves. For most of her life, not being hard and aggressive had worked against her survival. The men who wanted to "marry" her at the factory likely picked the smallest or most passive women to prey upon. And her husband attacked her as an easy, soft target.

Forbes wasn't sad for the defendant, nor was she impressed by how Kitty read her Bible during the jury selection. To Forbes, Kitty cared nothing for the verses she read. She was just using the Bible to make herself look good while the prosecutors asked potential jury members if they were willing to send Kitty to the gallows. For the state, a juror had to be comfortable with the death penalty in order to be accepted onto the panel.

"Are you willing to give the death penalty to this woman, even if she has a child?" the prosecutor asked each potential juror.

The thought of hanging must have unnerved Kitty, and she shot back with her characteristic tough-girl attitude. "Say," she joked to the reporters sitting within earshot. "I have as much chance of getting the rope as Malm has of getting angel wings when he croaks."

Forbes was not impressed with Kitty's rhyming abilities. She was more intent on the jury selection. That afternoon, the prosecution and defense were only able to agree on four jurors. One of the jurors, John Behmiller, was a veteran of murder trials. About two decades earlier, Behmiller was part of the jury that had convicted Adolph Luetgert, "the Sausage King of Chicago," who was accused of murdering his wife and dissolving her body in a vat of lye. The defense in that case argued that Luetgert's wife left the family after their sausage and packing business crashed into bankruptcy. The case dragged on for more than a year before the jury convicted Luetgert and gave him a life sentence. He died the following year in the penitentiary.

"Is there anything in that experience that would make you less fit to serve here as a juror?" the prosecuting attorney asked.

"Nothing," Behmiller assured the court. "Except that I don't want this case to be so long."

Kitty looked up from her Bible and smiled at the juror.

––––––––––

More than a week later, the gallery was packed with reporters waiting to hear the verdict against Kitty. The jury had retired to deliberate eighty minutes earlier. It was late in the evening and they wanted to finish the trial that had disrupted their lives for more than a week.

Everyone wanted the trial to conclude, except Kitty. The trial had gone as poorly as the robbery that led to this trouble. Her attorney's strategy was outmaneuvered by the two prosecutors. First, the prosecutors arrested Kitty's husband, Max Baluk, and had him testify they were still married. This eliminated any spousal testimony privilege that Otto Malm could have used to avoid testifying in her trial. When Otto did testify, he blamed Kitty for the murder. Then, the prosecutors found a woman who claimed Kitty bragged about the killing and showed off her favorite gun. The woman seemed delighted to testify, as if the two had a long-standing hatred. But they didn't really know each other, they only shared a room in a boardinghouse when Kitty was on the lam.

Kitty braced herself when word came the jury had reached a verdict. From inside the deliberation room, the foreman knocked on the door to signify they were ready. A current of anticipation ran through the room. The two prosecutors watched the jury file back into the courtroom. The foreman passed a sheet of paper to the clerk.

The court quieted. The clerk unfolded the piece of paper and paused to clear his throat. "We, the jury," the clerk read, "find the defendant, Katherine Baluk Malm, guilty . . ."

Kitty lowered her head and absorbed the verdict. She would either hang or live her life in Joliet prison. The plea bargain that she rejected was for only fourteen years in prison.

The clerk continued, focusing his attention on the words before him. ". . . guilty of murder in a manner and form as charged in the indictment, and we fix her punishment at—"

Kitty didn't want to know. She screamed and her howl interrupted the verdict.

The clerk paused for a moment and looked up at Kitty. Then he finished reading the verdict: ". . . imprisonment in the penitentiary for the term of her natural life."

Kitty's first emotion was rage, a seething anger at everyone who had brought her to this point. Otto. Max. The police. That woman from the boardinghouse. The prosecutors. Her lawyer and his stupid strategies. The jury. The reporters. She hated them all.

The bailiffs circled close to Kitty as a clear threat of hysteria surfaced. "Keep away!" she warned the bailiffs. "I don't want to see anybody!"

Kitty moaned and shook her head in disbelief. Then, she fainted, dropping to the courtroom floor.

Everyone in the courtroom was talking at once. The bailiffs moved to pick Kitty up from the floor. The judge banged his gavel and demanded order. And the deputy sheriffs stepped forward to collect the prisoner.

Kitty was placed in a chair and lifted to the elevator and brought down to the bridge. When she awoke, she was back in her cell. "My God!" She blurted. "What did they do?"

Before anyone could answer, Kitty fainted again. When she awoke, she found herself on her cot. She blinked and looked around her cell. It was luxury compared to the one that awaited in the Joliet Penitentiary. The prison was woefully outdated, and there was no indoor plumbing. She would be squatting over a chamber pot for the rest of her natural life.

As Kitty lay on her cot, she had to realize how few friends and allies she had in the world. Otto had turned on her. Max was in the process of filing for divorce. At least her mother, sister, and young daughter still loved her. And Kitty had Sabella.

In Sabella, Kitty had the comfort of a woman who also faced the end of her life. Both felt the unfairness of the city and its uncompassionate court system. Sabella's English was steadily improving into broken sentences, and she was learning to read and write. The two could commiserate together. Cry. Hug. Hold hands and pray for a better outcome. Sabella and Kitty would need this comradeship in the months to come. In early spring, the jail was about to be disrupted by two beautiful boyfriend killers. They were glamorous. They were guilty. And they were not the least bit sorry.

28

SLUMMING IN
THE POLICE STATION

March 12, 1924

FREDA LAW SAW THE TAXICAB from the window. It was near 2 AM, early Wednesday morning. Her husband, Walter, was finally home, no doubt too drunk to drive. He had called earlier, during dinner, and asked if she wanted to go out that evening. It was a cold night, just a few degrees above freezing, and it wasn't the type of weather that made her want to ignore her work and spend the evening at a speakeasy.

"I have to sew," Freda told her husband on the phone. The curtains she was making were soon due and she wanted to finish the project.

"I'm going into work," Walter lied.

Freda suspected Walter's plan for the evening actually involved time spent in a gin joint. He was an automobile salesman, and the showroom wasn't a twenty-four-hour business. Perhaps some interested buyer might stay until eight or nine o'clock finishing the paperwork for a purchase. But then, Walter was heading out without Freda.

Freda fed the couple's son, Walter Junior, gave him a bath, and put the three-year-old to bed. She turned her attention to sewing for a while, and then focused on Walter and when he might return.

Freda was not naive. Sweet, perhaps, but not naive. She'd had too much experience in life with sadness. She was an orphan by the age of five and had lived with her aunt and uncle. Within a few years, her uncle passed away and she lived with her aunt, renting a room in a South Side apartment. She married at the age of eighteen, but the marriage dissolved after her husband began his service in the Great War. Freda moved on to Walter Law, and her ex-husband quickly found himself a new wife.

Walter was taller than her ex-husband and had blue eyes. And he came from a good family. His father was a Southerner, a gentleman who treated Freda like a daughter. Walter's parents owned a building on Ellis Avenue, near the lakefront. The neighborhood was changing, and most of the tenants were black. Freda was not progressive in her thinking, and the change worried her, as if a drunken Walter might stumble home into a neighbor's fist. Freda did not yet realize the person who would cause her the most harm was a wealthy white woman.

Freda waited up, and she tightened when she saw the taxi's headlights flash against the street. She saw a figure approach the building and briefly turn toward the neighbor's door. *Walter is drunk*, she thought. *He's going to the wrong door.* But then the figure corrected his path and approached her door. There was a knock.

It wasn't Walter. It was the police. And they were sorry, they had very bad news to share. Walter was dead, killed just a few hours before. He was shot at close range and died on top of a steering wheel of an automobile. The car belonged to another woman. The police believed that woman was the shooter.

––––––––––

Freda sat in the Wabash Avenue police station and watched the police escort Belva Gaertner into the makeshift courtroom. Belva was dressed in a black coat with a fur collar and a matching fur hat. She wore seven diamond rings that glittered after being freshly scrubbed of Walter's blood.

Freda silently raged when she saw Belva enter the room. At thirty-eight years old, Belva was more than a decade older. Belva was a stylish woman and she knew how to work with cosmetics. But she was not a beautiful woman. She had drooping cheeks, bulging eyes, and a large, prominent nose. Her hair was ratty and there was a small pat of fat underneath her chin. For Freda, there was no dignity in seeing this was the woman with whom Walter had chosen to have an affair.

Belva seemed to giggle as the police led her to the table and sat her directly next to Harry Law, Walter's father. The old man was positioned between his dead son's tearful wife and his murderous mistress. If he wanted, he could have slapped the woman who shot his son. Pulled her hair. Knocked her nose out of joint. But he was expected, as was Freda, to remain calm despite the unreasonably close proximity. He obliged the expectation, regardless of Belva's clear sentiment that Walter's death meant nothing to her at all.

Belva sat casually at the table, chuckling to herself with disbelief that the police had the nerve to arrest her. She acted as though the police were her servants, who should have cleaned up the body, towed the car, and been on their way. To come into her apartment, question her, disrupt her aging mother, and then arrest her was simply uncalled for.

Genevieve Forbes sat in the police station's makeshift courtroom and studied the socialite. If Belva was ashamed, she refused to show it. Belva was a former showgirl, and now she was performing, acting as if the moment mattered nothing to her. Forbes jotted in her notepad that Belva seemed "sprightly." She suspected the socialite was amused by "slumming" in the police station.

Forbes's attention refocused on the widow. Freda's anger had dissolved into anguish. She pressed against her father-in-law, and the two cried together. It had been only hours since police had knocked on her door and revealed that her husband was both unfaithful and dead. Since that time, friends had visited the house and offered comfort, assuring her that the murderer would certainly hang for her crime. In her grief, Freda had initially felt an odd sense of sympathy for the woman who killed Walter. This woman, whoever she was, faced either the noose or a lifetime in prison. Either way, her life was over. Such sympathy dissipated when the mystery woman materialized into a shameless socialite.

Some friends of the Law family sat in the gallery among the reporters and talked freely among themselves, their voices heightened so Belva could hear. That "wicked woman" had lured Walter away from his "domestic duties." But Harry Law dismissed placing the blame only on Belva. He was ashamed of his son for not resisting her advances. Temptation, he reasoned, was not a modern or urban problem. He had seen it himself as a young man in North Carolina, and believed a husband was obligated to remain faithful to his wife.

"No, daughter," Harry murmured to Freda. "It's not that woman's fault entirely. Walter ought not to have gone out with anyone. He had a lovely wife and a fine baby. No, he did wrong and we know it." Harry looked small behind the table. He seemed old to Forbes, and frail.

As the inquest began, Belva seemed intent on destroying any confidence Freda Law had about her marriage or the memory of her husband. At times, Freda responded with tears. But in other moments, she leaned past her father-in-law and glared directly at Belva.

Belva was certain the awkwardness of the coroner's jury and the nasty glares from the widow were momentary discomforts. It wasn't her fault, she reasoned, that she was the other woman. Walter simply hated his wife.

"Walter never really did get along with his wife," Belva told the coroner's jury. "He often told me that if it weren't for his little boy, he'd never live with her."

Freda pushed back when asked about her husband. "He was so good," she testified. "And he was so fond of the boy, Walter Jr., the very image of his father. What will I tell the baby when he begins to ask questions? What will I tell him?"

Who was the jury to believe? The wife who claimed she never suspected her husband cheated? Or the mistress who boasted she saw the victim at least once a week, sometimes more? Belva seemed confident the jury would take her side, and she grew increasingly alarmed when witnesses were brought in to testify against her.

Belva clutched her purse as one of Walter's coworkers began to testify. Paul Goodwin was also a salesman at the Nash Automobile Company, and he knew Walter had been having an affair with Belva. Walter had confided in his friend that Belva was unpredictable and dangerous. She had threatened to kill Walter, Goodwin said, and Walter, believing she was capable of it, had thought about increasing his life insurance policy.

Belva called the story "bunk" and claimed her "Wallie" only took out the insurance policy after Freda visited a fortune teller and was told her husband would soon die. Then she added boastfully how Walter supposedly said he "would tie up the insurance so that his wife wouldn't get a penny of it. He said he'd have it all made out for his boy."

The coroner's jury wasn't convinced, even when Belva acted horrified at the accusation that she pulled a knife on Walter. "Me threaten him with a knife?" she repeated. "That's crazy. He was always a courteous gentleman to me. Why should I ever be angry with him?"

Belva wasn't credible. She was mean, and she wasn't sorry. The coroner's jury wasn't letting her go. They remanded her to a grand jury, and she was required to stay in Cook County Jail until the jury convened.

The police pulled Belva from the room so she could be transferred to Cook County Jail. Harry led Freda from the room so she could begin the process of planning her husband's burial. The reporters drained from the police station, and some headed to Hyde Park to call on Belva's wealthy ex-husband, William Gaertner.

Gaertner was two decades older than his ex-wife and still smitten with her. They had been married for only three years, and divorced for the past four, but he paid her way through life in exchange for a nightly phone call. When the reporters found him at home, they noticed a large portrait of Belva displayed prominently on the wall. Any money she needed, William promised, he could deliver.

That coroner's jury had some nerve. It was true Walter Law was found dead in Belva's car. It was true the two of them spent the evening at a speakeasy, drinking gin and dancing. And it was true police found Belva in her apartment, dazed and covered with Walter's blood. But she claimed she was innocent and couldn't remember a thing. How dare the coroner's jury remand her to jail?

Belva blamed the coroner's jury for being so nasty. "That was bum," she complained to a reporter. "They were narrow-minded old birds—bet they never heard a jazz band in their lives. Now, if I'm tried, I want worldly men, broad-minded men, men who know what it is to get out a bit. Why, no one like that would convict me."

Belva had quite a bit to say. It had been two days since her arrest, and it seemed as though she had yet to absorb her predicament. She had been transferred to the fourth floor of Cook County Jail like a criminal, cuffed and in a paddy wagon. She'd sat in the darkness of the automobile, looking for light from the slim windows that lined the top of the wagon, as all the others before her had done. When the vehicle pulled into the small, confined courtyard, procedure dictated that she was removed and led through the massive sliding door. And when the door locked behind her, she became an inmate like any other.

Belva settled into a cell with Kitty Baluk, who was impressed by the older woman. Belva had yet to receive her jail uniform, and for the time being, she wore her own fine clothing, which communicated she was a woman of privilege. Sabella Nitti, along with everyone else, likely glimpsed Belva's beautiful clothing and sparkling gems and assumed she was as lovely as the things she owned.

All her finery covered up how Belva Gaertner, at her core, would always be Belva Boosinger from downstate Illinois. A girl whose father had died young and whose poverty-stricken mother had no choice but to relinquish her children to the state. A girl raised in an orphanage designated for children of Civil War veterans. In Chicago, Belva became Belle Brown, a sought-after showgirl whose name meant beauty. As Belle, she performed in the cabarets of Chicago, donning exquisite costumes and intricate makeup. Over time, her projection of splendor and sensuality became her daily persona. People believed it.

One thing that separated Belva from the other inmates was her lack of emotion. She was irritated and sometimes remorseful, but she wasn't devastated. Kitty, Sabella, and many other women came into Cook County Jail damp with tears. Belva never sobbed or attempted suicide, whereas both Kitty and Sabella had painful, failed suicide attempts in their recent histories.

The women who were most desperate and distraught were willing to inflict great pain on themselves for the promise to end it all. These frantic emotions were felt by women who knew they could not control their judicial fate. Belva, in contrast, seemed outraged that the various players in the court system thought they had any control over her life.

The first night, Belva waited on her bed in the cell she was assigned to share with Kitty. Reporters swarmed the cell, taking turns sitting with Belva and lavishing her with the attention she felt she deserved. She let the reporters know that she was not one bit sorry. How could she be apologetic if she didn't remember any of the events?

"Why it's silly to say I murdered Walter," she mused. "I liked him and he loved me—but no woman can love a man enough to kill him. They aren't worth it, because there are always plenty more. Walter was just a kid—29 and I'm 38. Why should I have worried whether he loved me or whether he left me?"

The full situation seemed funny to her. The *Chicago Daily Tribune* reporter made note of her laughter and her "lengthy" musings on gin, guns, romance, and marriage. ". . . I wish I could remember just what happened. We got drunk and he got killed with my gun in my car. But gin and guns—either one is bad enough, but together they get you in a dickens of a mess, don't they?"

Forbes seemed skeptical in the story that ran the next day, but it wasn't as condemning as Sabella or Kitty's coverage. From the onset, Sabella was described as a depraved woman who brutally bludgeoned her husband. But Belva was permitted to express her innocence, and although Forbes noted she "chortled" in her jail cell, the story stopped short of blaming her for the crime. The accompanying photo on the back page showed Belva wearing a striped ensemble, her own clothing, that she likely put on before police brought her to the South Wabash police station. The irony of the horizontal stripes apparently escaped her.

Other reporters followed the same pattern. They described how Belva was indifferent to the damage she caused, but they stopped short of declaring her guilty. One newspaper described how she played cards and laughed in jail while Walter's family cried graveside. Another showed a photograph of Belva playing cards with Kitty. The two women sat close together at a table and posed so that their cards were revealed to the camera but not each other. They looked at each other and smiled as though they were having a delightful time.

Belva presented herself as an innocent good-time girl who had no animosity toward her former lover. She told reporters she remembered little about the evening, but she did remember the two joking how they should have a gun duel. She didn't elaborate on whether she thought the duel actually happened, but she left open the possibility of an accidental death.

Perhaps in her first night in Cook County Jail, Belva thought she had the situation in control. The next morning, the attorneys her ex-husband hired for her defense came to the jail and interrupted her delusions. They forbade her from further discussing the case with the press. Silence was an appropriate strategy—the Law family was hosting a private viewing and burial that same day, and the press was eager to compare the devastated family with the bemused Belva. The attorneys refused to let them do so.

The attorneys also ended her haughty and playful behavior. No more card playing, laughing, or seeming amused by the situation. After they left, Belva responded accordingly, organized a Christian choir, and gathered the other women each day to sing hymns. The press maintained their interest in the case, even if Belva was forbidden from delivering incriminating statements.

On the last day of March, the *Chicago Daily Tribune* ran Belva's picture as she attended a concert in the women's block. A civic group had arranged for a jazz band to play for the female inmates, and the event was an excuse for a story. In the photo, Belva sat in a row alongside Kitty Baluk and two other inmates. Kitty gave the band her attention, but the other two women seemed downright bored. One crossed her arms and looked down, as if she were busy worrying about her problems. The other shot an irritated glance at the camera. Belva sat upright with her hands folded neatly in her lap. She was showing the press, as she would the jury, that she was a lady. A lady incapable of murder.

For a while, the reporters took little further interest in the women of Cook County Jail. Belva had been instructed to ignore the press. Kitty was no longer news; her trial was over and she awaited transfer to the prison in Joliet. And Sabella was occupied with her chores and English practice as she waited to hear whether or not she would be granted a new trial. After the jazz band entertained the women in late March, there wasn't any news coming from the fourth floor of the jail. The reporters followed stories elsewhere, and life in the women's block reverted to the same routine.

Every day, Sabella scrubbed Belva's cell, tended to any of her laundry needs, and then collected a few coins from her. The two had settled into a lady-maid type of relationship that appeared mutually beneficial. Belva didn't have to lower herself to the indignity of chores, and Sabella had a small income.

In the mornings, the women formed a line for their meals. Then, the sound of Belva's Christian singing group was heard throughout the block. The rest of the day was spent trying to pass the time with their few sources of distraction. Books, card games, and letters were a brief escape from the tedium and uncertainty of jail.

The monotony broke in early April when the newspapers began reporting a new female slayer on the front page. The young woman was being held at the Hyde Park police station, and there was no doubt she would transfer to Cook County Jail as soon as a grand jury indicted her.

29

HULA LOU, THE GAL WHO CAN'T BE TRUE

SABELLA WOKE ON APRIL 5 to a cold, damp morning. The cell blocks never quite brightened without sunlight, and the inmates were trapped in a daylong sensation of dusk. It was the type of day that made napping easy, but Sabella was never one to take a nap, especially when there was work to do.

Sabella washed in her cell and tended to her morning chores, including those she did for Belva. In the midst of her chores, she passed the cell where the new inmate was housed. The evening before, the women's cell block had received the loveliest murder suspect the city had yet to see. Beulah Annan was twenty-five years old, slender, and radiant with dark red hair and bright blue eyes. Her eyelids were hooded and slightly downturned, which opened her eyes and made her seem innocent. She had a round face that gave her the appearance of being sweet, with full lips and a slender nose.

Sabella stopped in front of the redheaded woman's cell and listened to the agonizing sounds that came from within. Beulah sat on her cot with her back facing the hallway, sobbing softly. Sabella paused, perhaps remembering her own experience of sobbing in her dark cell.

Sabella knew the anguish of feeling as though she couldn't stop crying, even if she wanted to. And she knew she was not yet free from the threat of such misery returning. It had been seven months since the team of six had successfully argued for a stay of execution while the Illinois Supreme Court reviewed her case, but the court had yet to decide whether or not she and Peter deserved a retrial. If they sided with Judge David, then she would hang within weeks of the decision.

Sabella put her hand on the bar and peered inside the darkened cell. She wanted to comfort the redheaded girl, to tell her not to worry. "You pretty-pretty," Sabella assured. "You speak English. They won't kill you—why you cry?"

Beulah turned and looked at the Barese woman in the hallway. Sabella saw that Beulah was not alone in her cell; she was giving an interview to a reporter. The two inmates looked at each other and then Beulah turned her head dismissively. It was as though she only needed a moment to determine she was better than Sabella Nitti.

The judgment stung. Sabella retreated from the cell and went back to her chores. "Poor thing," Beulah said to the reporter, disguising her sense of superiority with a sympathetic tone. "She's a lost soul—nobody cares about her."

Beulah redirected the conversation back to herself, although Sabella's interruption was helpful. Beulah needed to distinguish herself as separate from the low-class murderesses who inhabited the cell block. Just one quick glance and any reporter could see Beulah had nothing in common with the Barese immigrant accused of bludgeoning her husband to death or the "tiger girl" who shot a night watchman to please her jailbird boyfriend.

Beulah, as she told it, was a victim. She had shot her secret boyfriend in self-defense. Or at least that was the version of events she recited to reporters. The shooting had occurred just two days earlier, on a Thursday afternoon while Beulah's husband was at work. Beulah's boyfriend, Harry Kalstedt, had slipped up the back steps of her apartment building in an attempt to avoid the attention of neighbors.

This type of indiscretion wasn't foreign to Harry or Beulah; neither of them were new to navigating infidelity. Cheating was simply what Beulah did when she was married. Her first marriage in her home state of Kentucky had fizzled when her husband, Perry Stevens, asked her to leave after her unfaithfulness became apparent. Perry likely suspected Beulah saw other men during their brief marriage. His suspicions were confirmed when Beulah was badly injured in a car accident. She was in the car of another man, speeding along the highway, when the car crashed into a telephone pole. Perry gained custody of their young son, and Beulah headed to Louisville, and then Chicago. Almost immediately, she married another Kentuckian, Albert Annan.

Al was handsome enough to qualify as Beulah's husband, and he was naive enough to believe his long days at work were for the benefit of his devoted wife. He was stout in stature and about an inch taller than average. A bachelor at age twenty-seven, Al seemed excited to be married to such a beautiful woman, and he envisioned their future together. He would work all hours, if necessary, to give his beautiful Beulah what she desired. He failed to realize that what his beautiful Beulah truly desired was the company of other men.

Harry knocked on the door frame and smiled when Beulah answered the door.

"Oh, hello, Anne," Harry said. "You all alone?"

The nickname was likely a take on Beulah's married name, Annan. Not only was Harry bold enough to have sex with another man's wife, but he also mockingly made reference to the deceived man's name.

Beulah answered the door wearing a camisole that clung to her curves and showed the shape of her breasts. She wore the camisole as they sat on the couch drinking wine in the early afternoon, while the rest of the city worked. Beulah downed more than two bottles of wine during this time, forgetting that her husband would be back in the evening and she would have to appear sober.

Buying wine was forbidden under prohibition, and Beulah desperately wanted what she couldn't have. She wanted Harry. She wanted hooch. And she wanted a more exciting life than sitting all afternoon in her apartment, waiting for Al to come home.

In her desperation for something new and exciting, Beulah became terribly predictable. She was flushed and excited, experiencing the brief euphoria a person feels with the first few drinks. But then her delight advanced into feelings of anger, mostly toward Harry.

Harry was as drunk as Beulah, and their conversation disintegrated into angry recriminations. Neither one was sober enough to understand what the other was trying to argue. They both took offense, and disagreement fused with confusion to bring hatred. It was a new sensation between them, but it was strong and it was real for the moment.

Harry and Beulah called each other names. Ridiculed. Threatened that their love for others meant more. Then they were on their feet and moving across the apartment in an angry dance of volatile hand gestures and staggering strides. When Beulah was in the bedroom, she grabbed the revolver Al kept near the bed. She pointed the gun at Harry, then she squeezed the trigger.

It only took one shot. The impact blasted Harry toward the wall. His back hit the wall, and he slid into a sitting position.

"My God!" Harry panted. "You shot me!"

Stunned, Beulah touched Harry, wetting her fingers with his blood. She backed away, crossed the room to the phonograph, picked up the needle, and positioned it on top of a record, leaving behind red prints. The phonograph crackled and then began to play the "Hula Lou," a fox trot about a Honolulu beauty with a roster of lovers. Beulah listened to the song on repeat, obsessively yearning for more of the song's upbeat rhythm.

Beulah had no plan of action, except to listen to the "Hula Lou" and feel the wine working its way through her body. She might have lost consciousness or simply been in a stupor. It was possible the alcohol numbed her emotions and Beulah didn't care what she had done to Harry.

More than two hours after the shooting, Beulah called the laundromat where both she and Harry were employed. She asked for him, and became irritated when her boss, Betty Bergman, said Beulah knew very well that Harry hadn't been in all day.

"What's the matter, Red? You sound kinda stewed," Betty accused.

"No, I haven't had a drink all day," Beulah lied. "I talk queerly because I'm trying to talk to you and read the telephone directory at the same time."

The two women hung up their extensions. Betty went back to the laundry's books, and Beulah looked at the pool of blood forming around Harry. She had no plan, and she let almost another hour pass before she called Al at the garage where he worked as a mechanic.

"I've shot a man, Albert!" she cried. She spit out a lie to explain why a man was in her home. "He tried to make love to me."

Al hung up the phone, urgently hailed a taxi, and sped north to his apartment, about eight miles away. When he stepped into the apartment, he found his home life shattered. A young, dark-haired man in his midtwenties was dead against the wall. The man wore only a short-sleeved shirt and pants. That meant, at one point in his visit, the man had taken off his overcoat and hat, and then peeled off his suit jacket and vest. Al looked at Beulah. She was wearing only a camisole. It was splattered with blood. Why was Beulah undressed and alone with a man? Why was the man undressed?

Beulah was hysterical, and Al believed her when she said a man from work had pushed his way into the apartment and tried to "make love" to her. She blubbered how she shot the intruder in self-defense.

Al picked up the phone to call the police. Beulah begged him to stop, and listened over his shoulder. When she heard the police sergeant pick up the extension, she grabbed the receiver and yelled into the phone, "I've just killed my husband!" She paused and then gave their address.

The South Wabash station responded by contacting the state's attorney's office as well as the Hyde Park station. When the detectives pushed open the apartment door, they expected to find a husband killed by his wife. Instead, a nearly nude woman in a blood-stained camisole was hysterical, and her husband bewildered. A fox trot record played in the background.

The first officer through the door glanced at his watch to note the exact moment of entry. The detectives scanned the crime scene and saw the victim was hunched against the wall. In the living room, they noted two wine glasses and empty bottles. It looked like a woman had shot her lover. She was clearly unstable, and the police first wanted to secure the area.

"Where is the gun?" Officer Thomas Torton demanded.

Al retrieved the gun and gave it to the officer.

The officers evaluated the room. It was vital that nothing be removed and no unauthorized person be allowed to enter. One of the officers approached the body and listened for breathing sounds. He announced to the room that Harry might still be alive. It was hard to tell; they needed a physician.

The physician arrived within fifteen minutes. Dr. Clifford Oliver knelt beside Harry's body and examined the young man. Harry's body was soft, and the warmth suggested the man had died only within the previous half hour. Later at the hospital, the doctors determined Harry had been shot in the heart. He had hemorrhaged and experienced massive shock.

The detectives moved around the room, taking notes and conferring with each other. There was blood on the phonograph, which suggested Beulah had touched her victim while he lay dying and then operated the machine. Did this beautiful woman, they asked themselves, listen to music while her victim lay dying?

Beulah grew increasingly hysterical as the police swarmed her apartment. She was being treated as the villain and she wanted to be the victim. All eyes were on her as the criminal suspect, and the scrutiny was overpowering. Beulah fainted, perhaps from fear or intoxication, but possibly as a way to appear helpless and victimized. When she blinked her eyes open, she was helped to her feet and brought into the kitchen by the crowd of men. She acted disorientated and frightened—a damsel in distress.

The pack of police shifted from the living room to the kitchen. Police procedure dictated who was called when a murder was reported, and even specified the order in which each person was notified. The finger print man was first—he needed to collect evidence without being disturbed. The photographer was second, followed by the coroner's physician, the state's attorney, the draftsman who sketched the crime scene, and the stenographer who transcribed the proceedings.

Assistant state's attorney Roy C. Woods stepped into the kitchen. Beulah evaluated Woods's black hair and hazel eyes. The prosecutor was in his midforties and had a full head of hair that he neatly parted on the side and slicked back. He wore small, wire-rim glasses, which, along with the cleft in his chin, made him appear distinguished. Woods was in his second year as an assistant state's attorney, and he had ambitions for the state senate. In just two years, he would indeed be elected to the state senate, a position he would keep for seventeen years before opening a law firm with his son.

The questioning began gently. "Don't you know me?" Woods asked mildly. He was a customer of the laundry where Beulah worked part-time as a bookkeeper. "Don't be afraid," Woods assured her. She looked at him with wide eyes, as though she were confused. "You shot a man in your own house. It's no crime," said Woods.

Beulah should have nodded and thanked Woods for his comfort. Instead, she decided his kindness was ripe for manipulation.

"Couldn't we frame it to make it look like an accident?" she blurted.

Woods instantly soured. "You don't frame anything with me," he warned.

Beulah was placed under arrest. The police allowed her to wear a jacket over her camisole for warmth, and she carelessly—or intentionally—left it unbuttoned, keeping the view of her bosoms in full view. She was loaded in the back of the police vehicle, and the driver pulled from the curb and drove east toward the lake.

Beulah was still drunk as the car turned onto Lake Park Avenue and rumbled south. It would take almost a day for the alcohol to leave her system. She likely did not realize the car's direction was indicative of the trouble she faced. If the car had driven west toward the Wabash Avenue station, then it would have meant the police were only going to ask her questions before releasing her. This was because the Wabash Avenue station didn't have women's quarters. Beulah was being driven south, to the Hyde Park station, the closest station with cells for women. She was in serious trouble.

At the Hyde Park station, Beulah held firm for hours with her story about nearly being assaulted. She reeked of body odor and booze, having spent almost a day in the same clothing. Yet her hair was stylishly waved and tucked behind her ear, and Beulah must have known the glimpse of camisole underneath the open jacket was alluring. When the newspaper photographers stepped forward to take her picture, Beulah was ready with a pose. With her overcoat slightly open and the camisole exposed, Beulah looked pensively in the distance. The look didn't convey guilt or remorse. It was as though Beulah had sighed and moaned "poor me" right before the shutter flashed.

While Beulah posed for the photographers, Al complained heavily. "I've been a sucker, that's all!" he told reporters. "Simply a meal ticket. I've worked 10, 12, 14 hours a day and took home every cent of my money. We'd bought our furniture for the little apartment on time and it was all paid off but $100. I thought she was happy. I didn't know . . ."

The day was endless. After midnight, the police tired of questioning Beulah at the station and tried bringing her back to the apartment to ask questions at the crime scene. Two assistant state's attorneys were present and they fired questions at Beulah. Beulah tried to remain firm that she had shot Harry in self-defense. But the crime scene suggested she'd killed Harry intentionally and waited hours to make sure he was dead.

"What about the blood on the phonograph record? What about the wine and gin bottles and empty glasses?" the prosecutors interrogated.

Beulah surveyed the apartment. The scene was incriminating.

"You're right, I haven't been telling you the truth," she admitted.

The details spilled out. "I'd been fooling around with Harry for two months," Beulah confessed. "This morning, as soon as my husband left for work, Harry called me up. I told him I wouldn't be home, but he came over anyway."

Everyone listened intently—the police, the reporters. Beulah admitted she drank half a gallon of wine with Harry. The more they drank, the more irritated they became with each other. Harry had asked earlier in the day to borrow money, and Beulah gave him a dollar. Now she resented Harry for asking.

"We sat in the flat for quite a time, drinking. Then I said in a joking way that I was going to quit him," Beulah said. "He said he was through with me and began to put on his coat. When I saw that he meant what he said, my mind went in a whirl and I shot him. Then I started playing the record. I was nervous, you see."

And Chicago saw the prettiest murderess ever locked up at Cook County Jail.

Almost a week later, the weather in Chicago had softened. The temperatures no longer hovered near freezing, and the warmth promised the arrival of spring. Although temperatures were mild, storms threatened, and the *Chicago Daily Tribune* again warned the atmosphere would be unsettled. But as Helen Cirese left her office on Clark Street and walked north to the Cook County Jail, she must have felt buoyant: the Illinois Supreme Court had finally made a decision in the Nitti case. It had reversed the verdict against Sabella and Peter and remanded the case to be reheard by a new judge and, if necessary, a new jury.

The court was firm in its opinion, ruling that the so-called evidence—the ring, the shoes, the contrived confession—that Smith and Romano had presented in the first trial was circumstantial and would be inadmissible in the retrial, and that the prosecution had taken advantage of defense attorney Eugene Moran's spiraling mental health. The case was not a proper application of Illinois law, and the supreme court would not allow it to stand.

As Cirese strode across the Clark Street Bridge, she did not yet know all the details of the decision. Someone on the team of six had made arrangements with the high court's clerk to send word of the opinion as soon as the judges read it from the bench, but the telegram was likely brief, simply stating the case was remanded. Sabella and Peter would not hang.

It would take days for the full opinion to be mailed to Cirese's office. She would learn a few details, along with the rest of the *Chicago Daily Tribune* readers, in the next day's paper. Tucked back onto page 21, next to one advertisement for coffee and another for moth-proof wool, the reporter relayed part of the high court's opinion that further investigation with competent counsel was required.

Cirese entered the jail and headed to the women's block to deliver the good news to Sabella. In the next building, Milton Smith and Michael Romano had likely received their own telegram regarding the verdict. It was easy to smile at the thought of those men feeling frustrated, perhaps even angry at how the supreme court decided against them. Cirese and the team were prepared for battle, and they knew their opponents had been dealt a fatal blow. In the state's attorney's office, the atmosphere was indeed about to become unsettled.

30

A DELICATE CONDITION

Prosecuting attorney Milton Smith surveyed the parade of murder suspects. What was happening to Chicago? Four cases on the docket that morning involved female suspects, one of whom was a grandmother in a petticoat. Smith stood at the prosecutor's table and looked at the crowded table across the aisle.

Belva Gaertner was the first case in front of Judge William Lindsay that morning. It was late April, but Belva sat bundled in both a jacket and a wrap. She wore a hat that slid low past her ears. She was quiet and reserved, and wore a pained expression. Smith had heard the murder charges against the socialite, but the case wasn't one of his assignments. He could use Belva's time in front of the judge to review his notes for the murder trial against the Montana family, or he could watch her attorneys in action. The same team who defended Belva also represented the entire Montana family, and the jury selection was expected to begin before lunchtime.

Smith knew Belva's attorney, Thomas D. Nash, a prominent defense lawyer who defended some of Chicago's worst criminals. A client didn't have to be innocent; he or she just had to be bankrolled. Belva was being financed by her ex-husband, who seemed determined to help his former wife avoid any consequence for the life she had taken.

The evidence against Belva was mounting. No surprise, her attorneys weren't ready to go to trial. They wanted more time for motions to exclude key evidence, and the case was continued for another week. Nash stepped back and refocused his attention on the Montana family. The five family members sat nervously next to each other, waiting for the trial that would determine their fate.

Nash was a relatively young man of thirty-eight, but his hair had turned completely white and he looked much older. He used his aged appearance to his advantage, presenting himself as wise and distinguished. Nash was the type of attorney who put on a show for the jury. Smith was the same, and the prosecutor had prepared a performance, describing how Chicago Police Officer Lawrence Harnett had merely been investigating complaints about a bootlegging operation at the Montana family grocery store when he was ambushed by three generations of the Montana family. The women in the family—even the old grandmother—had swung at the officer.

Smith likely expected Nash to put up a defense that the family thought they were being robbed. Nash indeed took such a strategy and later claimed his clients had been innocently at home when their grocery was raided—without a warrant—and they had feared for their lives. The seventeen-year-old grandson had shot the officer to save his family and end the attack.

The next case on the docket was called up. Beulah Annan, "Chicago's prettiest slayer," appeared before Judge Lindsay. Beulah seemed posed at all moments, as if she were waiting for the camera bulbs to flash. She wore a cloche hat that her husband had brought for her, as well as a light jacket and a wrap pinned around her neck. The case against the redheaded beauty was even more damning than the socialite's. Beulah had confessed to shooting her secret boyfriend in her apartment, but later tried to change her story with reporters. The case was assigned to two other attorneys in Smith's office, and they planned to ask the jury for the noose.

Beulah's husband hired William Scott Stewart, one of Chicago's slickest defense attorneys, for her defense. Only a few years earlier, Stewart had worked in the state's attorney's office and was quite successful at sending men to the penitentiary and the gallows. Smith and

Stewart had tried cases together as a team, and they were credited with sending Carl Wanderer, the wife killer, to the gallows. Stewart knew how prosecutors thought, he knew how Smith worked, and he was a dangerous opponent.

Stewart wasn't ready to proceed, and the case was continued for another week. The process was slow moving, and Beulah hadn't even been arraigned or entered a formal plea. If the delays continued, it might be months before Beulah's case was heard in front of a jury.

Sabella Nitti was next, and Smith came to attention. The woman before him was not the same defendant he had prosecuted the previous year. Last July, Sabella Nitti sat in Judge David's courtroom wearing carpet scraps on her feet. Her hair was greasy, streaked with gray and then pinned haphazardly on her head as if she hadn't thought to look in a mirror. She sat with her legs open and made disturbing grunting sounds.

A new woman sat at the defense table, surrounded by her pack of attorneys. Smith knew it was the girl attorney who was fixing her up—everyone knew it. And it was well known that Sabella was learning English from the other inmates and working on her reading skills. Defense attorney Helen Cirese wasn't hiding her clean-up effort from anyone. In fact, she seemed to be using it against the state's attorney's office to insinuate that pretty women were rarely charged with murder, and that the lawmen were deeply biased.

Smith looked across the room at Sabella. She wore a stylish black dress and high heels. Her hair was freshly colored, curled, and tucked under a light gray hat. She had a stack of papers in front of her and held a pen in her right hand. She looked as though she belonged at a ladies' luncheon or a country club event. She didn't look as though she belonged at a murder trial, except perhaps as a spectator.

Her entire demeanor had changed. Sabella sat quietly, folded into herself. She seemed optimistic about her day in court and she broke into a smile that spread cheerfully across her face. That was a terrible problem for Smith—Sabella Nitti seemed sweet.

Sabella had been in jail for almost a year and she still had a smile. The two women before her had been in jail for a matter of weeks and they wore sour expressions, as if the act of being charged with murder had somehow victimized them. The contrast simply wasn't helpful for Smith. It looked bad to the reporters in the gallery, who were most certainly taking notes on what each woman wore and how she acted.

If Smith stood close enough, he could hear that Sabella's English had advanced into basic sentences. Her accent was harsh, but she was improving on her previous tendency to add an "a" to the end of her words. She still used "me" instead of "I," but the defense could put her on the stand to testify in English if they chose.

It was a disaster for the prosecution. Sabella Nitti looked nice. She smelled nice. And she had proper American manners. It was almost as big of a blow to the state's case as the Illinois Supreme Court's decision the previous week.

Smith and the state's attorney had the option to agree to dismiss the charges. But a dismissal would feel like an admission of wrongdoing, and Smith didn't believe he was wrong in pursuing Sabella. He had to fight on in case there was a chance he might win and send her to the gallows.

Defense attorney Rocco DeStefano approached the bench. The defense was ready to go to trial. DeStefano motioned for separate trials for Peter and Sabella, and his motion was granted. Then, he motioned for a bail hearing to be set and assured the judge that funds were available should bail be granted. Judge Lindsay set the bail hearing for the following Saturday. The new trial was set for May 12.

Smith agreed to the trial date knowing he was not prepared. The state had nothing new on Sabella. His plan was to repeatedly ask for continuances until the judge forced the trial. County law forbade a case from being continued for more than four court terms because it hindered a defendant's right to a speedy trial. That meant Smith had the better part of the year to build his case against Sabella Nitti. Unless, of course, something more important came up.

The following weeks were troubling for Beulah. She appeared twice in court and nothing significant happened. She was just one of many defendants paraded in front of the judge for an arraignment, continuance, or pretrial hearing. There was a strict, clinical procedure in place, and Beulah was expected to conform to the process. There were no special privileges, and that didn't feel right to Beulah.

Beulah didn't like how schedules between the judges and the lawyers were fluid. Attorneys showed up at hearings just to ask for continuances. Sometimes, defendants sat in the courtroom waiting their turn, only to watch as another case ran longer than expected. When it came time to reschedule, the lawyers and the judge consulted their already packed calendars and found a day in the distance that suited all the parties involved.

Beulah saw how such scheduling nonsense happened to Sabella Nitti. The Saturday after Belva, Beulah, and Sabella appeared in court together, Sabella was set to return to Judge Lindsay's courtroom for a bail hearing. The day held huge potential for Sabella—her attorneys were ready to pay the $12,500 bond if the judge agreed to release Sabella on bail. Following the hearing, Sabella would have returned to her cell to collect her belongings and then walked into the late April sun.

But that Saturday the court was busy with the Montana family trial. The case was finally sent to the jury late Saturday night, and Judge Lindsay clearly wanted the trial to conclude. The entire family was acquitted and released onto Dearborn Street to find their way home.

In the excitement of the day's concluding trial, Sabella's bail hearing was rescheduled. Perhaps in June everyone could find time on their respective calendars to revisit the motion? Until then, Sabella Nitti was back in her cell for weeks, if not months. It was unnerving to the other inmates, particularly Beulah. When would *she* have her time in front of a jury? When might she expect to be released? Would a series of continuances and scheduling conflicts lock her in prison for the next year?

Beulah needed something to distinguish her from the other women. She needed to give the court a reason to see her as unique and to grant her special privileges not offered to any other inmate. She had an idea.

––––––

On May 8, defense attorney William Scott Stewart made an announcement. Beulah Annan was pregnant with her husband's child. "Her condition has no bearing upon the legality of the case," Stewart told reporters. "It would be a matter of executive clemency, once the sentence is passed. Or it might affect the jury."

The announcement affected the state's attorneys. It was terrible news, of course, that the beautiful Beulah was pregnant. The state planned to ask for the death penalty. A pregnant woman could not hang under state law because the execution took two lives, not one. If the prosecutors waited to try Beulah when she was in her third trimester, they risked having the jury see her swollen belly and sympathize with the expectant mother. If the state waited until after the baby was born, they risked the jury perceiving Beulah as a loving mother.

The best option was to expedite the case. If the state was ready, the defense was willing to proceed. The trial was expected to begin within two weeks. Given the woman's delicate condition, the state was willing to grant Beulah special privileges.

––––––

Judge Lindsay allowed the people from the motion pictures company in his courtroom. They set up special lights to illuminate the witness stand and positioned the camera to capture the pretty young defendant as she testified. Beulah was careful not to look at the camera as she spoke, and she turned her attention to the jury, as if she were begging them with each rehearsed answer to please let her go.

The camera lights flattered Beulah. Her attorneys insisted she not wear a hat so that the all-male jury could fully appreciate her beauty. The light made her skin appear pale and smooth, and her blue eyes glimmered.

Her attorney stood and approached the witness stand. He was careful to treat his client as a scared, expecting mother—the type of woman who needed the jury's protection.

"Did you shoot him?" he asked.

"I did," Beulah admitted to the jury.

"Why?"

"Because he was going to shoot me," Beulah answered with a soft voice that emphasized her sweet Kentucky accent.

Beulah and her attorney recounted a new version of the afternoon. It started with Harry visiting her apartment sometime in the morning to ask to borrow money. He returned a few hours later, drunk and carrying two quarts of wine. Beulah admitted she let him in, but then begged him to leave.

". . . he refused," she told the jury. "And he asked me to take a drink first. So I did—just to get him to leave. But still he wouldn't go, though I begged him to, told him my husband might come home and he would shoot us both."

The attorney nudged her along and asked how Harry had responded to such a threat. Beulah claimed he said, "To hell with your husband!" He then insisted she drink another glass of wine and play a jazz record.

Beulah paused for dramatic effect. "And then he said, 'Come on into the bedroom' and I refused and begged him to go. And finally, I told him . . ."

Beulah waivered, as if the memory was so painful she needed a moment to brace herself. Her attorney gently encouraged her to continue. She closed her eyes as if she were digging deep within for the strength to go on. "I told him of my—delicate condition," she said. "But he refused to believe me—and boasted that another woman had fooled him that way and that he had done time in the penitentiary for her. And I said, 'You'll do another!' and he said, 'You'll never send me back!' and I said, 'I'll call my husband and he'll shoot us both!'"

Beulah next claimed that Harry had guessed correctly that there was a loaded gun in the bedroom and strode across the apartment. Beulah pursued behind him, and they reached for the gun handle at the same time. Beulah snatched the gun and pointed it at Harry.

Harry stood back for a moment. He was angry, Beulah told the jury, and he threatened to kill her. Her attorney wanted to know what happened next.

"He started toward me," Beulah said. "And I pushed his shoulder with my left hand, and shot."

Beulah testified convincingly. It seemed realistic that such a beautiful young woman was menaced by such a persistent man. And she seemed quite traumatized by the ordeal. After Harry was shot, she claimed she sat beside his body, disorientated from the shock. Beulah denied having a relationship with Harry, and she suggested that the confession she gave to the police came after a long evening of interrogation and harassment. She stepped from the witness stand and returned to her seat at the defendant's table.

Beulah looked meaningfully at the jury, as if she knew each member personally. She was engaging them to focus on her and note her emotional responses to her attorney's closing statements. The reporters in the gallery saw her crying as sensational and performative. The timing of her tears was also suspicious. Beulah's eyes were dry as her attorney reviewed the sequence of events that led to Harry's death. But tears streamed down her face when her attorney described the mean police treatment she endured.

As Beulah cried at the table, her attorney described her as a "frail little girl" who had to contend with a "drunken brute." A few of the jury members nodded in agreement, conveying that yes, Beulah was indeed the true victim. Several others chewed their gum aggressively, clearly angry at the dead man's assault on a helpless woman.

The prosecutor begged the jury to not let a pretty woman "get away with it." The jury had to think about it. It took them almost two hours to acquit Beulah. She was free to leave, her entire ordeal lasting less than eight weeks. In a flurry, her belongings were whisked from the Cook County Jail, where Sabella still languished, and she was back in her apartment.

On Monday morning, the secretaries at the county courthouse filed the verdict in Beulah's case into record. At the same time, Beulah met with her attorney and signed paperwork to begin divorce proceedings against her husband. He was too slow, she complained. He didn't know how to dance and he didn't want to have any fun. "I want lights, music and good times . . . and I'm going to have them," she told the press who had been invited to watch her file for divorce. The pregnancy that had expedited her court date and helped persuade the jury was forgotten, as if it never existed.

31

GOLDFISH

ILTON SMITH WAS EXHAUSTED, but not from late nights spent building a new case against Sabella Nitti. Instead he was sidetracked by what would soon become known as the "trial of the century."

It was after midnight on Friday, May 30, and Smith sat alongside a college student named Nathan Leopold. The police weren't sure how the young man was involved in the kidnapping and murder of fourteen-year-old Bobby Franks. All they knew was that Nathan's eyeglasses had been found near the boy's body in a forest preserve. A search of Nathan's bedroom in his family's Hyde Park mansion also found an unregistered handgun and a letter to another graduate student at the University of Chicago. The letter was oddly written, alternating between irritation and desperate pleas that the other student not end the friendship.

The other student was Richard Loeb, and the police surmised the two had a homosexual relationship. The last week of May was not a good time in Chicago to be a person with a prior history of what the police called "unnatural acts." The police were rounding up anyone with past convictions—or mere charges—of homosexuality, sodomy, and other bedroom business illegal under 1924 law.

The detectives' interest in Nathan's sexual orientation was connected to how the body was found. The young victim's face and genitals were stained with brown, as if he had been wrapped in a rusty chain. His anus was dilated, and the police assumed the boy had been violated prior to his death.*

At the same time, the police were also rounding up owners of a popular automobile model with the color gray. Bobby Franks was last seen by a schoolmate climbing into a gray automobile on his way home from a pickup baseball game played in an empty lot near his Hyde Park home. Several unfortunate men were pulled into the police station for questioning. But none of the potential suspects endured as much abuse as the teachers at the posh private school Bobby had attended. Seven of his teachers were bombarded by police in the middle of the night and dragged from their beds. Several were held for days and routinely beaten with rubber hoses by the police. The rubber hoses didn't leave marks, which was necessary for the police to claim that suspects confessed of their own free will. Phone books were also helpful instruments. An interrogator slammed the suspect in the face with the phone book, and it rarely left a mark.

The police had a term for suspects who were beaten during inter-rogation. They called them "goldfish" and brought them to "goldfish rooms." A designated closet held the collection of rubber hoses of vari-ous lengths. The police alternated the beatings with interrogations from the detectives and state's attorneys. Smith and the other assistant state's attorneys ignored the teachers' bleary eyes and shaky voices. The teach-ers were in shock—they lived quiet lives and had limited exposure in their adult lives to violence. And then suddenly, they were pulled from their beds and beaten at regular intervals.

The trauma inflicted on the teachers was considered collateral dam-age. So what if one of them shook from fear in the weeks or months that followed? Who cared if any one of them jumped at loud noises for

---

* Forensic science now finds postmortem perianal dilation occurs in children who are not suspected to have been violated, and investigators are urged to look for other physical evi-dence. See John McCann, Donald Reay, Joseph Siebert, Boyd G. Stephens, and Stephen Wirtz, "Postmortem Perianal Findings in Children," *American Journal of Forensic Medicine and Pathology* 17, no. 4 (1996): 289–298.

decades afterward? It wasn't the police's problem if any of them suffered nerve damage or long-term injuries. Their complaints were insignificant; all that mattered was the crime was promptly solved.

The police seemed genuinely surprised when all the teachers maintained their innocence, despite multiple rounds of beatings. State's attorney Robert Crowe suspected the English teacher, and was sorely disappointed when a lawyer for the teachers secured their release from police custody. The questioning, Crowe thought, needed to continue, as did the whippings.

But then the police consulted area optometrists and eyewear retailers who confirmed that only one shop in the area sold the unique hinge found on the glasses near the victim. The shop directed police to Nathan Leopold, the nineteen-year-old son of a wealthy Hyde Park family. Crowe instructed his attorneys to tread carefully—no goldfish treatment. And when they brought the suspect in for questioning earlier in the afternoon, they brought him to a hotel downtown. They didn't want to risk offending his father. When it became clear Nathan was a strong suspect, he was brought to the Criminal Court Building attached to the jail.

In another room, the state's attorneys held eighteen-year-old Richard Loeb, the subject of the letter found in Nathan's room. The attorneys streamed from one room to the next, meeting in the hallway or a quiet office to compare notes and trade strategies. They needed one of the suspects to break and confess to the crime. Time was of the essence—the boys' fathers were certain to file a writ of habeas corpus to have their sons released from custody.

Milton Smith sat next to Crowe and another assistant state's attorney, Joseph Savage. Savage neatly parted his thinning dark hair in the middle and wore a three-piece suit with his shirt cuffs poking out from his jacket sleeves. He was a slender man with a small build and a meek appearance he knew how to use to his advantage. Savage also seemed refined, a quality that Crowe did not share. Crowe had a heap of hair on top of his head that was graying inconsistently. He had a hard, oval jaw and a broad forehead, both of which pushed his facial features to share a small space in the center of his face. At times, particularly when he was looking down to read a paper or check his timepiece, Crowe appeared quite handsome. He had a masculine, strong look to him. Other times, Crowe's face appeared wrongly crowded.

Smith, Crowe, and Savage faced Nathan Leopold and watched him inhale one cigarette after the next. The young man was calm and professional. He maintained eye contact with Crowe, as if he were at a job interview or a business negotiation. Nathan occasionally glanced at Smith and Savage, as if he were trying to make them feel included in the conversation.

The young suspect seemed unbreakable. He tolerated questioning past sunrise, and by 7 AM, Crowe was exhausted and frustrated. He ordered police to take Nathan and Richard to separate police stations so there was no chance they would learn the other was also detained. Both suspects were allowed to nap, have a meal, and then wash up in a sink. The prosecutors and the police had no such luxury. The press alerted both suspects' families to their detention, and Crowe was certain their fathers would demand their release.

Crowe instructed police to spread across the city in search of clues. They needed physical evidence and witnesses. Investigators interviewed neighbors, classmates, and the staff who worked inside the two families' mansions. They worked their media contacts to find out what reporters had learned. Any possibility was considered—the city was watching and the pressure was on the police and the prosecutors to produce a suspect, win a grand jury indictment, and hang the guilty man within a month.

———

Right before 4 AM on Saturday, assistant state's attorney Joseph Savage burst from the room where he was questioning Richard Loeb. He needed Crowe and a court reporter. Richard Loeb was ready to confess and he sat in the office, defeated and on the verge of tears. The slight young man wasn't whom Savage or any of the state's attorneys initially suspected in the kidnapping and murder of Bobby Franks. Richard was blond and handsome with a defined jaw and an easy laugh. He seemed to be a genius—he had graduated from the University of Michigan at the age of seventeen and was enrolled in a graduate program at the University of Chicago. He was good natured and well liked among his peers. He didn't seem like the murdering type.

The state's attorneys expected a killer to look like Sabella Nitti—foreign, dirty, or worn down from the hardships that led them to a life of crime. They expected a killer to lack refinement and have a tough edge to them, like Kitty Malm. Or they expected the killer to have an uncontrollable perversion. The English teacher they'd earlier suspected was a loner who struggled socially in the presence of women. The police were certain he was a homosexual, which they deemed to be both perverted and an indicator of the crime.

At first, Nathan and Richard didn't seem to share any of the obvious qualities with the killers the state's attorneys typically prosecuted. But when the police discovered the two boys were lovers, the investigators believed they'd hit upon a perversion that indicated the possibility of guilt. Physical evidence began lining up, and the state's attorney had a case against the two young men.

But Crowe wanted an undisputable case—a hanging case. And for that, he needed a confession. Crowe had worked Richard, but the young suspect had refused to break. Goldfish tactics weren't an option with a suspect whose family was wealthy and connected. Crowe broke instead. He was furious and exhausted, and he left the room steaming. Savage stayed behind to push Richard further, and within twenty minutes the kid cracked.

Crowe strode back into the interrogation room as Richard wiped away a tear. The weakness was reassuring. It was the start of a greater flood. Within a few short hours, Crowe transcribed confessions from each suspect. The confessions were almost identical. Both suspects admitted they had begun planning the previous November to kidnap and kill a young boy. They wanted to experience the act of murder, but, more importantly, they wanted the challenge of planning the perfect crime.

Both Nathan and Richard walked their interrogators through their planning stages. They secured a bank account under a fake name so they could rent a car for the day in question. They procured the chemicals needed to impair the victim and then disfigure his face and genitals beyond recognition. The chemical solution failed and left behind the brown discoloration the investigators initially mistook as residue from a rusty chain.

The boys admitted they had considered multiple victims, all of whom were wealthy students from a private school in Hyde Park. After each possibility slipped past, Richard recognized his young cousin, Bobby Franks, walking home from a baseball game and offered him a ride home. With Bobby tucked into the front seat, one of the boys beat his head with a chiseled hammer. His mouth was then stuffed with a cloth and he asphyxiated. But which suspect delivered the fatal blows? The only inconsistency in the confessions was who killed Bobby Franks. Both suspects blamed each other.

At least Crowe had a confession, though he wasn't near done. He knew the boys' fathers were capable of hiring the finest legal defense in all of Chicago. Crowe also knew he had a hanging case, and anything less than the death penalty would be a failure.

The city was riveted. The *Chicago Daily Tribune* assigned half a dozen reporters to the story, and the first six pages of the Sunday paper were devoted to covering the murder from every possible angle. The paper included maps, photographs, psychological analysis, and descriptions of how the two young murderers said they had killed "for the thrill of it."

No other case mattered. Almost every attorney on Crowe's staff was given an assignment. Whatever else the attorneys had on their dockets was not as important. Ask for continuances if necessary, push for settlements. Just help Crowe win.

On June 2, Belva Gaertner sat in her cell thinking about the next day. Jury selection was scheduled to begin the following morning. Within the next week, she would either be back in her South Side apartment or still in jail, awaiting sentencing. Belva reviewed in her mind what she planned to wear to the jury selection. She had a blue twill suit with a lacy frill down the front. For shoes, she'd wear high heels in patent leathers and gun metal gray hose. Her hat was stylish; she knew it would set her high above any defendant the court had yet to see. It was shaped like a helmet and had a ribbon that tied underneath her chin.

The hat mattered. Belva was meant to be seen and not heard during the trial. Her attorneys were holding firm that she couldn't remember a thing from the evening her married lover Walter Law was killed in her car, and there was no point in putting her on the stand. She wouldn't incriminate herself. Instead, the attorneys planned for Belva to sit demurely at the defendant's table and use her quiet charm to convince the jury she was incapable of such violence.

But no one in the building cared about Belva and her hat. At the moment, a twenty-two-year-old man, Charles Ream, was next door in the Criminal Court Building, stunning reporters with one of the most horrific stories the city had heard. The reporters in the room were speechless.

Charles, a young cab driver, was in Crowe's office to identify Nathan and Richard as the two men who six months earlier had kidnapped him, used a chemical agent to render him unconscious, and then castrated him. The assault left him forever changed. With the loss of his testosterone production, Charles lost muscle mass. He struggled to climb the flight of stairs up to Crowe's office and was understandably depressed.

The attack had occurred when Charles was on his way home from work. Two men pulled up alongside him and showed a gun. He was ordered into their car, and he complied.

"Well, they had everything planned, just as they did in the Franks case," Charles told a reporter for the *Chicago Daily Tribune*. "I was ordered to turn around in the seat, to put my head in the corner of the car and to put my hands behind my back. Instantly the coils of a small rope went around my wrists. Then a gag was pushed into my mouth and a rope was tied around my head, holding the gag firm."

Charles recalled how his assailants checked to make sure his blindfold was secure. And then he smelled a familiar odor of ether, an anesthetic.

"I knew what was coming," he said. "I have been around hospitals. The odor grew stronger—I dropped off to sleep."

Charles awoke in a prairie, about a mile from where Bobby's body was found. He was half naked and bloody from his testicles being sliced from his body. "I was in great pain," Charles remembered. "I managed to crawl to a nearby house and to notify the residents."

Charles knew he'd been mutilated. It wasn't until weeks later when the bandages were removed that the extent of the damage was revealed. He relived the attack constantly, and when he saw Nathan and Richard's photographs in the paper, he recognized his assailants immediately. Richard was slight to him, and it was surprising that such a soft fellow was involved in a kidnapping. Nathan was different, harder. Charles likened him to a West Side thug.

The trauma had not left Charles. He sobbed, his body convulsing. Others in the room tried to offer comfort, but Charles was too hysterical to respond. He dropped toward the floor in a faint, his fall broken by a reporter who grabbed his arm and steadied him. The reporters were stunned. Crowe's resolve was strengthened. He was dealing with monsters.

―――――――

On June 3, the grand jury convened to hear the charges against Nathan and Richard. Typically, an introduction of the evidence was sufficient for securing an indictment. Crowe was leaving nothing to chance. He wanted testimony on the record, and he planned on calling seventy-two witnesses. The grand jury hearing would take the full week, and Crowe was prepared to spend the energy and the time needed to ensure his case was on record.

Crowe's longtime legal nemesis, Clarence Darrow, was representing the defendants. For a sloppy old man who dressed in stained, crumpled clothes, Darrow was unbelievably slick. Crowe feared Darrow was planning a plea of not guilty by reason of insanity. One of Darrow's past clients, Emma Simpson, had shot her husband and gleefully admitted so much in court. After a brief stint in the insane asylum, she was released to her former life. Crowe had to fight against the possibility that Nathan and Richard would be enrolled in the fall semester at the University of Chicago, sitting in graduate classes as though their time in county jail was a field trip.

Elsewhere in the building, two assistant state's attorneys were given time off the Bobby Franks murder to try the case against Belva. Assistant state's attorney Samuel Hamilton scanned each potential jury member and watched how each man reacted to Belva and her finery. Especially that hat.

"Would you let a stylish hat make you find her 'not guilty'?" Hamilton asked.

"No," the potential juror assured, earning Hamilton's approval.

Belva's young, white-haired attorney, Thomas Nash, had his own concerns regarding the jury's judgments.

"Would you be prejudiced if it should develop that—er—the lady had been drinking that evening?" he asked.

The juror assured Nash that hooch wouldn't bias his decision. The rest of the jury members didn't come as easy. It was a slow process and the day only yielded four men for the jury. Assistant state's attorney Harry Pritzker avowed to reporters that he had put Kitty Malm behind bars, and he was capable of doing the same to Belva. "I hope to send her over the same road," he said.

The next day, Crowe plowed through his witness list, entering into record the testimony of Bobby's parents, the worker who'd found the young victim's body, the investigator who first noticed the eyeglasses, and Nathan's family chauffer. The presentation of the evidence was exhausting, and even if the grand jury members felt ready to vote, Crowe refused to relent until all testimony was entered into record.

Elsewhere in the Criminal Court Building, the jury in Belva's case was treated to a far speedier trial. Belva entered the courtroom in a light brown dress that showed off her slender body and slight curves. Today she wore a deep, chocolate brown hat that highlighted her brown eyes and a mink wrap at her neck. Her nails were freshly tinted a soft rose color and she held gloves in her hand, which she nervously twisted.

After the final jury members were selected, the state launched into its opening statement. From the defense table, Nash waved his hand dismissively. The defense was passing on the opening statement.

The prosecution had few witnesses to call. There was a waiter and the owner from the gin joint Belva and Walter visited a few hours before the murder. Walter's widow, Freda, was called to testify to establish corpus delicti—proof that a crime did indeed occur.

The defense responded only by poking holes in the prosecutor's case through cross-examination and dismissive, irritated objections. Nash did not call one witness, and he remained silent during the closing arguments. By 6 PM, the jury was in the deliberation room with little evidence to consider. Walter had been found dead in Belva's car, yet she claimed she was too drunk to remember what happened. And she always maintained that she had no vengeance against Walter, no motive to shoot him dead.

Belva smoked in the bull pen reserved for defendants waiting to hear their fate. The jury was less than six feet away in another room, but she couldn't make out what they said. It was torturous to know her fate was being decided by someone else.

The jury filed back into the courtroom around midnight with the verdict. The sheets of paper were passed to the clerk, and the courtroom fell silent, awaiting his announcement. "Not guilty," he read.

Belva, in her relief, burst into a hysterical laughter. She hugged Nash and then thanked the jury. Her excitement bubbled over, she was free. "O, I'm so happy!" she burst, as Freda watched from the gallery. "So happy! And I want to hurry out now and get some air!"

Belva flounced back to her jail cell to collect her belongings. Her sister accompanied her and excitedly escorted her home. Meanwhile, Freda stayed in the courtroom, sobbing in the arms of her own sister. "There's no justice in Illinois!" she cried. "No justice! Walter paid—why shouldn't she?"

Pritzker was equally annoyed. "Woman—just woman!" he muttered.

32

A HANGING CASE

FOR PROSECUTING ATTORNEY MILTON SMITH, the Nitti case was all but forgotten. Something much better had come along. He was assigned to combat the insanity plea that Robert Crowe was certain Clarence Darrow would enter on behalf of Nathan Leopold and Richard Loeb. The past few weeks had been a blur of meetings with criminal psychologists and an incessant search for the use of insanity defenses in other murder cases.

It was a plum assignment to be a prosecutor in the trial of the century. Smith prepared to directly examine the state's expert witnesses in psychology, and there was a possibility he might also take a portion of the closing statements. Professionally, it was the type of association that would one day advance his senate campaign. Voters would see him as hard on criminals, a protector of the population.

Smith had no time for Sabella's case, and assistant state's attorney George E. Gorman went to court on June 17 on the state's behalf. Gorman was there to serve as a messenger, and defense attorney Rocco DeStefano quickly realized the man was more of a placeholder than a roadblock.

"Do you have any new evidence?" Judge Lindsay asked the state.

Gorman reported that no, the state had not collected new evidence in the two months since Sabella was last seen in court. The bail sheets were brought forward, and Gorman had no reason not to agree to release Sabella on bail.

Judge Lindsay set the bond at $12,500. The papers were fetched from his bench and brought to the defendant's table. Someone pointed on the page as to where Sabella needed to sign. Sabella took hold of the pen and signed her name. The reporters took note—the previous summer, Sabella had grasped the pen as though she'd never held one in her life and scratched an *X* onto official court documents. In the autumn, defense attorney Helen Cirese had signed on behalf of her clients. But Sabella Nitti was now a literate English speaker, capable of signing for herself.

Cirese accompanied Sabella back to her cell to gather her things. Sabella said good-bye to the other women in the cell block, although her longtime companions were gone. Kitty had transferred to Joliet to serve her life sentence in prison. Beulah was at home on the South Side of Chicago, working on her divorce from Al. And Belva was in her ex-husband's Hyde Park mansion, moving toward a reconciliation that would prove short lived. Sabella was the last one, but her day had finally come. She was free.

Sabella didn't need to pause and remember the moment. She had spent more than fourteen months on the women's cell block, not including the three months she spent in jail on fornication and adultery charges. More than a year and a half of her life was wasted in this jail. Such abuse was impossible to forget, and Sabella had no need to take one last look around her old cell. She'd remember just fine.

Memories of jail time, for most who experience it, are tied to painful life events and personal failures that manifested in crime. There are a few exceptions—Belva only seemed inconvenienced by her incarceration, not devastated. Nathan and Richard also appeared relatively unshaken. Both young men were housed in a special cell block for young offenders. They had the support of families who brought them comfortable clothing and supplementary meals. And they enjoyed special privileges like playing baseball in the small yard.

Perhaps the limited stress Richard and Nathan initially felt was because they were responsible for their unenviable position. Belva was the same. She chose to leave her doting older husband to live in an apartment he subsidized. She decided to invite a married man into her motorcar for a night of gin drinking and cabaret shows. And although she refused to admit any guilt, she pulled the trigger and left a man for dead. Sabella had made no such choices, and held no power. Dasso and the other lawmen had pursued her relentlessly and tried to sacrifice her to the criminal court system.

The team of six knew the case was effectively over. Judge Lindsay warned the prosecution that the case was in the end stages, and resuscitation seemed impossible. The case was continued, but given the state's attorney's workload with the Bobby Franks murder, the continuance felt more like a mourning period for Smith, Dasso, and the others to cope with their loss.

Sabella's defense team waited outside the jail for her to emerge. When she stepped from the jail, DeStefano quickly sensed Sabella was shaky. It had been more than a year since she had left the confines of the jail. He looped his arm into hers and pulled her tight as they stepped out the back door of the jail. A pack of reporters stood near, watching Sabella take the brief steps between the jail door and the motorcar her defense team had arranged to whisk her away. Sabella blinked at the light and then seemed as though she might faint. DeStefano kept her upright and then tucked her into the car.

A reporter later wrote that Sabella returned to the truck garden farm she owned prior to her arrest. But the farm was long gone—James had plundered it the previous year. Anything she had was from the generosity of her defense team and her supporters. They were tasked with reuniting Sabella with her two daughters and helping them settle into an apartment in the city. Sabella was an industrious woman, and finding someone who wanted to hire her as a cleaning woman would not be difficult.

Helen Cirese and the defense team returned to court the next day to secure Peter's release. As he left the jail, Cirese paused and explained to reporters how Peter was also not returning to the farm. Sabella and Peter did not have plans to live together as they awaited their second trial. Cirese didn't supply further details, but it was clear the marriage was the result of Dasso's fornication and adultery charges, not a burning love that motivated them to kill.

––––––––––

The week after Sabella was released from jail, Crowe sent Smith, Savage, and Sbarboro to Geneva, Illinois, to attend an insanity hearing for the Lina Lincoln murder case. Geneva was forty miles west of the city, and the three attorneys had to travel by train, stopping several times at various stations to switch platforms and transfer to connecting lines. The journey likely took several hours and required Smith and his colleagues to spend multiple nights in a hotel near the courthouse.

It was a case that Crowe insisted they understand. Lina Lincoln and her brother, Byron Shoup, had disappeared in January 1923. Police entertained the possibility that Lina and Byron had run away from the home they shared with Lina's husband, Warren. More than a year later, Warren told police he found Lina and Byron having sex. He claimed he'd shot and killed Byron with the revolver he was carrying. He then went to the shed and retrieved a rifle. Lina was naked and searching for a hiding spot. Warren said he shot her as she ran into the bedroom.

Warren then proceeded to decapitate both corpses and place his victims' heads into a block of concrete. The concrete blocks served for several months as porch supports, until Warren brought them to the garbage dump. He later led investigators to the site and encouraged them to dig until the blocks were found. "Getting warm," Lincoln called, as if they were playing a hiding game. "Getting warmer."

The defense claimed Lincoln was insane, an accusation he long contested. Crowe wanted his attorneys to be well schooled on the various possibilities as to how an insanity plea might be tried. He ordered Smith and the others to Geneva to watch the hearings. Smith, Savage, and Sbarboro complied and journeyed to the western town to take notes on how the Kane County prosecutor responded to the plea.

In the Kane County courtroom, Smith saw a defendant who looked decades older than his forty-six years. Warren Lincoln's pale skin appeared as though it had stopped producing the melanin it did in his younger years. The top of his head was bald and smooth, and creases formed around his eyes. His actions in the previous year certainly suggested he was insane. He claimed his wife and her brother had an incestuous relationship. He decapitated his victims and stuffed their headless bodies into a massive furnace. And he faked his own murder and tried to start a life elsewhere.

The insanity defense was a risk. Insanity had to be determined in a jury trial. If the jury found the defendant was insane, the payoff was a stint in the mental asylum that might last a few short months. The jury also had the power to sentence the defendant to death. Pleading guilty avoided such a risk. When a defendant pleaded guilty, the trial was waived and a sentencing hearing in front of a judge was held. The judge did have the authority to sentence the guilty person to death, but most were given jail terms.

Crowe was fairly confident that a jury would find Nathan and Richard sane and order them to the gallows. But he didn't trust Darrow, the defense attorney, to be predictable, and he prepared his team for battle. As soon as his three assistants returned from Geneva, he directed them to meet daily with a team of psychologists. For the previous forty days, the two young defendants had been marched in front of a team of a dozen forensic psychologists employed by the defense. The psychologists measured every aspect of Nathan's and Richard's bodies and asked endless questions. The science at the time believed certain hormonal secretions or thickness in the bones resulted in pathological behavior, and Darrow ordered his team to fully evaluate the young men.

Nathan and Richard went along willingly. Although Nathan denied he was insane, he seemed to enjoy the attention from the interviews, and he openly shared his sexual fantasies about being a powerful slave to a needy king. The psychologists related this fantasy to his relationship with Richard. At times, Richard had pretended to be drunk and helpless while Nathan had sex with him. At other times, Richard had played the king who designed their criminal plans to steal or shatter store windows. The psychologists weren't as certain how to translate Nathan's fantasy that he was a German officer in the Great War who participated with his troops in the violent rape of a beautiful French woman. Nathan admitted he initially wanted to kidnap, rape, and kill a young girl, but Richard didn't allow it. They settled on kidnapping and murdering a boy.

Crowe's attorneys didn't have access to the same psychological information as the defense. The state's psychologists had briefly interviewed the defendants before the grand jury indictment. But the room was packed with attorneys, investigators, and court reports, and it wasn't the type of private conversation that revealed the inner workings of a killer. The interview only confirmed the two men were sound of mind and understood the consequences of their actions.

Darrow's advantage put Crowe on the defense. In mid-July, Crowe ordered Smith and three other attorneys to begin an intensive study in forensic psychiatry. Every day, Smith and the other attorneys attended what the press called "insanity school" with four state psychologists who planned on testifying the defendants were sane. The goal was to have the assistant state's attorneys so well-versed in psychology and the law that they could dominate any move the defense made.

Smith was supplied with college textbooks to read each evening, and each day he spent two hours sitting in lectures. He had almost no time to investigate Sabella's case, and there was no available manpower in the prosecutor's office to turn her case over to another attorney.

Smith likely expected no sympathy from the team of six. Less than a year before, Sabella's defense team had a brief ninety-five days separating the verdict and her execution date. Almost half of that time was squandered by Moran's bumbling appeals. When the team of six members were able to step in as Sabella's representation, they'd had to run like hell to make up for lost time. In between court filings, they had mere days to race around Chicagoland to interview various witnesses and collect affidavits about key evidence not included in the first trial.

Those bursts of urgency surely kept the attorneys in the office long after closing time. There were likely many nights that the team rode the streetcar home on the late night "owl" schedule or just slept with their heads on their desks. They had pushed through because they wanted it. Smith no longer had the same drive against Sabella that once motivated him.

The team of six still had their drive, and they planned to overpower Smith just as Darrow was pushing on Crowe. As the summer coursed into autumn, Smith maintained his focus on the Bobby Franks murder. Smith's responsibilities heightened when Darrow encouraged his clients to change their pleas from not guilty to guilty. Such a strategy meant the two defendants would not have a jury trial, but a sentencing hearing before the judge. Darrow would then use the hearing to present his case that both young men were insane.

The strategy infuriated Crowe. It was brilliant, but completely wrong. Only a jury could determine insanity, yet Darrow was parading his psychological experts in front of the judge. The sentencing hearing stretched for weeks, and it wasn't until the early autumn that Nathan and Richard were given life sentences. For Darrow, it was a victory because his clients were not sentenced to death. For the prosecution, the victory resembled a loss.

———————

Sabella had herself a new fur coat, or at least a coat that was new to her. The luxury item was likely a second-hand coat. Either defense attorney Helen Cirese had secured the coat for her client or Margaret Bonnelli, the wife of defense team member Nuncio Bonnelli, had. Either way, Sabella Nitti was beginning to resemble Belva Gaertner in her court appearances. Sabella had silk stockings and fine, clean clothes.

Cirese encouraged her client to speak with the media. Sabella had the right to complain about how she was treated by the courts, and to express the terror she experienced. The press took note, and described her as a woman in her recovery from her torturous experience. Her once gray hair that was considered dirty was reframed as a symptom of the stress she'd endured during her horrifying ordeal.

Cirese was actively using Belva and Beulah to exonerate her clients. Both of those women were terribly guilty and not one bit sorry. But they were beautiful and the criminal court system had a bias for lovely ladies. Cirese encouraged Sabella to speak with reporters and repeat the lines they had rehearsed together. Sabella was to remind the reporters that she was not guilty, and her homely appearance was responsible for the guilty verdict.

"Pretty woman always not guilty," Sabella criticized.

It sure seemed that way to Milton Smith, who must have hated the idea of losing yet another case. The year had been a disappointment. Beulah was acquitted, and then Belva. Kitty Malm was only given life in prison and avoided the gallows. And both of Bobby Franks's killers were also spared the noose with life sentences. But in early December, Smith and the state's attorney dropped the charges against Sabella. They didn't have any new evidence, and the court was pressuring them to produce new evidence or end the ordeal.

The court had forced the prosecutors to concede, but Smith never relented. He remained proud of the conviction he earned in 1923 and boasted the accomplishment for the rest of his professional life. So what if he was wrong, and the supreme court called the trial an injustice? Winning isn't always about being right.

EPILOGUE

ALL THAT JAZZ

THE COLLECTIVE MEMORY PUSHED to forget Sabella Nitti. It was easier to focus on Belva and Beulah and their respective court victories. Maurine Watkins, a reporter for the *Chicago Daily Tribune*, left the newspaper in the following years and wrote a play, *Chicago*, about two fictional ladies of the gun who resembled Belva and Beulah. Within a few years, tickets to the play sold out. In the 1970s, the play was turned into a smash Broadway musical. In time, the musical came to represent 1920s Chicago—a fictional time of jazz, speakeasies, and gin. There was an innocent immigrant in the background of both stories, and she represented Sabella's unfortunate story.

In 2002, a movie version of *Chicago* was released starring Renee Zellweger and Catherine Zeta-Jones. The doomed immigrant was a small part of the storyline, and the character was written as a Hungarian, not an Italian, who was accused of a crime that resembled the charges against Sabella and Peter. During a musical number, "Cell Block Tango," the innocent woman sang her story in Magyar:

Mit keresek én itt? Azt mondják, a híres lakóm lefogta a férjem, én meg lecsaptam a fejét. De nem igaz. Én ártatlan vagyok. Nem tudom, miért mondja Uncle Sam, hogy én tettem. Próbáltam a rendőrségen megmagyarázni, de nem értették meg.

Translated, her words told the story of Sabella Nitti:

They say my famous boarder held down my husband while I chopped off his head. But it isn't true, I am innocent. I don't know why Uncle Sam says I did it. I tried to explain at the police station but they didn't understand me.

In the final scene of the movie *Chicago*, the characters based on Beulah and Belva—Roxy and Velma—performed a musical review for a packed audience. The song, "Nowadays," celebrated the freedoms of the 1920s. "But nothing stays," they crooned. "In 50 years or so, it's gonna change you know." Then, they dropped their fur coats and performed a dance number.

The real-life versions never enjoyed being such sensations. Sabella's friend Kitty Malm contracted pneumonia in 1931 and died at the Joliet Penitentiary at the age of twenty-eight. Beulah Annan also met an untimely demise. After her trial, she divorced Al and married a boxer in 1927, whom she claimed beat her mercilessly. In early 1928, she used a fake name and entered a fresh air sanatorium for the treatment of tuberculosis. She died within a few weeks, and it took the newspapers at least a week to report her passing. Belva Gaertner also struggled with violence in the years following her trial. She remarried William Gaertner but was viciously physical with the older man. He ended the marriage, and she left Chicago. Belva traveled throughout Europe and settled in Southern California near her younger sister.

Sabella's life seemed to improve in the years after the trial. She moved into an apartment in Chicago with her two young daughters and worked as a housecleaner. Her dreams of opening a store never materialized, but a modern apartment with running water, electricity, and heat must have felt like heaven.

In the 1930 census, Sabella listed herself as a widow and continued to call herself "Nitti." Peter never appeared on any other record in Cook County. It was possible he died after the trial, or he might have sensibly left the area for good. Clearly, Sabella and Peter were not the passionate lovers that Dasso accused them of being. It was more likely that they were scared friends who married to avoid further fornication and adultery suspicions. After the charges were dropped, the two had no reason to continue the marriage.

Sabella remarried in the early 1930s to another Barese immigrant. They moved to Southern California, where she died more than twenty years later, at age seventy-seven. Records indicate that Charley followed her to Southern California, and there appeared to be a continued relationship between the mother and son who had suffered in Cook County together.

Sabella's daughters remained in the Chicago area, married, and raised families. Whether Sabella maintained contact with her older two sons is unknown. Both men served minimal time in the penitentiary for a robbery they attempted together in 1924, but their whereabouts after that are not known. One might hope that in the sunshine of Southern California, Sabella found the peace she so rightfully deserved.

Genevieve Forbes continued writing for the *Chicago Daily Tribune*. While covering the Leopold and Loeb trial, she met her husband, a fellow reporter. She went on to cover politics for the paper, as she always intended to do. Forbes later resigned from the paper when her close friendship with Eleanor Roosevelt irritated the publisher.

In the end, the lawyers won—with the exception of Moran, whose mental illness brought him into long-term care. The others all experienced promotions, appointments, and upward movement. Several members of the team of six became judges or magistrates. Helen Cirese continued in her law career and served as a magistrate in Oak Park for fifteen years. She broke numerous barriers, first serving as a committee head for various law associations and then taking on the top leadership roles. She practiced law until the early 1980s and died while vacationing in Florida. Both DePaul University and the Justinians have scholarships in her honor.

The prosecution in Sabella's case continued to function as legal authorities in the decades that followed. Their careers were dotted with advancements and honors. Milton Smith became a state congressman, and Paul Dasso continued his work as the deputy sheriff until his retirement. Both Smith's and Dasso's obituaries noted their involvement with the Nitti trial and boasted how they were part of the team that secured a death sentence for the first woman in Cook County. They never relinquished their suspicions against Sabella and Peter.

There have been other defendants like Sabella in the past. And there will be more to come. They will face their own versions of Dasso and Smith. They'll find themselves falling into unraveling safety nets. They'll land in a courtroom similar to Judge David's—with a jury eager to convict based on assumptions tied to appearance, race, class, and ethnicity. Who steps forward to defend them will be of great consequence. Will it be someone as incompetent and hapless as Eugene Moran? Or as brave as Helen Cirese and the steeled team of six?

ACKNOWLEDGMENTS

Fɪʀsᴛ, I ᴛʜᴀɴᴋ ᴍʏ editor at Chicago Review Press, Lisa Reardon, for championing this project. Thank you for helping me pull Sabella from the shadows so her story could finally be told.

Thank you to Dr. Sabrina Pasztor for her Hungarian translation. I also thank Dr. Martin Maiden with the University of Oxford for helping me determine the profound differences between Barese and the other Italian dialects. And thank you to Dr. Laura Fulginiti for answering my question regarding the arteries and deciphering age.

Dr. Dominic Candelero with Casa Italia Chicago generously shared images with me as well as expertise. I also thank John Devona with the Western Springs Historical Society for his time and insight. Thank you to Jessica DePinto, past president of the Justinian Society for Italian-American Lawyers, for her support of and interest in my book.

I also thank the librarians at the Oak Park Public Library. Many times, they helped me fumble with the microfilm. They also had brilliant ideas on how to deepen my search, and I am grateful to have such a great resource in my hometown.

Dr. Federica Forniciari read my earlier work and helped me develop my narrative nonfiction skills. She also read my entire dissertation, and I can't think of a better *vero consulente*.

Shelby Sheehan also read my earlier work, and I can't thank her enough for her constructive criticism, support, ideas, and friendship.

Adriane Stoner-Vosko and Jeremy Vosko were early supporters of this work. They were two of the first people to see The Binder, and their genuine enthusiasm let me know I had something real.

Renee Powers has heard every detail of this book, and I can't thank her enough.

Dr. Catherine Knight Steele has been a constant source of support. She always saw the potential for this work and encouraged me to be enthusiastic, even when the challenge felt overwhelming.

I also thank Antara Das and Dr. William Gartside for the many layers of support and guidance they have provided. From pictures to visual media to encouragement—everything they could do to help, they did. Thank you my friends.

Writing, selling, and preparing this book took more than two years. Telling people that you are writing a historic nonfiction book sounds a bit like a pipedream. On occasion, people would look at me with a slight smile as if they knew my hopes were about to be dashed. But many people supported me and did not act as though my goal was pie in the sky. Specifically, I thank my family—Adina, Uncle Glen, Uncle Joe, Aunt Marda, and Aunt Michelle for their support. Thank you Tana, Suzie, and Natalie for your enthusiasm, support, and for serving as my audience for my presentation.

I dedicated this book to Tana for many reasons. She was born in Tuscany in 1926, lost her mother at the age of nine, and was liberated by the Buffalo soldiers as a teenager. Tana is tough, smart, and kind. She is one of the best people I know. Thank you, Tana, for all your kind words and support as I wrote and sold this book.

Additional gratitude goes to my parents-in-law, Rosa and Michael. I also thank my parents, Joel and Francine, for prioritizing my development as a student and a writer. Children with hearing problems often struggle with reading and math concepts, and my mother was determined to see her daughter succeed. My parents worked overtime to give me the gift of fluid reading and a love for writing. I thank them for the years of proofreading, rewrites, practice spelling tests, and double checking of the homework. (I only partially thank them for that math workbook from the summer of 1985.) Mostly, I thank them for making me feel empowered as a student, when I easily could have felt stupid or defeated.

I also thank Mia the Chihuahua and Daisy the toy fox terrier for their expert companionship.

Last, I thank my husband, Michael Lucchesi. I researched and wrote this book while I finished my dissertation. I felt as though I was treading water for months, if not years, and I admit I was somewhat of a complainer. I would not have reached either goal without his support. You are, Michael, the best person I know.

To all my family and friends—I'm sorry for bringing up the contents of chapter eight during mealtimes.

Grazie mille.

Thank you, thank you, thank you.

CHRONOLOGY

1922

JULY 29: Francesco Nitti goes missing from his family's farm in Stickney, Illinois.

SEPTEMBER 14: Cook County deputy sheriff Paul Dasso arrests Francesco's wife, Sabella Nitti, and a farmhand, Peter Crudele, at the family farm on charges of adultery and fornication. Unable to post bail, Peter and Sabella must remain in jail while waiting for a magistrate to hear the charges.

SEPTEMBER 19: The Cook County State's Attorney's Office begins investigating Francesco Nitti's disappearance as a murder.

SEPTEMBER 29: A grand jury determines there is not enough evidence to advance a murder case.

DECEMBER 6: Sabella and Peter are released from Cook County Jail after a magistrate dismisses the adultery and fornication charges.

1923

MARCH 9: Possibly fearful of another adultery charge, Sabella and Peter marry.

MAY 9: A worker discovers a decayed corpse in a drainage ditch in Stickney, Illinois. Peter, Sabella, and sixteen-year-old Charley Nitti are arrested for murder.

JULY 3: The murder trial against Sabella, Peter, and Charley begins.

JULY 7: Judge David forces prosecutors to drop the charges against Charley.

JULY 9: A jury finds Peter and Sabella guilty and fixes the sentence at death.

JULY 14: At the sentencing hearing, Judge David upholds the verdict and sets October 12, 1923, as the execution date.

AUGUST 4: Team of six appears in court as Sabella and Peter's new defense team.

SEPTEMBER 25: Illinois Supreme Court agrees to review Sabella and Peter's trial. Execution is stayed.

1924

APRIL 14: Illinois Supreme Court rules Sabella and Peter deserve a new trial.

MAY 12: Sabella and Peter appear in court separately with their defense team to begin pretrial hearings.

JUNE 16: Sabella is released from jail on bail.

JUNE 17: Peter is released from jail on bail.

DECEMBER 2: Prosecutors agree to drop charges against Sabella and Peter.

NOTES

1. That Means a Hanging!

In the early afternoon through *"That means a hanging!"*: Genevieve Forbes, "Death for Two Women Slayers," *Chicago Daily Tribune*, July 10, 1923.

He hardened his jaw: Ibid.

"dumb, crouching, animal-like": Forbes, "Death for Two Women Slayers."

"Deputy Dasso": Ibid.

The foreman, Thomas Murtaugh: Ibid.

"We, the jury," Vogel read: People of the State of Illinois v. Peter Crudelle, Isabella Nitti, and Charles Nitti (People v. Nitti), Supreme Court of Illinois Case Files, 1820–1970, case no. 15740 (1924).

Peter stared ahead: Forbes, "Death for Two Women Slayers."

Vogel moved the papers: Ibid.

"We, the jury, find": People v. Nitti.

She hadn't understood: Forbes, "Death for Two Women Slayers."

"Motion for a new trial" through *"Denied"*: People v. Nitti.

Forbes watched as the Italian women: Forbes, "Death for Two Women Slayers."

Sabella saw her oldest son: Ibid.

2. Give Them the Extreme Penalty

Prosecutors Milton Smith and Michael Romano: Forbes, "Death for Two Women Slayers."

More than two dozen times: "2 Women Sentenced to Die," *San Francisco Chronicle*, July 10, 1923.

At twenty-six, Romano: Obituary, *Illinois Bar News*, April 1953.

His fiancée, Cecilia Volini: Cook County, Illinois Marriage Indexes, 1912–1942, record no. 0997322.

Cecilia's father was a prominent physician: Council of the Chicago Medical Society, *History of Medicine and Surgery and Physicians and Surgeons of Chicago* (Chicago: Biographical Publishing Company, 1922).

Cecilia even went with him: "Camillo Eugene Volini, MD," accessed January 2015, www
.camilloeugenevolini.com.

Romano stepped to the side: Forbes, "Death for Two Women Slayers."

part of the two-attorney team: "Wanderer Grilled on Robber Shooting," *Chicago Daily Tribune*, July 8, 1920.

Some newspapers opined: "War Insanity Seen as a Probable Cause for Wife Slayer's Deeds," *Washington Post*, July 13, 1920.

A few months later: "Wanderer to Hang at Dawn," *Chicago Daily Tribune*, September 30, 1921.

Still single, Smith: US Census 1920, roll T625_311, page 7B, enumeration district 576, image 798.

At that point: US Census 1940, roll T627_1009, page 2A, enumeration district 103-2805.

The stamp read: People v. Nitti.

Sabella waited in her cell: Jail life descriptions from Frank Loomis, *Cook County Jail Survey*, report to the Board of County Commissioners, 1922.

Almost half the men executed: "Cook County Hangings: 1840–1927" in Ed Baumann, *May God Have Mercy on Your Soul: The Last Moments of 171 Convicted Killers Who Paid the Ultimate Price* (Chicago: Bonus Books, 1993).

Several states began: Mark Essig, *Edison and the Electric Chair* (New York: Walker Books, 2003).

this technique was demonstrated: Craig Brandon, *The Electric Chair: An Unnatural History* (Jefferson, NC: McFarland, 2009).

more US states were requiring: Christopher Kudlac, *Public Executions: The Death Penalty and the Media* (Westport, CT: Praeger, 2007).

Public behavior at these events: Ibid.

Private executions were meant: Vic Gatrell, *The Hanging Tree: Execution and the English People 1770–1868* (Oxford University Press, 1994).

3. I'll Tell Her If I Have To

Cook County Jail warden: Forbes, "Death for Two Women Slayers."

Anyone building a case: Photos of Westbrook from Chicago History Museum, digital collection, *Chicago Daily Tribune* negatives; height and build descriptions from WWI draft card, Cook County, IL, roll 1504087, draft board 86.

The following year: "Terry Druggan Ordered to Pay $1,000," *Belvidere Daily Republic*, May 2, 1927.

dimly lit cells: Descriptions of jail from Loomis, *Cook County Jail Survey*.

Not being able to read: US Census 1920, roll T625_363, page 10B, enumeration district 209, image 326.

in the midst of her chores: "Woman Ignorant of Death Award," *Ada Weekly*, July 12, 1923.

Sabella found her lawyer: Forbes, "Death for Two Women Slayers."

the cells in Cook County Jail: Description taken from photos of Cook County Jail, Chicago History Museum, digital collection, *Chicago Daily Tribune* negatives.

Sabella's face brightened: "Murderess Swoons When Informed She Must Die for Slaying Ex-husband," *Joplin Globe*, July 11, 1923.

Although the translator was a native: "Illinois Deaths and Stillbirths, 1916–1947," index, FamilySearch, Salt Lake City, UT, 2010.

"*I'll tell her if I have to*": Forbes, "Death for Two Women Slayers."

Forbes stood in the hallway: Ibid.

Sabella could not breathe: "Mrs. Crudelle Collapses When Told of Fate," *Freeport Journal-Standard*, July 10, 1923.

She prays in Sicilian: "Wife First to Hear Verdict in Illinois That She Must Hang," *San Francisco Chronicle*, July 10, 1923.

"*cruel, dirty, repulsive woman*": Forbes, "Death for Two Women Slayers."

4. Send a Woman to the Gallows? How Could You?

"*My fam-lee*": Genevieve Forbes, "Guards Gloat over Miseries of Immigrants," *Chicago Daily Tribune*, October 22, 1921.

She began working her way: Linda Steiner and Susan Grey, "Genevieve Forbes Herrick: A Chicago Tribune Reporter Covering Women in Politics," paper presented at Association for Education in Journalism and Mass Communication annual meeting, Gainesville, FL, August 1984.

On the Monday evening after: Forbes, "Death for Two Women Slayers."

But the story she filed through *was rational and just*: Genevieve Forbes, "Jury Foreman's Wife Rebels at Nitti Verdict," *Chicago Daily Tribune*, July 11, 1923.

Mrs. Murtaugh's two younger sisters: US Census 1920, roll T625_312, page 12A, enumeration district 125, image 685.

Her mother was actually dead: US Census 1910, Carbon, PA, roll T624_1321, page 23B, enumeration district 0029, FHL microfilm 1375340.

On the Monday through *she confessed to him*: "Woman Hurrying from Scene of Crime Is Sought," *News-Herald* (Franklin, PA), February 27, 1923.

Frederick had paid for: "Death at Apex of Triangle," *Logansport Pharos-Tribune*, February 27, 1923.

One Chicago editorial: "Shadow of Executioner on Their Walls," *Iowa City Press-Citizen*, July 14, 1923.

The papers reported: "Mrs. Anna Buzzi Jokes with Relatives," *Lebanon Daily News*, July 10, 1923.

The newspapers continued: "Woman to Hang with 'Star Boarder,' Wed After Killing," *Hutchinson News*, July 13, 1923.

Sabella stood and bowed: "Woman Under Death Sentence Tries Suicide," *Manitowac Herald-Times*, July 11, 1923.

5. Gone

Every seventeen years: "What a 17 Year Locust Looks Like," *Chicago Daily Tribune*, June 9, 1922.

warned readers to cover: Garden Notes, *Chicago Daily Tribune*, June 11, 1922.

Sabella was just fifteen: US Census 1930, roll 452, page 9A, enumeration district 0832, image 910.0, FHL microfilm 2340187.

She gave birth to Vincenzo: US Census 1920, Stickney, IL, roll T625_363, page 10B, enumeration district 209, image 326.

She lost an infant: Proof of heirship, Probate Court of Cook County, Estate of Francesco Nitti, October 30, 1923, case no. 84083, doc. 216, page 84083.

But then Francesco left: US Immigration, 1907 to New York City, microfilm serial T715: 1897–1957, microfilm roll 0915, line 13, page 18 (1916); Arrival: New York, New York, microfilm serial T715: 1897–1957, microfilm roll 2483, line 5, page 33.

rented a plot of land: Farm life descriptions from James Nitti testimony, People v. Nitti; and from the listing of the property in Probate Court of Cook County, Estate of Francesco Nitti, case no. 84083.

Sabella didn't know the joy: Descriptions of the Nitti family home and furnishings from proof of heirship, Probate Court of Cook County, Estate of Francesco Nitti, case no. 84083, doc. 216.

Francesco was violent through *"how it is to work on the farm"*: People v. Nitti.

For the next two weeks through *Francesco was not in bed*: Ibid.

6. The Crime in Dasso's Head

On September 14, 1922: The Weather, *Chicago Daily Tribune*, September 14, 1922.

In 1898, a former cook through *lashing to stop*: "Uses Paddle on the Boys," *Chicago Daily Tribune*, December 4, 1898.

The city was horrified: "Pay Visit to Bridewell," *Chicago Daily Tribune*, January 8, 1898.

The city council appointed: "Effort to Remove Dasso," *Chicago Daily Tribune*, April 11, 1899.

After a two-hour, closed-door meeting: Obituary, *Chicago Daily Tribune*, February 6, 1942.

Sabella watched as Dasso sped in: Arrest records and proceedings from Dasso testimony, People v. Nitti.

He was instead arresting Sabella: The Revised Laws of Illinois, Eighth General Assembly, 1833.

Dasso theorized that Peter and Sabella: People v. Nitti.

Sabella and Peter were residents: *The Centennial History of Illinois*, vol. 5 (Centennial Commission, 1917).

Neither Sabella nor Peter had the money: Ibid.

it was easy to detain: Joseph Tybor and Jerry Thorton. "Alleged Tryst Revives Rare Adultery Law," *Chicago Tribune*, July 11, 1997.

7. The Widow's Award

James was handsome: Description of James from photograph in "Child Tells How Father Was Slain," *Chicago Daily Tribune*, September 21, 1922.

intricate touches throughout the building: Description of elevator and Stock Exchange Building from "Looking After Louis Sullivan: Photographs, Drawings, and Fragments," Art Institute of Chicago official website, accessed October 20, 2015, www.artic.edu/aic /collections/exhibitions/LouisSullivan/index.

The Stock Exchange Building had a trading floor: *Chicago Central Business Directory* (Chicago: Winters Publishing Co., 1922).

He wandered past the communal bathrooms: Ibid.

These were standard questions: All testimony from table of heirship, Probate Court of Cook County, Estate of Francesco Nitti, October 27, 1922, case no. 84083.

By the time the court through *two kerosene cans*: Appraisement, Probate Court of Cook County, Estate of Francesco Nitti, January 9, 1922, case no. 84083.

Moran came to battle: Eugene A. Moran, notice to W. W. Witty, Probate Court of Cook County, Estate of Francesco Nitti, case no. 84083.

The judge agreed: Judge Henry Horner, order, Probate Court of Cook County, Estate of Francesco Nitti, January 13, 1923, case no. 84083.

She had no home to return to: People v. Nitti.

A week later, Moran sent: Horner, order, Probate Court of Cook County, Estate of Francesco Nitti.

he slipped up to Michigan: People v. Nitti.

8. We Laid Him on the Prairie

About a dozen men: Page 40 photograph, *Chicago Daily Tribune*, May 10, 1923.

an aging bricklayer: US Census 1920, roll T625_357, page 11B, enumeration district 2276, image 372.

found the body: "Boy Tells How 'Star Boarder' Slew His Father," *Chicago Daily Tribune*, May 10, 1923.

The police magistrate: US Census 1920, Stickney, IL, roll T625_363, page 8B, enumeration district 209, image 322.

His previous civic involvement: *Denní Hlasatel*, March 8, 1916.

David Abram, the undertaker: US Census 1910, Greenfield, IL, roll T624_290, page 16A, enumeration district 0050, FHL microfilm 1374303.

and also studied: Illinois State Department of Health, List of Licensed Embalmers, 1913.

an elevated grate: Eisele testimony, People v. Nitti.

Hidden within the basin: Roden testimony, People v. Nitti.

"We are in a fix": Ibid.

The crowd waited: Ibid.

"Is the finger" through *"Nobody else gets this"*: Ibid.

Roden collected a gold band: Ibid.

Abram's undertaking business: US Census 1920, Berwyn, IL, roll T625_357, page 1A, enumeration district 3, image 613.

The body was placed on a worktable: Abram testimony, People v. Nitti.

From the waist up through *difficult to gauge*: Ibid.

a badly decomposed body through *may have been round*: Hatton testimony, People v. Nitti.

Deputy Sheriff Paul Dasso: Dasso testimony, People v. Nitti.

It was late afternoon: James Nitti testimony, People v. Nitti.

James had come by: Ibid.

James had just come from the undertaker's: Taken from both Dasso and James Nitti testimony, People v. Nitti.

The Volpes had agreed: "In Jail, Asks for Children," *Ogden (UT) Standard*, July 31, 1923.

Charley stood at the front window: James Nitti testimony, People v. Nitti.

Sabella knew something was wrong: Dasso testimony, People v. Nitti.

Dasso had never seen: Ibid.

"I have a lot of trouble": Ibid.

9. Unraveling the Safety Nets

Varney was tall and heavily built: WWI draft card, Cook County, IL, roll 1439747, draft board 15.

At forty-six, Varney: *American Machinist* 51, nos. 1–13 (1919).

The day after the body was found: "Boy Tells How," *Chicago Daily Tribune*.

10. You Would Have Wanted It Too

one of eight children: US Census 1900, roll 286, page 13A, enumeration district 1024, FHL microfilm 1240286.

During his law career: "Contemptuous Larry," *Chicago Daily Tribune*, January 31, 1875.

Moran kept an office: WWI draft card, Cook County, IL, roll 1503829, draft board 47.

Moran often handled divorces: "Charges Bribery in Divorce," *Inter Ocean*, April 23, 1913.

Moran placed a help wanted advertisement: "Balm for All Ye Redheads," *Chicago Daily Tribune*, May 7, 1913.

Moran was arrested and charged: "Eugene A. Moran Is Held on Charges . . . ," *Inter Ocean*, April 22, 1913.

The Inter Ocean concluded the story: Ibid.

11. I Ought Not Tell You How to Try Your Case

Eugene A. Moran identified himself: People v. Nitti.

The women's block: Ione Quinby, "Mrs. Gaertner's Powder Puff Is Seen as a Victory Aid," *Chicago Evening Journal*, June 4, 1924.

Sabella slouched in a chair: Genevieve Forbes, "Dialect Jargon Makes 'Em Dizzy at Nitti Trial," *Chicago Daily Tribune*, July 7, 1923.

The state called Mike Travaglio: People v. Nitti.

Smith began the direct through *"Yes, I knew him"*: Mike Travaglio testimony, People v. Nitti.

Moran stayed silent: Ibid.

Smith sensed through *"He was pretty good"*: Ibid.

Smith continued to ask: Ibid.

"And what was his general" through *"identification," Smith said*: Ibid.

The prosecution claimed through *the body was Francesco Nitti*: Ibid.

Moran sensed the testimony through *"Cross-examine," Smith announced*: Ibid.

"And with whom": Ibid.

"Have you got any interest" through *"Charley told"*: Ibid.

"Unless counsel insists": Ibid.

Instead, Moran launched through *"the way it was now"*: Ibid.

That was enough through *"That is all"*: People v. Nitti.

12. You Don't Know What Burdens I Am Carrying

The People of the state of Illinois called through *Smith conceded. "Yes"*: People v. Nitti.

Smith began the direct through *"I will withdraw it"*: James Nitti testimony, People v. Nitti.

"There is nothing to show" through *"answering the question"*: Ibid.

Judge David overruled through *"you contemplate going"*: Ibid.

The jury filed out through *would all come together*: People v. Nitti.

about twenty years younger: Cook County, IL, Marriages Index, 1871–1920, record no. 0820523.

She was a Wisconsin native: Jean Martin, "I'll Put My Noose to Tightrope Use, and Gaily Prance upon It," anecdotes from friends, Connie Moran Papers, Chicago History Museum, F38DA.M791.

Connie was a small woman: Photograph in Connie Moran Papers, Chicago History Museum, F38DA.M791.

Advertising during the 1920s: William Leiss, Stephen Kline, and Sut Jhally, *Social Communication in Advertising: Persons, Products, and Images of Well-Being* (Scarborough, Ontario: Nelson Publishers, 1990).

The couple lived together: John Walley, letter to Herman Kogan, editor at *Chicago Daily News*, July 20, 1964, Connie Moran Papers, Chicago History Museum.

Connie left for France: Connie Moran Papers, Chicago History Museum, 1985.0708.

One friend described her letters: Robert Faherty, "A Thought from Paris," anecdotes from friends, Connie Moran Papers, Chicago History Museum, F38DA.M791.

Moran moved into the Milwaukee Sanitarium: US Census 1930, Wauwatosa, Milwaukee, WI, roll 2599, page 21A, enumeration district 0374, image 870.0, FHL microfilm 2342333.

The sanitarium treated patients: C. Ochler (relative of Connie Moran), electronic correspondence with author via Ancestry.com, March 3, 2015.

When Moran was released: US Census 1940, roll T627_1008, page 6A, enumeration district 103-2748.

When Moran died: Obituary, *Chicago Daily Tribune*, December 20, 1940.

13. The White Widow

Moran wasn't the only attorney: "Judge David Dies at 74; on Bench 21 Years," *Chicago Daily Tribune*, February 18, 1938.

Judge David worked tirelessly: "Judge David Works on 68th Birthday," *Chicago Daily Tribune*, October 28, 1931.

The judge's industrious nature: "Judge David Dies at 74."

He had fading brown hair: "Judge Joseph David and Judge Claire C. Edwards Sitting in a Courtroom in Waukegan, Illinois" (photograph), 1923, Chicago History Museum, digital collection, *Chicago Daily Tribune* negatives, DN-0075919.

the Hyde Park home: State of Illinois, death certificate for Emma David, June 28, 1924, no. 17370.

They were German immigrants: US Census 1910, roll T624_246, page 6B, enumeration district 0334, FHL microfilm 1374259.

Few worked outside the home: Marion Harland and Virginia Terhune Van de Water, *Marion Harland's Complete Etiquette: A Young People's Guide to Every Social Occasion* (Indianapolis: Bobbs-Merrill, 1914).

many women in Southern Italy: "La Famiglia: 1890–1910," *The Italian-Americans*, PBS, aired February 17, 2015.

The foreign powers that had ruled Southern Italy: Ibid.

The region was also centuries behind: Phyllis H. William, *South Italian Folkways in Europe and America; A Handbook for Social Workers, Visiting Nurses, School Teachers, and Physicians* (New Haven, CT: Yale University Press, 1938).

married before the age of sixteen: Ibid.
a virtuous woman stayed at home: Ibid.

14. Do You Love Your Mother?

They swiftly flowed through the testimony: James Nitti testimony, People v. Nitti.
In his testimony, James claimed through *"that is enough"*: Ibid.
"You don't know anything" through *"That is all"*: Ibid.

15. Just the Bare Skull

Dr. Edward Hatton was tall: Physical description from WWI draft card, Cook County, IL, roll 1613655, draft board 56.
It was a confidence: Ludvig Hektoen, "The Coroner in Cook County," *Illinois Crime Survey*, 1928.
Chicago newspapers had accused: Edward H. Hatton, "Report Concerning the Work of the Coroner's Office of Cook County," presentation to Committee on Medicolegal Problems of the Division of Medical Sciences, National Research Council, Washington, DC, 1926.
He had been with the office: Hektoen, "Coroner in Cook County."
He would speak at conferences: Hatton, "Report Concerning the Work."
He was a relatively new physician: Minnesota 1903 directory in John Dalby, comp., *Rice County, Minnesota Directories, 1888–1953*.
"Doctor, did you make a postmortem" through *"and 50 on the other"*: Hatton testimony, People v. Nitti.
a Chicago attorney was briefly questioned: People v. Nitti.
"Did you know Frank Nitti" through *The jury heard for a second time*: Abram testimony, People v. Nitti.
Neither attorney knew what to do: Eisele testimony, People v. Nitti.
Eisele knew things that no one asked him: People v. Nitti.

16. He Took the Body on His Back

Dasso set the scene through *David ignored the defense attorney*: Dasso testimony, People v. Nitti.
Smith started with the trousers through *leave the question*: Abram testimony, People v. Nitti.
There was something about the cross-examination through *Judge David agreed*: People v. Nitti.
Judge David listened through *served as the interpreter*: Dasso testimony, People v. Nitti.
Romano's parents were from Laurenzana: Rocco V. Romano, passport application, US Passport Applications, 1795–1925, National Archives and Records Administration, Washington, DC, Passport Applications, January 2, 1906–March 31, 1925, collection no.: ARC identifier 583830/MLR no. A1 534.
He was the son and brother of Liguri: *L'Italiat*, September 7, 1919.
Her dialect, Barese: Dr. Martin Maiden, e-mail message to author, March 25, 2015.
Romano's dialect was no more helpful: Ibid.
She likely understood Standard Italian: Dr. Tullio Telmon, e-mail message to author, March 31, 2015.

17. Oh, Dough

Judge David told the stenographer: People v. Nitti.

James answered a few easy questions through *"Pete paid it," James admitted:* James Nitti testimony, People v. Nitti.

Instead, he tried to compare through *"of his own like'":* Ibid.

During Moran's cross-examination through *"evidence," he said:* Dasso testimony, People v. Nitti.

Moran read Dasso's statement through *"Yes, I do":* Ibid.

Dasso did have his theories through *to describe Sabella:* Ibid.

The confusion in the courtroom: People v. Nitti.

She was the godmother: Sabella Nitti testimony, People v. Nitti.

There was a story through *the judge refused:* Anna Volpe testimony, People v. Nitti.

After lunch, the new interpreter: People v. Nitti.

Louis Roden, the Berwyn city employee: Roden testimony, People v. Nitti.

Roden stepped down: People v. Nitti.

"I'm not going to waste any time": Ibid.

Desant translated swiftly through *the judge shamed:* Anna Volpe testimony, People v. Nitti.

Desant was dismissed: People v. Nitti.

Frank Allegretti, another attorney: Photograph and biography from *Chicago Bar Association Record*, March 25, 1924.

Allegretti had a full head of dark hair: Physical description from WWI draft card, Cook County, IL, roll 1504081, draft board 86.

The questioning resumed through *"wished her well now":* Anna Volpe testimony, People v. Nitti.

The courtroom was too noisy: People v. Nitti.

The questioning proceeded through *"That is dry bread":* Anna Volpe testimony, People v. Nitti.

Saturday morning through *the first witness, Peter Crudele:* People v. Nitti.

The testimony began: Peter Crudele testimony, People v. Nitti.

Moran tried to establish through *"Take the witness":* Ibid.

Smith refused: People v. Nitti.

Charley had grown his hair long: Physical description from photograph, 1922, Chicago History Museum, digital collection, *Chicago Daily Tribune* negatives, DN-00750751.

Now sixteen, his face: Physical description from "Mrs. Nitti Denied Right to Keep Children in Jail," *Chicago Daily Tribune*, July 31, 1923.

Moran began questioning through *"No further cross-examination":* Charles Nitti testimony, People v. Nitti.

18. Sabella on the Stand

Moran addressed the court through *"children were bumming":* Sabella Nitti testimony, People v. Nitti.

Smith's assumption that the market was closed: City of Chicago, *Fulton-Market Landmark District*, report to the Commission on Chicago Landmarks, April 2014, www.cityof chicago.org/content/dam/city/depts/zlup/Historic_Preservation/Publications/Fulton _Randolph_Market_District_Prelim_Sum.pdf.

the market wasn't open: Ibid.

Smith's insinuation through *punishment from the court*: Sabella Nitti testimony, People v. Nitti.

Judge David ordered calm through *"That is all," Moran agreed*: Ibid.

Both sides rested through *witness for the state*: People v. Nitti.

The man did not have much through *"That is all," he told the courtroom*: James Volpe testimony, People v. Nitti.

19. Don't Think of Her as a Woman

The jury was led out through *the close of court*: People v. Nitti.

the home he shared with his mother: 1920 US Census, Chicago, IL, roll T625_330, page 2B, enumeration district 1106, image 719.

He looked in the mirror: Physical description from photograph in *The Syllabus* (Northwestern University yearbook), 1921.

It was an unusually cool day: The Weather, *Chicago Daily Tribune*, July 9, 1923.

His face was soft: Physical descriptions from photographs in Chicago History Museum, *Chicago Daily Tribune* archives.

"May it please Your Honor" through *was firmly established*: People v. Nitti.

Romano began by detailing through *twenty-two-year sentence*: *Reports of Cases at Law in Chancery Argued and Determined in the Supreme Court of Illinois*, vol. 282 (Bloomington, IL: Supreme Court of Illinois, 1918).

Romano read from the case law through *"punishment of death"*: People v. Nitti.

20. The Guilt of Others

She described Sabella: Analysis of Forbes's stories in the *Chicago Daily Tribune*, July 1923.

Sabella spent the time in her cot: "Woman Sentenced Would Kill Self," *Daily Independent* (Murphysboro, IL), July 11, 1923.

They believed she wasn't guilty: Genevieve Forbes, "Mrs. Nitti's Tragedy Melts Hearts of Women in Jail," *Chicago Daily Tribune*, July 12, 1923.

Most female murder suspects: Analysis of Northwestern University's Chicago Homicide database.

Anna McGinnis was the most recent: "Own Stories of Sisters Prove Slayings," *Chicago Daily Tribune*, June 15, 1923.

They were the "comrades" through *trying to be "psychologists"*: Forbes, "Mrs. Nitti's Tragedy."

Women's club committees through *help Sabella with her appeal*: "Club Women Plan Efforts to Save Murderess' Neck," *Springfield (MO) Leader*, July 15, 1923.

Other women argued differently: "Brains Saved Women's Lives," *Cincinnati Enquirer*, July 16, 1923.

"Can beauty be convicted?": *Evening Tribune*, July 16, 1923.

The other side embraced the verdict: "Death Is Penalty for Equal Rights," *Ogden Standard-Examiner*, July 16, 1923.

She was panicked and crying through *He spent the next hour*: "October 12 Is Set as Date to Hang Woman Slayer," *Chicago Daily Tribune*, July 15, 1923.

Moran further argued: "Sentence Mrs. Crudelle to Be Hanged on October 12," *Evening Independent*, July 15, 1923.

The gallery buzzed with excitement: "October 12 Is Set," *Chicago Daily Tribune*.

Judge Cleland was sixty-one: Edward F. Roberts, "McKenzie Cleland of the Municipal Courts," *Chicago Daily Tribune*, August 23, 1908.

As a judge, Cleland was compassionate: Ibid.

Judge Cleland was a bony man: Photograph, University of Iowa Libraries, digital.lib.uiowa .edu/tc.

"May I say a word" through *"a mother to hang"*: "October 12 Is Set," *Chicago Daily Tribune*.

Judge David was outraged through *"The motion is overruled"*: Ibid.

Judge David took no responsibility: Ibid.

The Judge refused further discussion: Ibid.

Sabella knew few English words: Ibid.

Peter leaned down: Ibid.

She broke free: "Woman Tries to Jump down Shaft," *Ogden Evening Standard*, July 15, 1923.

21. Eighty-Nine and Ninety

One of his paintings depicted: Based on an image of Dasso's 1925 painting retrieved from an online auction website.

In the span of his career: Obituary, *Chicago Daily Tribune*, February 6, 1942.

The only thing a condemned man expected: Descriptions of the execution process from Baumann, *May God Have Mercy on Your Soul*.

Dasso had attended the execution: Ibid.

On a painfully cold January day: "Doane Driver Is Shot Down by Auto Thief," *Chicago Daily Tribune*, January 19, 1918.

But he was seemingly immune: "Influence Used to Free Thief of Murder Charge," *Chicago Daily Tribune*, January 21, 1918.

"I'm innocent as usual": "Speedy Justice at Last Grips Immune Killer," *Chicago Daily Tribune*, January 22, 1918.

At the time of the killing: "Lawyers in Dear Hearing Seek to Quit," *Chicago Daily Tribune*, February 7, 1918.

Dear's lawyers claimed: "Dear's Defense: Intoxication," *Chicago Daily Tribune*, February 21, 1918.

And then two witnesses said: "Woman and Man Say They Saw Dear Kill Wolfe," *Chicago Daily Tribune*, February 22, 1918.

His young wife: "Dear's Defense," *Chicago Daily Tribune*.

Margaret sensed his impending doom: "Dear Sentenced to Hang for Wolfe Murder," *Chicago Daily Tribune*, March 2, 1918.

Dear waited in jail: "Dear and Three Bandits Break Jail," *Chicago Daily Tribune*, September 13, 1918.

He stood by through *"a cigarette do me?"*: "Dear Cries for Dope to Deaden His Waning Life," *Chicago Daily Tribune*, June 27, 1919.

Dasso arranged for the reverend through *a guard explained*: Baumann, *May God Have Mercy on Your Soul*.

It was just after 9:30 through *disposing of the body*: Ibid.

The gallows that awaited Sabella: James Janega, "Grim Bit of History for Sale," *Chicago Tribune*, October 18, 2006.

A fifth noose: Elizabeth Dale, "The People Versus Zephyr Davis: Law and Popular Justice in Late Nineteenth Century Chicago," *Law and History Review* 17, no. 1 (1999): 27–56.

The gallows were erected: Elizabeth Dale, *The Rule of Justice: The People of Chicago v. Zephyr Davis* (Columbus: Ohio State University Press, 2001).

The platform to the gallows: Description of the gallows from photograph in *Chicago Tribune*, June 17, 1977.

She would have the distinction: "Cook County Hangings" in Baumann, *May God Have Mercy on Your Soul*.

The execution of George H. Painter: Baumann, *May God Have Mercy on Your Soul*.

After the First World War: "History of the Death Penalty," Death Penalty Information Center official website, accessed April 27, 2015, www.deathpenaltyinfo.org/part-i -history-death-penalty.

22. The Surratt Effect

more than three hundred women: "History of the Death Penalty," Death Penalty Information Center.

Colonial history was filled with examples: Analysis of "Executions in the U.S. 1608–2002: The Espy File," Death Penalty Information Center official website, accessed April 27, 2015, www.deathpenaltyinfo.org/executions-us-1608-2002-espy-file.

Mary Surratt was about forty-two: Kate Clifford Larson, *The Assassin's Accomplice* (New York: Basic Books, 2008).

Surratt's execution had a chilling effect: Analysis of "Executions in the U.S.," Death Penalty Information Center.

After her sentencing, Mary Surratt: Larson, *Assassin's Accomplice*.

Moran was running to save Sabella: "In Jail, Asks for Children," *Ogden (UT) Standard*, July 31, 1923.

several women's groups: "Claims Illinois Cannot Execute Woman Slayer," *Fort Wayne Sentinel*, July 28, 1923.

The attempt failed miserably: "Mrs. Nitti Fails to Get Freedom on Court Writ," *Chicago Daily Tribune*, July 29, 1923.

Attorney Florence King: "Doomed Woman Hopeful," *Joplin Globe*, July 17, 1923.

others publicly announced their support: "5 Lawyers Make New Attempt to Save Mrs. Nitti," *Chicago Daily Tribune*, April 5, 1923.

23. Dust of the Feet

Helen Cirese waited for the elevators: Author analysis of area maps, office rental advertisements.

one of five women: DePaul University commencement speech, June 18, 1920, Helen Cirese Papers, Special Collections, UIC Library.

After graduation she'd had to wait: "Girl Wins Degree at Law but Must Wait a Year to Practice," *Chicago Daily Tribune*, June 17, 1920.

a newspaper ran her photograph: Photos of the Day, *Warren (PA) Tribune*, April 14, 1925.

She was first-generation American: 1920 US Census, Oak Park, IL, roll T625_361, page 11B, enumeration district 143, image 768.

They settled in north Oak Park: Description of home from author site visit; 1920 US Census, Oak Park, IL, roll T625_361, page 11A, enumeration district 143, image 767 330330.

author Ernest Hemingway: Hemingway and Cirese as classmates from *Tabula* (Oak Park and River Forest High School yearbook), 1917; Hemingway's hatred for mother from Ernest Hemingway, letter to Charles Scribner, August 27, 1949, in *Ernest Hemingway: Selected Letters 1917–1961* (New York: Scribner, 1980).

In late 1921, several dozen Italian lawyers: Anthony Scariano, "A Brief History of the Justinian Society," Justinians Society of Lawyers official website, accessed October 20, 2015, https://justinians.org/history/.

he had worked his way up: Bailiff from WWI draft card, Cook County, IL, roll 1613517, draft board 42; judge from 1940 Census, Cook County, IL, roll T627_972, page 7A, enumeration district 103-1611.

Bonelli was a short man: Bonelli description from WWI draft card.

staring into the eyes of angry murderers: Based on analysis of *Chicago Daily Tribune* articles about cases that appeared before the judge.

Albert N. Gualano: "Albert Gualano for Judge," *True Republican*, April 5, 1930.

a new defense team: Team of six list from People v. Nitti.

She was panicked through *portray her clumsy efforts*: "October 12 Is Set," *Chicago Daily Tribune*.

Forbes also enjoyed mimicking: Forbes, "Mrs. Nitti's Tragedy."

When Cirese stood outside Sabella's cell: Helen Cirese Papers, Special Collections, UIC Library.

Margaret Bonelli, the wife: Cook County, Illinois Marriage Indexes, 1912–1942, record no. 0693564.

She knew loss: 1910 US Census, Washington DC, roll T624_151, page 21A, enumeration district 0089, FHL microfilm 1374164.

One time, a Chicago Daily Tribune reporter: "Slayer Gets Stay of Execution" (standalone photo), *Chicago Daily Tribune*, September 25, 1923.

On August 4, day twenty-six: "5 Lawyers Make New Attempt," *Chicago Daily Tribune*.

the "dean" of the Italian community: "A Victory for Rocco DeStefano," *Vita Nuova*, July/August 1930.

Success came easy to him: Dominick Candeloro, *Italians in Chicago* (San Francisco: Arcadia Publishing, 2001).

He was also notably regal: DeStefano physical description from WWI draft card, Cook County, IL, roll 1613518, draft board 42; passport application 33868, US Passport Applications, January 2, 1906–March 31, 1925, National Archives and Records Administration, Washington, DC, roll 1606, certificates 33750–34125 (May 11, 1921–May 12, 1921).

When DeStefano presented his motion: "5 Lawyers Make New Attempt," *Chicago Daily Tribune*.

24. You've Got Me

Anna Schiner, a notary public: People v. Nitti.

Cirese started in Stickney through *was afraid for his life*: Ibid.

Team members spread out through *She had to get to court*: Ibid.

"If the court please" through *slipping it into the record*: Ibid.

"The evidence in this case": "Denies New Trial to Doomed Nitti Woman and Mate," *Chicago Daily Tribune*, August 30, 1923.

25. *Given Under My Hand and Seal*

The team had filed a writ through *what they needed—time*: People v. Nitti.

Peter understood immediately: "Stay of Execution Is Granted to Crudelles," *Fort Wayne Daily News*, September 25, 1923.

Cirese brought a hairdresser: Ione Quinby, "Husband Killers Find Rouge Is Great Lawyer," *Decatur (IL) Herald*, March 20, 1931.

Around Sabella's hairline: Description of Sabella from document analysis of photographs of Sabella Nitti from May 1923 and June 1924.

The newspapers took note of Sabella's makeover: Ione Quinby, "Nitti-Crudeli Benefitted by Prison Period," *Davenport Democrat and Leader*, March 24, 1924.

The papers made mention of the "jail school": Genevieve Forbes Herrick, "Jail Can Really Do a Lot for a Woman," *Chicago Daily Tribune*, June 3, 1927.

26. *Monkey Meets a Tiger*

Kitty Baluk pushed open the wood door: "Mrs. Malm Surrenders, Admits Share in Slaying," *Chicago Daily Tribune*, November 28, 1923.

Kitty and Otto had tried to rob: "Killed by Thief; Seeks Girl," *Chicago Daily Tribune*, November 5, 1923.

Kitty looked around the station: Ibid.

Assistant state's attorney John Sbarboro: "Mrs. Malm Surrenders," *Chicago Daily Tribune*.

The warrant for her arrest: "Issue Warrant for Mrs. Malm, Charge Murder," *Chicago Daily Tribune*, November 27, 1923.

Police already had Otto Malm: "Longing for Baby Brings Mother's Surrender in Strange Chicago Murder Tangle," *New Castle Herald*, December 8, 1923.

a series of convoluted confessions: "Quiz Killers Face to Face," *Chicago Daily Tribune*, November 29, 1923.

She had short hair: Description of Kitty from a photograph in "Confesses in Fatal Shooting," *Chicago Daily Tribune*, November 28, 1923.

Sbarboro was a tall man: Description of Sbarboro from WWI draft card, Cook County, IL, roll 1503828, draft board 46.

Dean O'Banion's $10,000 funeral: Description of funeral expenses from Probate Court of Cook County, Estate of Dean C. O'Banion, 1924, case no. 101951.

"What's your name?": "Mrs. Malm Surrenders," *Chicago Daily Tribune*.

Kitty had been only seventeen: "Illinois Deaths and Stillbirths, 1916–1947," index, FamilySearch, Salt Lake City, UT, 2010.

and already pregnant: Cook County, IL, Birth Certificates, 1878–1922, film no. 1379016.

when she married: Cook County, Illinois Marriage Indexes, 1912–1942, record no. 0899060.

"What is your address?" through *"What kind of gun did you have?"*: "Mrs. Malm Surrenders," *Chicago Daily Tribune*.

Kitty didn't fall for it: Ibid.

She didn't seem the violent murderess: "Chicago Police Seek Gun Girl," *Lincoln Star*, November 25, 1923.

She was a "two gun woman": George Britt, "Mother Love May Send Wolf Woman to the Gallows," *Huntington Herald*, December 5, 1923.

Kitty's story contradicted Otto's confession: "Mrs. Malm Surrenders," *Chicago Daily Tribune*.

how she had avoided arrest: "Mother Love Stronger than Fear of Gallows," *Fort Wayne Sentinel*, November 28, 1923.

He brought the information to his boss: "Quiz Killers," *Chicago Daily Tribune*.

Sbarboro ordered the guards: "Indict Them All," *Chicago Daily Tribune*, December 5, 1923.

Local high school students cooked: "Turkeys to Vie with Prayers for Thanksgiving," *Chicago Daily Tribune*, November 29, 1923.

Over at the Hudson Avenue police station through *"Then, my baby came"*: Genevieve Forbes, "Savage Mother Cries Out from Gun Girls' Soul," *Chicago Daily Tribune*, November 29, 1923.

Max indeed appeared to be twice as old: Physical description from photograph, February 1924, Chicago History Museum, digital collection, *Chicago Daily Tribune* negatives, DN-0076735.

In her interview with Forbes through *"won't be no other"*: Forbes, "Savage Mother Cries Out."

Kitty was desperate through *West Chicago police station*: "Malm Woman Tries Suicide in Her Cell," *Chicago Daily Tribune*, December 1, 1923.

A twelve-year veteran: Chicago Civil Service Commission, *Annual Report*, vol. 17 (Chicago Civil Service Commission, 1911).

Whalen was a large woman: Physical description from "Leaders in Elopement Plot," *Chicago Daily Tribune*, February 13, 1923.

Kitty asked the matron through *"kill myself sure as hell"*: "Malm Woman Tries Suicide," *Chicago Daily Tribune*.

By the time Kitty was transferred: "Indict Them All," *Chicago Daily Tribune*.

Kitty became the most engaged: Description of Sabella and Kitty's friendship from Douglas Perry, *The Girls of Murder City: Fame, Lust, and the Beautiful Killers Who Inspired Chicago* (New York, Viking: 2010).

27. My God! What Did They Do?

Kitty dressed for the occasion: Genevieve Forbes, "Angel Wings for Malm If I Hang, Says Lone Kitty," *Chicago Daily Tribune*, February 19, 1924.

especially Genevieve Forbes through *fates to be determined*: Ibid.

The morning was a plea hearing: Ibid.

Judge Walter P. Steffen: "Steffens Feats," *Chicago Daily Tribune*, March 10, 1937.

Steffen was still young: "Wally Steffen, Noted Athlete and Judge Dies," *Chicago Daily Tribune*, March 10, 1937.

"How do you plead?" through *"Say, that's a hot one"*: Forbes, "Angel Wings for Malm."

Her assurance seemed to grow through *agree on four jurors*: Ibid.

One of the jurors: "Luetgert Held on Wife-Murder Charge," *Chicago Daily Tribune*, May 18, 1897.

The defense in that case: Linda L. Kleplinger, *Fundamentals of Forensic Anthropology* (Hoboken, NJ: Wiley, 2006).

"Is there anything": Forbes, "Angel Wings for Malm."

More than a week later: Genevieve Forbes, "Mrs. Malm Has Collapse After State Surprise," *Chicago Daily Tribune*, February 22, 1924.

The trial had gone as poorly: "First Testimony Expected Today in Malm Trial," *Chicago Daily Tribune*, February 20, 1924.

When Otto did testify: Forbes, "Mrs. Malm Has Collapse."

Kitty braced herself through *"don't want to see anybody!"*: "Guilty; Malm Girl Gets Life,"
      Chicago Daily Tribune, February 27, 1924.
Kitty moaned through *lay on her cot*: Ibid.

28. Slumming in the Police Station

Freda Law saw the taxicab: Genevieve Forbes, "Other Woman's Gems Shine as Widow
      Sneers," *Chicago Daily Tribune*, March 13, 1924.
It was a cold night: Weather, *Chicago Daily Tribune*, March 12, 1924.
"I have to sew": Forbes, "Other Woman's Gems."
Freda fed the couple's son: Ibid.
She was an orphan: 1910 US Census, Cook County, IL, roll T624_242, page 5B, enumera-
      tion district 0191, FHL microfilm 1374255.
married at the age of eighteen: Cook County, IL, Marriages Index, 1871–1920, record no.
      1030535.
but the marriage dissolved: WWI draft card, Cook County, IL, roll 1613517, draft board 41.
Walter was taller: WWI draft card, Cook County, IL, roll 1452384, draft board 03.
His father was a Southerner through *There was a knock*: Forbes, "Other Woman's Gems."
Freda sat in the Wabash Avenue police station: Ibid.
Belva seemed to giggle through *into a shameless socialite*: Ibid.
Some friends of the Law family: Ibid.
"Walter never really did" through *ex-husband, William Gaertner*: Ibid.
Gaertner was two decades older: Cook County, IL, Marriages Index, 1871–1920, record
      no. 1030679.
When the reporters found him: Forbes, "Other Woman's Gems."
Belva blamed the coroner's jury: "No Sweetheart Worth Killing—Mrs. Gaertner," *Chicago
      Daily Tribune*, March 14, 1924.
Belva Boosinger: Illinois Statewide Marriage Index, file no. 00006503.
A girl raised in an orphanage: US Census 1900, roll 323, page 1B, enumeration district
      0136, FHL microfilm 1240323.
designated for children: Civil War Pension Index, General Index to Pension Files, 1861–1934,
      National Archives and Records Administration.
Belle Brown: "Shot Dead in Woman's Auto," *Chicago Daily Tribune*, March 12, 1924.
The first night, Belva waited: Ibid.
The full situation seemed funny: Ibid.
But Belva was permitted: Ibid.
The accompanying photo: "Jail Doesn't Worry Her," *Chicago Daily Tribune*, March 14, 1924.
One newspaper described: "One Grief Stricken; One Smokes, Laughs, and Plays Card,"
      Belvidere Daily Republican, March 15, 1924.
Another showed a photograph: "Three Women Smilingly Await Trials That Might Mean
      Death," *Altoona (PA) Tribune*, March 21, 1924.
Belva presented herself: George Britt, "Bootlegger Had No Pints," *Iowa City Press-Citizen*,
      March 15, 1924.
the attorneys her ex-husband hired: "Bury Slain Man, Belva Gaertner Silent in Jail," *Chicago
      Daily Tribune*, March 15, 1924.
The attorneys also ended: "Mrs. Gaertner Leads Jail Women in Song," *Chicago Daily Journal*,
      March 14, 1924.

On the last day of March: "Play Jazz to Soothe Feelings of Women Slayers," *Chicago Daily Tribune*, March 31, 1924.

Every day, Sabella scrubbed: Perry, *Girls of Murder City*.

29. Hula Lou, the Gal Who Can't Be True

a cold, damp morning: Weather, *Chicago Daily Tribune*, April 5, 1924.

The evening before: "Mrs. Nitti Consoles Beulah: 'Lady Slayer' Told Not to Worry for 'Beauty Will Win,'" *Chicago Evening American*, April 5, 1924.

Beulah Annan was twenty-five: Maurine Watkins, "Beulah Annan Sobs for Life She Took," *Chicago Daily Tribune*, April 6, 1924.

Sabella stopped in front through *"nobody cares about her"*: "Mrs. Nitti Consoles Beulah," *Chicago Evening American*.

Her first marriage: Watkins, "Beulah Annan Sobs."

Perry gained custody: Cook County, IL, Marriages Index, 1871–1920, record no. 1030723.

He was stout: WWI draft card, Jefferson County, KY, roll 1653508, draft board 4.

"Oh, hello, Anne": Perry, *Girls of Murder City*.

Beulah answered the door: Description of the murder from Maurine Watkins, "Seeks Death for Most Beautiful Slayer," *Chicago Daily Tribune*, April 4, 1924.

More than two hours after the shooting: Maurine Watkins, "Jury Finds Beulah Annan Is 'Not Guilty,'" *Chicago Daily Tribune*, May 24, 1924.

"I've shot a man": Watkins, "Seeks Death."

A young, dark-haired man: Description of victim from WWI draft card, Cook County, IL, roll 1439693, draft board 12.

Al picked up the phone: "Woman Plays Jazz Air as Victim Dies," *Chicago Daily Tribune*, April 4, 1924.

The first officer through the door: Stewart P. Moss, *Chicago Police Manual* (Chicago: Flood, 1923).

The detectives scanned the crime scene: "Woman Plays Jazz Air," *Chicago Daily Tribune*.

"Where is the gun?": Watkins, "Jury Finds Beulah Annan."

The officers evaluated the room: Moss, *Chicago Police Manual*.

One of the officers approached: Watkins, "Beulah Annan Sobs."

He had hemorrhaged: State of Illinois, death certificate, no. 9489.

Beulah grew increasingly hysterical: Watkins, "Jury Finds Beulah Annan."

Police procedure dictated: Moss, *Chicago Police Manual*.

Beulah evaluated Woods's black hair: Physical description from WWI draft card, Cook County, IL, roll 1439759, draft board 13.

The prosecutor was in his midforties: "Noted Lawyer Assailed at Assembly Hearing," *Chicago Daily Tribune*, March 28, 1929.

Woods was in his second year: Paul Brown, "Barr Left off Chairmanship List in Senate," *Chicago Daily Tribune*, January 26, 1927.

a position he would keep for seventeen years: "Woods, Woods, Brown & Salter Form Law Firm," *Chicago Daily Tribune*, January 22, 1939.

The questioning began gently: Watkins, "Jury Finds Beulah Annan."

"Couldn't we frame it": Ibid.

station didn't have women's quarters: Loomis, *Cook County Jail Survey*.

At the Hyde Park station through *"I didn't know . . ."*: Maurine Watkins, "Demand Noose for 'Prettiest' Woman Slayer,'" *Chicago Daily Tribune*, April 5, 1924.

The day was endless through *"I was nervous, you see"*: Ibid.

the weather in Chicago had softened: The Weather, *Chicago Daily Tribune*, April 14, 1924.

Someone on the team: Description of court opinion announcements courtesy of the Illinois Supreme Court Historic Preservation Commission.

She would learn a few details: "Supreme Court Saves Mrs. Nitti from Gallows," *Chicago Daily Tribune*, April 15, 1924.

30. A Delicate Condition

Belva Gaertner was the first: Genevieve Forbes, "Women Slugged or Held Cops? Jurors to Say," *Chicago Daily Tribune*, April 23, 1924.

her attorneys weren't ready: "Trials of Belva and Beulah are Continued Again," *Chicago Daily Tribune*, May 2, 1924.

Nash was a relatively young man: US Census 1920, roll T625_313, page 11A, enumeration district 190, image 1039.

Nash indeed took such a strategy: Genevieve Forbes, "Family of Five Placed on Trial for Cop's Death," *Chicago Daily Tribune*, April 22, 1924.

The next case on the docket: "Least Stylish of Court Ladies Only Happy One," *Chicago Daily Tribune*, April 22, 1924.

one of Chicago's slickest defense attorneys: "William Scott Stewart Dies Broke, Alone," *Chicago Daily Tribune*, March 20, 1964.

The process was slow: "Trials of Belva and Beulah," *Chicago Daily Tribune*.

The woman before him: Description of Sabella Nitti in court from "Least Stylish," *Chicago Daily Tribune*.

She had a stack of papers: "Ladies Day," *Chicago Daily Tribune*, April 22, 1924.

Her entire demeanor had changed: Ibid.

Sabella's English had advanced: Description of Sabella's English progression is based on analysis of newspaper articles including "Song the Only Anodyne for Woman Who Lives in the Shadow of the Gibbet," *Sheboygan Press Telegram*, January 8, 1924.

Defense attorney Rocco DeStefano: "Least Stylish," *Chicago Daily Tribune*.

County law forbade: Maurine Watkins, "Beulah Annan Awaits Stork, Murder Trial," *Chicago Daily Tribune*, May 9, 1924.

that Saturday the court was busy: "Jury Clears Montanas of Harnett's Death," *Chicago Daily Tribune*, April 25, 1924.

On May 8: Watkins, "Beulah Annan Awaits Stork."

If the state was ready: Maurine Watkins, "Beulah Wants No Delay of Murder Trial," *Chicago Daily Tribune*, May 10, 1924.

Judge Lindsay allowed through *"my left hand, and shot"*: Watkins, "Jury Finds Beulah Annan."

Beulah looked meaningfully through *on a helpless woman*: Ibid.

The prosecutor begged the jury: Ibid.

The jury had to think: "Beulah Annan Fades Away to Seclusion," *Chicago Daily Tribune*, May 25, 1924.

On Monday morning: "Spurns Husband Who Saved Her from Gallows," *Houston Post*, July 13, 1924.

31. Goldfish

It was after midnight: Nathan F. Leopold Jr. statement, May 31, 1924, People of the State of Illinois v. Nathan F. Leopold Jr. and Richard Loeb, Cook County Criminal Courts Files, case nos. 33623 and 33624 (1924).

All they knew: "How Eyeglasses Throw New Light on Franks Case," *Chicago Daily Tribune*, May 30, 1924.

A search of Nathan's bedroom: "Richard Loeb as Best Friend, Letter's Theme," *Chicago Daily Tribune*, May 31, 1924.

The other student was Richard Loeb: Simon Baatz, *For the Thrill of It: Leopold, Loeb and the Murder That Shocked Chicago* (New York: Harper Perennial, 2008).

But none of the potential suspects: "Frees Franks Teachers," *Chicago Daily Journal*, May 28, 1924.

The rubber hoses: Mark H. Haller, "Historical Roots of Police Behavior: Chicago, 1890–1925," *Law and Society Review*, 1976, 303–323.

The police seemed genuinely surprised: "Kidnap Rich Boy; Kill Him," *Chicago Daily Tribune*, May 23, 1924.

The questioning, Crowe thought: "Frees Franks Teachers," *Chicago Daily Journal*.

But then the police consulted: John Herrick, "Search for New Thrill Motive Asserts Killers," *Chicago Daily Tribune*, June 1, 1924.

The shop directed police: Leopold statement.

his thinning dark hair: Joseph Savage description from Getty Images, image no. 459191472.

Crowe had a heap of hair: Crowe description from Getty Images, image no. 524441147.

Smith, Crowe, and Savage faced Nathan Leopold: Statement description from Leopold statement.

The young suspect seemed unbreakable: Orville Dwyer, "Clinch Youths' Confessions," *Chicago Daily Tribune*, June 1, 1924.

Savage burst from the room: Ibid.

Crowe strode back: "Young Millionaires Tell How They Killed Franks," *Chicago Daily Journal*, May 21, 1924.

They secured a bank account: Leopold statement.

They procured the chemicals: Orville Dwyer, "Clinch Youths' Confessions."

The boys admitted: "Four Boys on Kidnapping List," *Chicago Herald and Examiner*, June 1, 1924.

The city was riveted: John Herrick, "Search for New Thrill Motive."

On June 2, Belva Gaertner: Maurine Watkins, "Mrs. Gaertner Has Class as She Faces Jury," *Chicago Daily Tribune*, June 4, 1924.

At the moment through *and steadied him*: Morrow Krum, "Identifies Slayers as Gland Thieves," *Chicago Daily Tribune*, June 3, 1924.

On June 3: "Crowe Has Witness List Ready for Grand Jury at Once," *Chicago Daily Tribune*, June 3, 1924.

Crowe's longtime legal nemesis: "Woman Slayer of Husband Found Guilty," *Chicago Daily Tribune*, July 15, 1921.

Elsewhere in the building through *"over the same road"*: Watkins, "Mrs. Gaertner Has Class."

Elsewhere in the Criminal Court Building through *"Woman—just woman!"*: Maurine Watkins, "Jury Finds Mrs. Gaertner Not Guilty," *Chicago Daily Tribune*, June 6, 1924.

32. A Hanging Case

George E. Gorman went to court: "Mrs. Crudelle, Back on Nitti Farm, Rejoices," *Chicago Daily Tribune*, June 17, 1924.

Gorman reported that no: Ibid.

Nathan and Richard also appeared: Nathan Leopold, *Life Plus 99 Years* (New York: Doubleday, 1958).

DeStefano quickly sensed: "Mrs. Crudelle, Back on Nitti Farm," *Chicago Daily Tribune*.

Helen Cirese and the defense team: "Crudelle, Mrs. Nitti's Aid, Released on $12,500 Bond," *Chicago Daily Tribune*, June 18, 1924.

As he left the jail: "Respite Obtained for the Crudelles," *Jacksonville (IL) Daily Journal*, June 18, 1924.

The week after Sabella was released: "Lincoln Test Trial in Leopold Case," *Chicago Herald & Examiner*, June 23, 1924.

Lina Lincoln and her brother: Phillip Kinsley, "Lincoln Faces Death or Asylum: Victims' Heads Found Within Cement," *Chicago Daily Tribune*, January 27, 1924.

The defense claimed Lincoln through *start a life elsewhere*: "Officers' Theories in Aurora Mystery Are at a Variance," *Dixon Evening Telegraph*, May 4, 1923.

Crowe was fairly confident: "Insanity School for Crowe Aids in Franks Case," *Chicago Daily Tribune*, July 13, 1924.

Nathan and Richard went along: Karl M. Bowman and Harold S. Hulbert, *Report of Preliminary Neuro-Psychiatric Examination (Nathan Leopold Jr)*, Northwestern University Archives.

In mid-July, Crowe ordered: "Insanity School," *Chicago Daily Tribune*.

Smith maintained his focus: Genevieve Forbes, "Call 100 Franks Witnesses," *Chicago Daily Tribune*, July 22, 1924.

Sabella had herself a new fur coat: Description of Sabella from "Woman Hopes to Get Freedom on Clothes," *Ironwood Daily Globe*, November 14, 1924.

Epilogue: All That Jazz

Sabella's friend Kitty Malm: "Kitty Malm Tiger Woman Slayer Dies in Joliet Cell," *Milwaukee Sentinel*, December 27, 1932.

Beulah Annan also met an untimely demise: "Beulah Annan, 'Cook County's Most Beautiful Slayer,' Dead," *Evening Independent*, March 14, 1928.

Belva Gaertner also struggled: State of California Death Index, 1940–1997, Sacramento, CA, State of California Department of Health Services, Center for Health Statistics.

In the 1930 census: US Census 1930, roll 452, page 9A, enumeration district 0832, image 910.0, FHL microfilm 2340187.

Sabella remarried in the early 1930s: Cook County, Illinois Marriage Indexes, 1930–1960, record no. 1662070.

They moved to Southern California: State of California Death Index, 1940–1997, Sacramento, CA, State of California Department of Health Services, Center for Health Statistics.

Sabella's daughters remained: Philomena F. DelMedico, Social Security Death Index, 1935–2014.

Helen Cirese continued in her law career: "Helen Cirese Endowed Scholarship," AcademicWorks official website, accessed October 20, 2015, https://depaul.academicworks.com/donors/7.

INDEX